THE
WORLD
OF
MYTH

THE
WORLD
OF
MYTH

{AN ANTHOLOGY}

† DAVID ADAMS LEEMING †

NEW YORK OXFORD
OXFORD UNIVERSITY PRESS

Oxford University Press

Oxford   New York   Toronto
Delhi   Bombay   Calcutta   Madras   Karachi
Petaling Jaya   Singapore   Hong Kong   Tokyo
Nairobi   Dar es Salaam   Cape Town
Melbourne   Auckland

And associated companies in
Berlin   Ibadan

First published in 2014 by Oxford University Press,
198 Madison Avenue, New York, New York 10016-4314

First issued as an Oxford University Press paperback, 1992

Library of Congress Cataloging-in-Publication Data
Leeming, David Adams, 1937-
   The world of myth / David Adams Leeming. -- Second [edition].
     pages cm
   Includes bibliographical references and index.
   ISBN 978-0-19-931636-6
   1. Myth. 2. Mythology. I. Title.
   BL312.L444   2013
   201'.3 -- dc23
                                                    2013027571

10 9 8 7 6
Printed in the United States of America

✦ For Pam, Margaret, Juliet, and Paul ✦

PREFACE
TO THE SECOND EDITION

✦

This collection of world myths, although comprehensive, is not intended to be exhaustive and might well be supplemented by a good general encyclopedia or dictionary of mythology. The myths selected are representative of the cultures in question, with some emphasis on myths that have influenced the creative arts in Western culture. These myths are used to illustrate a process by which an approach to myth is gradually revealed. This approach, essentially archetypal in nature, will be of particular use to students of literature and the other arts. It should also be of interest to a general, nonacademic audience, as it stresses the connections between myth and our own everyday lives.

Many thanks to the following indviduals: Christian Bauer, Sierra College; William Clements, Arkansas State University; Maggie DiVito, Columbus College of Art and Design; Edward Karshner, Robert Morris University; Preselfannie Whitfield McDaniels, Jackson State University; Joseph Nagy, University of California, Los Angeles; Meena Nayak, Northern Virginia Community College; Kathleen Nicklaus, Polk State College; and Susan A. St. Peters, Riverside City College.

In this revised second edition I have responded to my readers' suggestions by adding significantly to the various sections to make them still more comprehensively representative of the world's many cultures and by adding more myths that use feminine metaphors to speak to our collective concerns. To make the myths more accessible, I have in many cases retold the myths myself or chosen more contemporary translations.

D. A. L.
2013

ABOUT THE AUTHOR

✦

David Leeming received his B.A. in English from Princeton University and his Ph.D. in comparative literature from New York University. For eight years he taught at Robert College in Istanbul, Turkey, and traveled widely in Greece and the Middle East, developing his interest in mythology. He is an Emeritus Professor of English at the University of Connecticut in Storrs, where he taught for twenty-six years. He has written many books on mythology in addition to *The World of Myth*, including *Mythology, the Voyage of the Hero*; *A Dictionary of Asian Mythology*; *Goddess: Myths of the Female Divine* (with Jake Page); *God: Myths of the Male Divine* (with Jake Page); *Jealous Gods and Chosen People: The Mythology of the Middle East*; *Myth: A Biography of Belief*; *The Mythology of Native North America* (with Jake Page); *Gods, Heroes, and Kings: The Battle for Mythic Britain* (with Christopher Fee); *A Dictionary of Creation Myths* (with Margaret Leeming); and most recently, *The Oxford Companion to World Mythology* and *Medusa*. He has also written biographies of James Baldwin, Beauford Delaney, and Stephen Spender, and he has edited the Springer *Encyclopedia of Psychology and Religion*.

CONTENTS

✦

PART FOUR   PLACE AND OBJECT MYTHS   275

✦ Albin-Guilot, packing the Venus de Milo

INTRODUCTION
THE DIMENSIONS OF MYTH
✦

In common parlance, a myth is an "old wives' tale," a generally accepted belief unsubstantiated by fact. Thus, it is a myth that professors are absentminded or that women are intuitive rather than rational. We also classify as myths the stories of gods and heroes of cults in which we do not believe, tales that once had religious significance. The stories of the exploits of Zeus and Hera, Theseus, Perseus, and Odysseus are in this sense myths. Collections of the myths of particular cultures are called mythologies: the exploits of the characters just mentioned form parts of Greek mythology; the stories of Osiris and Isis are part of Egyptian mythology. We also use the word "mythology" to refer to the academic field concerned with the study of myths and mythologies. We can also speak of myth as an abstract reality, like religion or science.

In the Western world, myths have traditionally been tales of "pagan" (i.e., non-Judeo-Christian) religions. We speak of Egyptian and Greek myths and sometimes of Hindu and Buddhist myths, but until recently even atheists have rarely spoken of Jewish or Christian myths. Yet if "myth" has always implied falsehood, if we have not believed in Zeus or the Golden Fleece, we have accepted the mythical tales of cultures we value—especially Greco-Roman culture—as somehow important and worth teaching our children. One of the assumptions of this book is that Greco-Roman myths (and those of other cultures) are not only worth teaching but are essential to our education.

The English word "myth" is derived from the Greek *mythos*, meaning word or story. Human beings have traditionally used stories to describe or explain things they could not explain otherwise. Ancient myths were stories by means of which our forebears were able to assimilate the mysteries that occurred around and within them. In this sense, myth is related to metaphor, in which an object or event is compared to an apparently dissimilar object or event in such a way as to make its otherwise inexplicable essence clear. Thus, when Yeats speaks of "Two girls in silk kimonos, both / Beautiful, one a gazelle," the girl in the poem is, in fact, not a gazelle, but something true about her grace and her presence is conveyed when the image of a gazelle is substituted in our minds. In the same way, something of the sense of loss and death we may feel in winter is conveyed by the story of the abduction of Persephone. In short, both as story and as extended metaphor, myth is the direct ancestor of what we think of today as literature. The meaning of myths, like the meaning of any literature, is, as Northrop Frye has said, "inside them, in the implications of their incidents" (*Fables of Identity,* p. 32).

But, as has already been implied, in its explanatory or etiological aspect, myth is also a form of history, philosophy, theology, or science. Myths helped early societies understand such phenomena as the movement of the sun across the sky and the changing of the seasons, as well as such events as the ancient struggle for the control of the Dardanelles and such mysteries as the Creation and the nature of the gods. Myths also served as the basis for rituals by which the ways of humanity and those of nature could be psychologically reconciled. Many of these myths and rituals are still operative in the world's religions. The anthropologist or sociologist will properly study a myth as the expression of a social ethos. For example, the Sumerian myth of Inanna perhaps indicates a matriarchal tradition, whereas the myths of Narcissus and Hyacinth might suggest a practice of ritual human sacrifice.

In recent times we have gradually broadened our understanding of myth. Psychologists, linguists, and anthropologists have taken us beyond an appreciation of myths as primitive literature, science, or history to a realization of their importance in our own lives today. When we study mythology now, we tend to concern ourselves with basic assumptions that define a person, a family, or a culture—with the informing reality that resides at the center of being. We find ourselves talking not only about pagan tales but also about national, religious, and aesthetic essences. We find architects like Bruno Zevi discussing the mythic implications of architecture, or scientists discussing Newtonian mythic structure as opposed to that of "the new physics." We can refer to the common millennial myth that pervades the Judeo-Christian and Marxist traditions or to the myth of the American Dream. In each case we are considering something intangible, perhaps not literally real, that is nevertheless "true" in some higher sense. In other words, we have come to think of myths as conveyors of information rather than odd examples of pagan superstition, and we have learned that the mythic tales of particular cultures are masks for a larger, less tangible mythic substructure that we all share.

Throughout recorded history, the stories and patterns that we call myths have dominated human experience. The great anthropologist and mythographer Claude Lévi-Strauss speaks of myth as a " language, functioning on an especially high level where meaning succeeds practically at 'taking off' from the linguistic ground on which it keeps rolling" (*Structural Anthropology,* p. 210). If the purpose of our existence in the larger organism we call Earth is to make that organism conscious of itself, we have tended to do so by means of myths—contained in stories, songs, rituals, and paintings—that accomplish such real tasks as the justification of power, authority, ideologies, and political acts. God, personified as the patriarchal figure with the long white beard, is not merely a superstition but the embodiment of a myth, possessing real power, who has dominated our spiritual and temporal world for millennia. He inhabits not only our churches and temples but our male-dominated governments, families, and schools, from London to Djakarta. Similarly, the story of the quest has been used to justify not only denial of physical needs for the sake of spiritual growth but even murder and genocide.

Joseph Campbell has written that "the chronicle of our species, from its earliest page, has been not simply an account of man the tool-maker, but—more tragically—a history of the pouring of blazing visions into the minds of seers and the efforts of earthly communities to incarnate unearthly covenants" (*The Masks of God*, I, p. 3). Thus, myths are not to be regarded lightly. Mythologist Bruce Lincoln speaks of myth as "ideology in narrative form," suggesting that myth can be used to justify violence of one group against another (*Theorizing Myths*, p. 147).

The stories in this book are cultural versions of universal tendencies. They are sometimes funny, occasionally bizarre, but they must always be taken seriously. One culture's cleansing ritual, based on myth, can become another culture's holocaust. Never was this dangerous aspect of myth so obvious as in Germany during the Third Reich, when Hitler used Germanic myths, particularly as popularized by Wagner in his operas, to justify the concept of an Aryan master race in a German fatherland.

A more positive impetus for the reemergence of myth as a phenomenon to be taken seriously was provided by a host of anthropologists and psychologists around the turn of the century who saw in myth a rich source of material for their study of human nature. Such names as Sir James Frazer, E. B. Tylor, Franz Boas, Bronislaw Malinowski, Adolf Bastian, and Ernst Cassirer come to mind, as do those of the two great founders of modern psychology, Sigmund Freud and Carl Jung. The emergence of psychology as a science has probably done more than any other recent development to remind us of the significance of myth in our own lives. Both Freud and Jung recognized motifs and patterns that were common to the mythic and subconscious worlds. Such phrases as "Oedipus complex" and the "Elektra complex," which arise from Freudian psychology, are now a part of our general vocabulary. Jung, in particular, made use of myths in his approach to questions of self-realization, stressing the existence of archetypes, or inherent psychic tendencies, in our "collective unconscious"—tendencies that take form as motifs or themes common to individual dreams and tribal myths. Among such archetypal themes are the femme fatale, the journey quest, the figure of the wise old guide, and many others.

The connection between dreams and myths is crucial for a proper understanding of the significance of the latter. An assumption of modern psychology popular at the turn of the century was that dreams are a symbolic language by which information about the dreamer is conveyed. More specifically, with the help of an analyst—a sort of modern-day shaman—the individual can find reflected in dreams messages drawn from the inner self, the self buried beneath the debris of childhood training, adult repression, and mental prejudice. When the dreams of an individual are studied as a whole, a pattern—a personal mythology—emerges. When the dreams of many individuals are compared, a universal dream language, a language of dream symbols, takes form.

Like the dreams of an individual, the myths of a given group are created unconsciously, as it were. As Claude Lévi-Strauss has written, "Myths are anonymous. . . . They exist only as elements embodied in a tradition," they develop on their own, they come from "nowhere" (*The Raw and the Cooked*, p. 18). Yet few anthropologists would deny that to read a culture's myths is to glean information about that culture—about its inner identity, hidden beneath the mask of its everyday concerns. To go one step further, when we study the world's mythologies and discover the archetypal patterns (also common to our individual dreams) that essentially unite those mythologies, we study what we might reasonably call the dreams of humankind, in which we find information about the nature of humanity itself. In a real sense, the world reveals its inner self through its common mythology.

When we study a dream or a myth, or a series of dreams or myths, we are simultaneously studying difference and commonality. On the surface of a dream we find material reflecting the dreamer's immediate circumstances and environment. The setting and the characters of the dream will contain mysteries, to be sure, but they will also reflect people and places known to the dreamer. By the same token, the external surface of a myth is likely to reflect the experience of the culture in question. American Indian myths are populated by ravens, buffalo, and other North American animals, while in East Indian myths we find elephants and cobras. But at a deeper level, the dreams of an African, the myths of a Native American, and those of an East Indian are unified by a common symbolic and archetypal "language" or "deep structure."

This psychological analogy can be taken one step further. Just as dreams help us to determine our identity as individuals and tribal myths help to establish a tribe's identity, so world mythology, considered as a whole, is the eternal story of humanity's quest for self-fulfillment in the face of entropy, the universal tendency toward disorder. Whether the hero of a myth is Indian, Norse, African, or Polynesian, whether he or she is on a quest for nirvana, self, the Kingdom of God, or the Golden Fleece, this figure is on a universal human quest for identity and individuation, as Joseph Campbell and Mircea Eliade, two of our most influential modern mythologists, have so eloquently taught us. This is a quest that we all understand, for only humans are endowed with the ability to be conscious, at any given time, of the universal scheme of things, of *mythos*, of the beginning, middle, and end of a given process. In that sense we are all ultimately questers, voyagers on the mythical "road of life," the "path," the "Tao."

A question that inevitably arises in connection with mythology is that of authorship. Who wrote the myths, or, more accurately, who first told them? Almost invariably the answer must be the people themselves. The myth, like its close relative the fairy tale, has its origins in the collective "folk" mind. Perhaps it was individual priests or shamans who gave some specific form to the "primitive" speculations concerning the reason for spring, the origin of earth, and the nature of death, but the essential similarities within those various forms, irrespective of chronology and geography, indicate a collective authorship, the human mind wrestling en masse with the mysteries, attempting to make earth conscious of itself. Of course, much later there arose great literary mythmakers, early poets who, like the shamans, medicine men, and priests, were somehow individually inspired—even possessed—to the point that they could achieve self-identity only by breathing a new conscious literary life into the old tales. These poets were, like the folk mind itself, true mythmakers to the extent that they found new ways to convey the universal human story in terms suited to their own cultures. It was at about the time of Homer—himself a figure of mythic proportions—that human beings began to associate particular names with their mythmakers. We do not know the name of the poet of the Gilgamesh epic, through which much of Sumerian mythology is known to us. There are many literary versions—which were eventually written down—of Indian, Chinese, Egyptian, and Hebrew myths as well, but we do not know their authors. If there was a historical Homer, he can be called the first identifiable mythmaker, unless it was the Indian counterpart of Homer, the legendary Vyasa, who was said to have composed the *Mahabharata*. The Greek poet Hesiod is among the first truly historical mythmakers, renowned for his descriptions of the mythological past in such works as the *Theogony*.

After Homer the mythmakers become more consciously literary, better known, and further removed from their folk sources. The Romans, primarily Virgil (the *Aeneid*) and Ovid (the *Metamorphoses*), are perhaps more accurately described as professional poets than as mythmakers; the creators of the oral epic tradition, such as Homer and Vyasa, were still straddling the folk world and the self-conscious literary world. In the *Odyssey,* Homer gives us a brief portrait (perhaps a self-portrait) of one of these inspired voices of the folk mind, a mythmaking minstrel at the court of the Phaiakians, who in his songs gave new form and life to the ancient tales of prehistory:

> The herald came to hand leading the beloved minstrel whom the Muse
> did especially love: yet had her gifts to him been mixed, both good and

evil. She had taken from him the sight of his eyes, and given him a power of harmony. . . . Then the Muse pricked the musician on to sing of the great deeds of heroes, as they were recounted in verses whose fame had already filled the skies. . . .

(Homer, *Odyssey VIII*, trans. T. E. Lawrence
[New York: Oxford University Press, [1932] 1991], pp. 105–106)

Like the Homer of legend, Demodocus, the minstrel described, is blind. He may lack sight, but he possesses insight, being closer to the gods, as it were, and to the folk imagination than to what we usually think of as "literature." In the *Odyssey* itself, Odysseus is certainly a literary hero, but he is also a mytho-religious figure whose journey is firmly rooted in a ritual pattern involving loss, descent, and rebirth. In this sense he resembles Job in the Old Testament or the Pandava brothers in the *Mahabharata*. In a way, the early poetic mythmakers told stories that the collective mind already knew. In those stories humanity could see itself in proper perspective; creation could step back and look at itself. It should be pointed out here that the modern artist is a direct descendant of the ancient mythmaker. The true artist explores the inner myth of life in the context of a particular local experience. If the story of Odysseus is humanity's story of loss and rebirth leading to transformation, so is *War and Peace* in a nineteenth-century Russian context and so, perhaps, is Picasso's *Guernica* in a twentieth-century European one.

In this book the great mythic tales of the world are introduced and arranged in such a way as to make the universal tale they tell as clear as possible. Four types of myths serve as the organizing principle: cosmic myths, theistic myths, hero myths, and place and object myths. Cosmic myths are concerned with the great facts of existence (e.g., the Creation, the Flood, the Apocalypse). The theistic myths involve cultural hierarchies (e.g., the Twelve Olympians, the Egyptian gods, and archetypal deity forms). Hero myths, perhaps the best known, are stories dealing with individuals (e.g., Cuchulainn, Odysseus, Theseus, Jesus, Gilgamesh). Place and object myths concern either mythical places (e.g., the Underworld, the Labyrinth) or objects (e.g., King Arthur's sword, the Golden Fleece).

As we explore the world of myth, we should remember that we are journeying not through a maze of falsehood but through a marvelous world of metaphor that breathes life into the essential human story: the story of the relationship between the known and the unknown, both around and within us, the story of the search for identity in the context of the universal struggle between order and chaos. The metaphors themselves may be Indian, Greek, Native American, or Egyptian. The story they convey belongs to us all. It is what Joseph Campbell called "the wonderful song of the soul's high adventure" (*The Hero with a Thousand Faces*, p. 19).

SELECT BIBLIOGRAPHY

✦

The following works are intended as background reading not only for this introduction but also for the subject of mythology as a whole. Additional bibliographical listings may be found at the end of each section of the book.

A

Armstrong, Karen. *A Short History of Myth*. Edinburgh: Canongate, 2006.

B

Barbour, Ian G. *Myths, Models, and Paradigms: A Comparative Study in Science and Religion*. New York: Harper & Row, 1976.

C

Campbell, Joseph. *The Hero with a Thousand Faces*. Princeton, NJ, [1959] 1968.
———. *The Masks of God*. 4 vols. New York, 1970.
Cassirer, Ernst. *Language and Myth*. New York, 1946.

D

Doty, William G. *Mythography: The Study of Myths and Rituals*. Second edition. Tuscaloosa: University of Alabama Press, 2000.
Douglas, Mary. *Thinking in Circles: An Essay on Ring Composition*. New Haven, CT: Yale University Press, 2010.

E

Eliade, Mircea, ed. *The Encyclopedia of Religion*. 16 vols. New York, 1987.
———. *Myth and Reality*. New York, 1963.
———. *Patterns in Comparative Religion*. New York, 1958.
———. *The Sacred and the Profane*. New York, 1959.

F

Freud, Sigmund. *Totem and Taboo*. New York, 1918.
Frye, Northrop. *Fables of Identity: Studies in Poetic Mythology*. New York, 1963.

H

Hamilton, Edith. *Mythology*. New York, [1942] 1953.

Harrison, Jane. *Mythology*. New York, 1963.

Hillman, James. *The Myth of Analysis: Essays on Psychological Creativity*. New York, 1978.

J

Jung, Carl Gustav. *The Archetypes and the Collective Unconscious*. Princeton, NJ, 1959.

———. *Symbols of Transformation*. Princeton, NJ, 1956.

L

Leeming, David A. *Myth: A Biography of Belief*. New York: Oxford University Press, 2002.

———. *The Oxford Companion to World Mythology*. New York: Oxford University Press, 2005.

———, ed.*Encyclopedia of Psychology and Religion*. 2 vols. New York: Springer, 2010.

Lévi-Strauss, Claude. *Myth and Meaning*. New York, 1979.

———. *Myth and Memory: Cracking the Cycle of Culture*. Schocken reprint, 1995.

———. *The Naked Man: Introduction to a Science of Mythology*. New York, 1981.

———. *The Raw and the Cooked*. Trans. John and Doreen Weightman. New York, 1969.

———. *Structural Anthropology*. New York: Basic Books, 1963.

Lincoln, Bruce. *Theorizing Myths: Narratives, Ideology, and Scholarship*. Chicago: University of Chicago Press, 1999.

Luke, Helen M. *Woman Earth and Spirit: The Feminine in Symbol and Myth*. New York, 1987.

S

Segal, Robert. *Myth: A Very Short Introduction*. New York and Oxford: Oxford University Press, 2004.

W

Walker, Barbara. *The Woman's Encyclopedia of Myths and Secrets*. New York, 1983.

THE
WORLD
OF
MYTH

Geographical Distribution of Sources in *The World of Myth*

NORTH AMERICA
Native North America (Onondagan): Star Woman and Earth Divers
Native North America (Acoma): Goddesses and the Emergence
Native North America (Hopi): Emergence to the Fifth World
Native North America (Cherokee): Sun Goddess
Native North America (Inuit): Sedanative
North America (Lakota Sioux): White Buffalo Woman
Native North America (Penobscot): Corn Mother
Native North America (Maida): Coyote
Native North America: Water Jar Boy
Native North America (Hopi): The Kachinas
Native North America (Apache): The Vagina Girls

MESO-AMERICA
Meso-America (Aztec-Mexica): Coatlicue the World Mother
Meso-America (Mayan): The Popol Vuh
Mexico: Our Lady of Guadaloupe
Meso-America (Toltec/Aztec): Quetzalcoatl

SOUTH AMERICA
South America (Incan): Viracocha and the Giants

WESTERN EUROPE
Darwin: Origins
Ireland and Wales: Danu-Don
Ireland: Cuchulainn
Europe: King Arthur
Europe: Parcival and the Holy Grail
Europe: Mary
Europe: The Chapel Perilous
Iceland (Norse): The World Parent of the Eddas
Iceland (Norse): Ragnarök
Iceland (Norse): The Aesir and the Vanir
Iceland (Norse): Odin
Iceland (Norse): Loki
Iceland (Norse): Yggdrasil

NORTH AMERICA

MESO-AMERICA

SOUTH AMERICA

GREECE AND ROME
Greece: Hesiod's *Theogony*
Greece-Rome: Deucalion and Pyrrha
Greece: Originators and Olympians / Children of Zeus
Rome: The Renamed Olympians
Greece and Rome: Adonis and Aphrodite
Greece: Dionysos
Greece: Hermes Steals the Cattle
Prometheus
Pandora
Tiresias, Echo, and Narcissus
Hyacinth and Ganymede
Eros and Psyche
Daphne and Apollo
The Eumenides
Zeus and Europa
Greece: Theseus
Greece: Herakles (Hercules) and the Twelve Labors
Greece: Antigone
Greece: Jason and the Golden Fleece
Rome: Aeneas
Greece and Rome: Orpheus and Eurydice
Greece: Odysseus
Greece: Alcestis
Greece and Rome: Lands of the Dead
Greece and Rome: Troy
Greece: Delphi
Greece: Tiresias
Greece: Daedalus and Icarus

SOUTH/SOUTHEAST ASIA
India: The Sacred Words
India: Manu
India: The End of the Kali Age
India: The Triad
India: Krishna-Vishnu as Brahman
India: Krishna and the Gopis
India: Indra and the Parade of Ants
India: The Buddha
Indonesia (Ceram): Hainuwele
India: Rama and Sita
India: Draupadi
India: Mount Meru
India: The Cosmic Tree

EAST ASIA
China: Cosmic Egg and Yin and Yang
China: Yü
Japan: Amaterasu
Japan: Izanami and Izanagi
China: Fusang

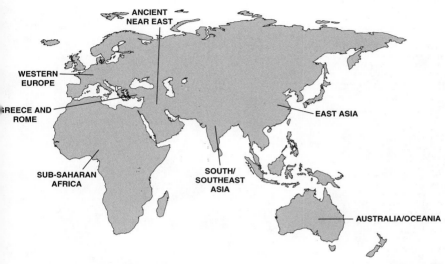

SUB-SAHARAN AFRICA
Africa (Boshongo-Bantu): Bumba's Creation
Africa (Bushman): Mantis
Africa (Fon): Legba
Africa (Kikuyu): Wanjiru

AUSTRALIA/OCEANIA
Australia (Aboriginal): The Pleiades
Australia (Aboriginal): Erathipa
Hawaii: Pele and Hiiaka

ANCIENT NEAR EAST
Egypt: Ex Nihilo Beginnings
Mesopotamia (Babylon): Enuma Elish and the World Parent
Israel: Genesis and the Talmudic Lilith
Iran (Persia): Aryan and Zoroastrian
Mesopotamia (Sumer-Babylon): Utnapishtim (Ziusudra)
Israel: Noah
Iran (Zoroastrian): Yima
Egypt: Hathor, Blood and Beer
Israel: The Day of Yahweh
Asia Minor (Christian): The Book of Revelation
Iran (Zoroastrian): The Savior Saoshyant
Arabia (Muslim): End of the World
Mesopotamia (Sumer): Gods of the Elements
Egypt: The Ennead
Israel: Yahweh
Mesopotamia (Sumer): Inanna (Ishtar)
Egypt: Osiris and Iris
Asia Minor (Phrygia): Attis
Mesopotamia (Sumer): Enki and the Me
Iran: Persia (Mithras)
Israel: Jonah
Arabia: Muhammad and the Night Journey
Mesopotamia: Gilgamesh
Israel: Jesus
Egypt: Osiris
Israel-Palestine
Asia Minor: (Phrygia): The Agdos Rock
Arabia: Muhammad's Cave

✦ Creation from the Egyptian *Book of the Dead*

PART 1 ✦

COSMIC MYTHS

C osmic myths are myths of the cosmos (Greek *kosmos*, meaning "order"). They belong to a science called cosmology, the study of the order of the universe as a whole. Under this category can be included such myths as those of Creation and the Fall, the Flood, and the end of the world. Each culture has its own mythic cosmology. Each cosmology reflects the experience of the culture that produced it. At the same time, all cosmologies reflect a universal human concern with the outer boundaries of existence. In our cosmologies, we humans have established ourselves at the very center of time-space. The cosmic myths give us purpose and significance in the larger perspective of the universe itself. In creation stories we are given a context; in flood myths we express a cosmic basis for the pervasive idea of the cleansing sacrifice; in apocalypse myths we relate to the immortality of human consciousness against the background of universal physical decay.

THE CREATION

A myth of creation, a *cosmogony* (Greek *kosmos,* meaning "order," and *genesis,* meaning "birth") is a story of how the cosmos began and developed. Typically, though not always, cosmogonies include the creation of the world, the creation of humankind, and the fall of humankind from a state of perfection, or the struggle in heaven between various groups of immortals.

Each person's birth is the subject of a story that is somehow revealing about that person. The events surrounding one's birth are a celebration of the miracle of individuality. The same applies to cultural myths of origin. Origin stories are sacramental—outward and visible signs of an inner truth about the individual or culture in question. Mircea Eliade has called the creation myth the "narration of a sacred history," the story of the "breakthrough of the sacred" into time *(Myth and Reality,* p. 6).

That the creation story is a metaphor for birth is indicated further by the frequent presence in cosmogonies from around the world of the motifs of the primal egg or the primal waters. These essential female symbols remind us that it is the Great Mother, perhaps breathed on by an intangible ultimate source, who gives form to life. It is she who is the *prima materia* without which life cannot be born:

> The mother of us all
> the oldest of all,
> hard,
> splendid as rock
> ("The Hymn to the Earth," *Homeric Hymns,* trans. Charles Boer, p. 5)

In the analogous mythic motif of the hero's birth, even God, if he chooses to participate in the human experience, must be born of a Maya or a Mary or an Isis, the living embodiment of Creation itself.

For us, the creation myth, like the myth of the hero's birth, inevitably has a psychological meaning. In the fact that cosmos is born out of chaos or nothingness, or the fact that a hero is born of a virgin, we find a metaphor for the awakening of consciousness from the unconscious. In the creation myths themselves, the creation of the human being is a necessary step. In the Judeo-Christian Genesis myth, for example, we find explicitly stated what is nearly always implied in creation myths, the idea that human beings are created to be namers, to apply their godlike powers of consciousness to recording creation and thereby providing it with significance.

The creation myth, then, establishes our reason for being, the source of our significance. As such, it is often used to help individuals or groups to regain health or order. When we are broken, we return to our origins to become whole again, whether on the psychiatrist's couch or in the shaman's hut. So it is that the ancient Sumero-Babylonian creation myth, the *Enuma Elish,* was read aloud at the Babylonian New Year festival. And so it is that many curing ceremonies, such as the Navajo and Buddhist sand-painting ceremonies, begin with the recitation of the creation myth. The sand painting is itself a mandala, a sacred circle representing creation in its original wholeness. When the patient sits in the sand painting and has the creation myth recited over him by the shaman (medicine man), he is returning to the womb of nature in the hope of being reborn into nature's wholeness, of reenacting the creation myth in his own life. But if the goal of life is to be a part of nature's wholeness, why must humans (or warring immortals) fall from grace so soon after creation? The answer would seem to lie in the nature of the created world. Life, by definition, implies death. To be alive is to be imperfect, to be on an evolving path toward death, toward the entropic equilibrium of chaos. To be in the world is to be a part of the life-defining struggle to create order out of chaos. The bodies we live in, the chairs we sit in—all in the process of decaying—are models of that struggle and, as such, models of creation. Works of art are even more obviously so. A poem lives insofar as its form holds chaos at bay, and its very being is a celebration of the skill that enables it to do so. The fall from grace at the end of the creation story perhaps suggests this necessary freedom of the created sphere of time and space from the formless perfection of the supreme source.

In his *Alpha: The Myths of Creation,* religion scholar Charles Long describes five basic creation myth types: creation from nothing (ex nihilo creation); creation from a preexisting chaotic mix of primal realities such as a cosmic egg (creation from chaos) or primeval waters; creation from the union, separation, division, or sacrifice of primordial parents (world parent creation); creation from an opening in the earth (emergence creation); and creation resulting from a dive into the depths of the primordial waters (earth diver creation). It is, of course, true that these types often overlap in particular myths. The types can, however, help us to recognize universal patterns in the process by which humans have tried to understand the origins of their world.

EGYPT: Ex Nihilo Beginnings

The Egyptian cosmogony developed in various directions over the centuries between the beginning of the Old Kingdom in c. 3000 B.C.E. and the end of the ancient civilization in the third century C.E. Our sources for Egyptian mythology are the ancient Pyramid Texts inscribed in hieroglyphs on inner chamber walls of Old Kingdom (3000–2200 B.C.E.) pyramids, the somewhat later

Coffin Texts of the Middle Kingdom (2134–1660 B.C.E.), and the *Book of Going Forth by Day* (often called the *Book of the Dead*), an early New Kingdom work (c. 1550 B.C.E.) that is derived from the earlier texts.

The central priestly source for the Egyptian creation myth is the cult of Atum or Re, the sun god of Heliopolis (near Cairo). In the various versions of the myth we find an original spirit or Word; the High God as a creating eye (the sun); a deity called Khoprer or Khepri (meaning "form") emerging from the "chaos" of primeval waters or a cosmic egg; a High God creating ex nihilo in an androgynous act of masturbation; and a world parent creation through the god Shu's separation of Sky (Nut) and Earth (Geb). We also find a primeval mound of earth, sometimes in fusion with the sun—a combination perhaps symbolized by the great pyramids themselves. We are not surprised to learn that rituals and myths of the Creation were repeated by the ancient Egyptians at funerals as well as at coronations and other important rites of passage.

What follows is a series of fragments that convey some idea of the Egyptian sense of the Creation. Many of these motifs of the Egyptian cosmogony are found in the creation myths of later cultures.

> I am the Eternal Spirit,
> I am the sun that rose from the Primeval Waters.
> My soul is God, I am the creator of the Word.
> Evil is my abomination, I see it not.
> I am the Creator of the Order wherein I live,
> I am the Word, which will never be annihilated
> in this my name of "Soul."
>
> · · ·
>
> The Word came into being.
> All things were mine when I was alone.
> I was Rê in [all] his first manifestations:
> I was the great one who came into being of himself,
> who created all his names as the Companies of the
>   [lesser] gods,
> he who is irresistible among the gods.
> The battleship of the gods was made according to what I said.
> Now I know the name of the great god who was therein.
> [An early gloss adds, "Perfume of Rê is his name."]
> I was that great Phoenix who is in Heliopolis,

who looks after the decision of all that is.
[An early gloss adds, "That is Osiris, while as to all that is, that is
    eternity and everlastingness."]

. . .

I fulfilled all my desires when I was alone,
before there had appeared a second to be with me in this place;
I assumed form as that great soul wherein I started being creative
while still in the Primeval Waters in a state of inertness,
before I had found anywhere to stand.
I considered in my heart, I planned in my head how I should make
    every shape
—this was while I was still alone—I planned in my heart how I
    should create
other beings—the myriad forms of Khopri—and that there should
    come into being their children and theirs.
So it was I who spat forth Shu and expectorated Tefnut
so that where there had been one god there were now three as well
    as myself
and there were now a male and a female in the world.
Shu and Tefnut rejoiced thereat in the Primeval Waters in which
    they were.
After an age my Eye brought them to me and they approached me
    and joined my body, that they might issue from me.
When I rubbed with my fist my heart came into my mouth in that
    I spat forth Shu and expectorated Tefnut.
But, as my father was relaxed . . . ages . . . serpents . . .
I wept tears . . . the form of my Eye; and that is how mankind came
    into existence.
I replaced it with a shining one [the sun] and it became enraged with
    me when it came back and found another growing in its place.
                    [R. T. Rundle Clark, *Myth and Symbol in Ancient Egypt*
                            (London, 1959, 1978), pp. 77, 79, 93.]

MESOPOTAMIA: *Enuma Elish* and the World Parent

One of the world's oldest written creation myths is the Babylonian *Enuma Elish*
("When on high"), composed no later than the reign of Nebuchadrezzar in the
twelfth century B.C.E. and perhaps much earlier. It is in part a creation myth and
in part a celebration of the high god Marduk. As a creation myth, it contains
several familiar motifs: the emergence of order from chaos, the primal waters

as a source of creation, a war in heaven, the emergence of a king god, and the creation of earthly matter from the body of the first mother, the world parent. The war in heaven is repeated in many cultures, perhaps most notably in the war between the Olympians and the older Titans in Greek mythology, in which Zeus, like Marduk, emerges in the end as undisputed king of the universe.

The *Enuma Elish* begins:

"When on high [*enuma elish*] heaven and earth had not yet been named."

It goes on to relate how Apsu, the primordial freshwater, and Mummu (Mother) Tiamat, the great saltwater body, "commingled" and so produced the silt deposits Lahmu and Lahamu, which we call "land." The union of Lahmu and Lahamu led to the first family of gods, Anshar and Kishar and their son Anu, who in turn fathered a young family of deities led by Ea. Ea and his brothers reveled in their existence and roamed over the commingled waters, creating wild winds that disturbed their ancient grandparents Apsu and Tiamat. When Apsu made plans to curb the play of the young gods, he was killed by them. This infuriated Apsu's mate, Tiamat, and she created horrifying monsters to help her take revenge. Anshar, Anu, and Ea made battle against these monstrous forces but were unable to subdue them. Meanwhile, Ea's consort Damkina gave birth to the great god Marduk, whom Ea called "my son, the Great Sun."

Seeing that his father and the others would lose the battle, the young Marduk sensed an opportunity. He offered to conquer Tiamat if he could be named King of the Gods and the Universe. After testing his powers over the skies, the gods agreed to Marduk's conditions, and Marduk, now the powerful storm god, took up his thunderbolt and charged the furious waters of Tiamat. The ancient goddess herself had taken the form of a monstrous dragon of the deep. In a terrible struggle, Marduk, the new sky god, defeated the ancient mother of the primordial waters and "divided her like a shell-fish" to form Heaven and Earth. Marduk then proceeded to turn what had been the chaotic creation presided over by Apsu and Tiamat into an ordered process by which Tiamat became a de facto world parent.

Out of her head Marduk made a mountain. Her eyes became the Tigris and Euphrates Rivers, her breasts hills, her nostrils reservoirs. Marduk then established Babylon as his temple city and the unified home of the gods. Out of the blood of Tiamat's son—some say lover—Qingu, Marduk had Ea create humans, who would do the work that the gods preferred not to do.

ISRAEL: Genesis and the Talmudic Lilith

The watery chaos or "deep" (*tehom*) of the Hebrew creation story, part of which was probably composed during and soon after the Babylonian captivity (that is, during the sixth and fifth centuries B.C.E.), owes something to the concept of Tiamat in the Babylonian *Enuma Elish*. If the Tiamat–*tehom* connection is not clear in the official Hebrew creation story, it is evident enough elsewhere in Hebrew scripture. When we read these words from Psalm 89 (9–10), we are reminded of the Babylonian wars in heaven and of the creative splitting of the primal mother, the world parent:

> Thou rulest the raging of the sea: when
> the waves thereof arise, thou stillest them.
> Thou hast broken Rahab in pieces, as one
> that is slain; thou hast scattered thine
> enemies with thy strong arm.

But if the Babylonian creation myth was meant to establish the rule of Marduk, the Hebrew Genesis seems to be more concerned with the establishment of humanity's role in the universe. Genesis is, in fact, made up of two somewhat distinct myths. Genesis I contains the version composed probably as late as the fifth century B.C.E.; Genesis II is a much earlier text, perhaps as early as 950 B.C.E. The differences to be particularly noted are those that concern the creation of the first humans. The story of the first humans in both of the Genesis versions continues to affect the relationship between men and women today.

Chapter 1

In the beginning God created the heaven and the earth.

2 And the earth was without form, and void; and darkness *was* upon the face of the deep. And the spirit of God moved upon the face of the waters.

3 And God said, Let there be light: and there was light.

. . .

26 And God said, Let us make man in our image, after our likeness: and let them have dominion over the fish of the sea, and over the fowl of the air, and over the cattle, and over all the earth, and over every creeping thing that creepeth upon the earth.

27 So God created man in his own image, in the image of God created he him; male and female created he them.

28 And God blessed them, and God said unto them, Be fruitful, and multiply, and replenish the earth, and subdue it: and have dominion over the fish of the sea, and over the fowl of the air, and over every living thing that moveth upon the earth.

29 And God said, Behold, I have given you every herb bearing seed, which is upon the face of all the earth, and every tree, in the which is the fruit of a tree yielding seed; to you it shall be for meat.

30 And to every beast of the earth, and to every fowl of the air, and to every thing that creepeth upon the earth, wherein there is life, I have given every green herb for meat: and it was so. . . .

Chapter 2

Thus the heavens and the earth were finished, and all the host of them.

2 And on the seventh day God ended his work which he had made; and he rested on the seventh day from all his work which he had made.

. . .

7 And the Lord God formed man of the dust of the ground, and breathed into his nostrils the breath of life; and man became a living soul.

8 And the Lord God planted a garden eastward in Eden; and there he put the man whom he had formed.

9 And out of the ground made the Lord God to grow every tree that is pleasant to the sight, and good for food; the tree of life also in the midst of the garden, and the tree of knowledge of good and evil.

10 And a river went out from Eden to water the garden; and from thence it was parted, and became into four heads.

. . .

15 And the Lord God took the man, and put him into the garden of Eden to dress it and to keep it.

16 And the Lord God commanded the man, saying, Of every tree of the garden thou mayest freely eat:

17 But of the tree of the knowledge of good and evil, thou shalt not eat of it: for in the day that thou eatest thereof thou shalt surely die.

18 And the Lord God said, It is not good that the man should be alone; I will make him an help meet for him.

19 And out of the ground the Lord God formed every beast of the field, and every fowl of the air; and brought them unto Adam to see what he would call them: and whatsoever Adam called every living creature, that was the name thereof.

20 And Adam gave names to all cattle, and to the fowl of the air, and to every beast of the field; but for Adam there was not found an help meet for him.

21 And the Lord God caused a deep sleep to fall upon Adam, and he slept: and he took one of his ribs, and closed up the flesh instead thereof;

22 And the rib, which the Lord God had taken from man, made he a woman, and brought her unto the man.

23 And Adam said, This is now bone of my bones, and flesh of my flesh: she shall be called Woman, because she was taken out of Man.

24 Therefore shall a man leave his father and his mother, and shall cleave unto his wife: and they shall be one flesh.

25 And they were both naked, the man and his wife, and were not ashamed.

Chapter 3

Now the serpent was more subtil than any beast of the field which the Lord God had made. And he said unto the woman, Yea, hath God said, Ye shall not eat of every tree of the garden?

2 And the woman said unto the serpent, We may eat of the fruit of the trees of the garden:

3 But of the fruit of the tree which is in the midst of the garden, God hath said, Ye shall not eat of it, neither shall ye touch it, lest ye die.

4 And the serpent said unto the woman, Ye shall not surely die:

5 For God doth know that in the day ye eat thereof, then your eyes shall be opened, and ye shall be as gods, knowing good and evil.

6 And when the woman saw that the tree was good for food, and that it was pleasant to the eyes, and a tree to be desired to make one wise, she took of the fruit thereof, and did eat, and gave also unto her husband with her; and he did eat.

7 And the eyes of them both were opened, and they knew that they were naked; and they sewed fig leaves together, and made themselves aprons.

8 And they heard the voice of the Lord God walking in the garden in the cool of the day: and Adam and his wife hid themselves from the presence of the Lord God amongst the trees of the garden.

9 And the Lord God called unto Adam, and said unto him, Where art thou?

10 And he said, I heard thy voice in the garden, and I was afraid, because I was naked; and I hid myself.

11 And he said, Who told thee that thou was naked? Hast thou eaten of the tree, whereof I commanded thee that thou shouldest not eat?

12 And the man said, The woman whom thou gavest to be with me, she gave me of the tree, and I did eat.

13 And the Lord God said unto the woman, What is this that thou hast done? And the woman said, The serpent beguiled me, and I did eat.

14 And the Lord God said unto the serpent, Because thou hast done this, thou art cursed above all cattle, and above every beast of the field; upon thy belly shalt thou go, and dust shalt thou eat all the days of thy life:

15 And I will put enmity between thee and the woman, and between thy seed and her seed; it shall bruise thy head, and thou shall bruise his heel.

16 Unto the woman he said, I will greatly multiply thy sorrow and thy conception; in sorrow thou shalt bring forth children; and thy desire shall be to thy husband, and he shall rule over thee.

17 And unto Adam he said, Because thou hast hearkened unto the voice of thy wife, and hast eaten of the tree, of which I commanded thee, saying, Thou shalt not eat of it: cursed is the ground for thy sake; in sorrow shalt thou eat of it all the days of thy life;

18 Thorns also and thistles shall it bring forth to thee; and thou shalt eat the herb of the field;

19 In the sweat of thy face shalt thou eat bread, till thou return unto the ground; for out of it wast thou taken: for dust thou art, and unto dust shalt thou return.

20 And Adam called his wife's name Eve; because she was the mother of all living.

21 Unto Adam also and to his wife did the Lord God make coats of skins, and clothed them.

22 And the Lord God said, Behold, the man is become as one of us, to know good and evil: and now, lest he put forth his hand, and take also of the tree of life, and eat, and live for ever:

23 Therefore the Lord God sent him forth from the garden of Eden, to till the ground from whence he was taken.

24 So he drove out the man; and he placed at the east of the garden of Eden Chĕr´-ū-bims, and a flaming sword which turned every way, to keep the way of the tree of life.

[Genesis 1:1–3, 26–30; 2:1–2, 7–10, 15–25; 3.]

In the *Babylonian Talmud*, a series of rabbinic commentaries written between 200 and 500 C.E. on various aspects of Jewish tradition, an alternative creation story involving Adam's "first wife," Lilith, emerges. Lilith probably came from the Mesopotamian tradition of the Sumerian goddess Ninli or Lilitu, whom the Babylonians associated with disease and ill winds. She would have been known to the Jews in exile in Babylon.

According to the story, on the first day God threw a huge stone into the void and it became the earth. On the second day God created the angels and on the third plants, trees, and Eden. The fourth day was for the stars and planets, the fifth for the creatures of the sea and air, including the Leviathan, and on the sixth day he created the beasts of the earth. On the sixth day he also discussed the creation of humans with the angels, but when some of the angels objected, God caused them to be consumed by fire. God now sent the angel Gabriel to collect soil from the four corners of the world, soil that would be used to form the humans. When the earth rejected Gabriel's mission on the grounds that humans would despoil the world, God reached down and collected the soil himself. Out of this soil he planned to make the first man, Adamah (Adam). When the angel Samael (Satan) and his followers objected to this creature of the soil having a soul, God threw them into Hell. Now he could create Adam and breathe life into him.

Adam noticed that the other animals had mates and wanted one for himself, so God used some soil to create Lilith as a mate for him. Lilith insisted on her equality with Adam, even demanding to be allowed to be "on top" when they made love. When Adam complained, Lilith left him and went to live with demons. Now God made Eve for Adam, and the happy couple wore nothing but shoulder bands bearing God's name. But Satan and Lilith had darker plans for them.

INDIA: The Sacred Words — creation through sacrifice

Like many cultures, India has a variety of creation myths. These are to be found in the Vedas, Brahamanas, and Upanishads, the sacred texts of the Hindus. They contain many familiar motifs: the creator god (Brahma or Prajapati), creation by the "spilling" of the creator god's seed, the sacrifice of a single world parent into two, the cosmic egg, the cosmic eye, the primal waters, and many others. A dominant theme is the emergence of reality as Mind (*manas*) or Soul (*atman*) from nothingness.

The most ancient of the Indian creation myth fragments are to be found in the oldest of the sacred written words, the *Rig Veda*, composed at least as early as 1500 B.C.E. One story tells us that the male power—the phallus of Heaven itself—reached out to and impregnated his own daughter, Earth. So it is that Heaven is our father and Earth our mother.

Another *Rig Veda* creation narrative is a world parent myth. Here the world parent is the thousand-headed, thousand-footed primal man Purusha, who enveloped Earth and was the universe itself, three-quarters immortal and one-third mortal. The gods performed a sacred sacrifice on Purusha, and his bottom quarter became the world. Out of his sacrifice came the plants and animals, the rituals, and the sacred words, the Vedas themselves. His mouth, the source of the sacred words, became the wise Brahmin priest caste and the god Indra. His arms became the warrior caste, his thighs turned into the common people, and his feet the lowest order. His mind became the moon, his eye the sun, his breath the wind. From his head the sky emerged, from his feet the earth.

A myth in another text, the *Shatapatha Brahmana*, relates how the creator, now known as Prajapati, broke out of a cosmic egg floating in the primeval waters. Once free of the egg, Prajapati spoke, and his words became the sky, the Earth, the seasons. He created the gods and the "darkness of Earth" with his hot breath. The *Aitareya Brahmana* contains a world parent elaboration of the Prajapati myth, revealing that the creator, in the form of a stag, committed incest with his daughter. The gods witnessed this outrageous act and created the wild Rudra (later Shiva) to punish the creator. When Rudra struck the progenitor with his arrow, Prajapati became a constellation of stars, and his spilled seed, heated by the fire god Agni, became many aspects of the created world.

In the later writings, the Upanishads, the creator has become the god Brahma, the third part of a trinity with the destroyer Shiva and the preserver Vishnu. In the *Chandogya Upanishad* of c. 600 B.C.E., a cosmic egg breaks into two parts containing all of the elements of creation, including Brahma, the sun, toward whom all things rose.

✦

In the *Barhadananyaka Upanishad*, the primal man as Purusha takes the form of the Soul, Atman—the ultimate Oneness within, the inner reality of the ultimate reality, Brahman. When Atman looked about into the void, he said, "I am," and Atman-Purusha was suddenly afraid. But when he reflected on his aloneness, he realized there was nothing to fear. Still, he wished not to be alone and so broke into two parts, becoming at once husband and wife. The couple produced humankind. But now the woman became concerned. "How," she wondered, "can he engender me from himself and how can we then engender others together?" Full of shame, the woman turned herself into a cow. But the man became a bull and found his other half and cattle resulted. Still ashamed, the woman became a mare and later a she-goat and even a she-ant, but the man mated with her as a stallion, a billy-goat, and even an ant. So it was that the creatures of the world were formed.

One *Rig Veda* hymn sings of the necessity of opposites; Being requires Non-Being. The wise, says the *Veda*, say that Being and Non-Being became one in the beginning and that the order of creation emerged from the original chaos. But finally, the Vedic poet asks, who really knows how creation came about? Maybe the creator himself does not know.

IRAN (PERSIA): Aryan and Zoroastrian

The Aryan invaders who moved into Iran and India in the third millennium B.C.E. shared a great many mythological traditions. An early Persian creation story is similar to several Vedic ones in India. It tells how the world was created when the fertility or solar god Yima, a Purusha-like primal figure, used a golden arrow to make his sister Earth pregnant. Because he married his sister, he was punished by the other gods. The old Aryan traditions were absorbed and changed with the development of Zoroastrianism in Iran (Persia), a religion founded by Zoroaster (Zarathustra), who was born in the sixth century B.C.E. The holy book of Zoroastrianism, the *Avesta*, emphasizes the importance of joining with the high creator god Ahura Mazda against his nemesis, the evil Angra Mainyu. The following creation myth is a retelling from a twelfth-century text, the *Bundahishn*. The creation story here is reminiscent more of the Jewish and Christian concept of creation than of the old Indo-Iranian or Aryan-Vedic traditions. When Zoroaster reformed the old Aryan and Mazdian religion, he moved away from an emphasis on the old gods and instead emphasized the duality of nature and the moral choice facing humans.

In the beginning there was only the essential duality. Ahura Mazda (Ohrmazd) was the good, Angra Mainyu (Ahriman) was the evil. In order to combat his evil opposite, Ahura Mazda created a spiritual rather than a physical world, waiting for 3,000 years before creating a perfect tangible world at the center of which was a perfect human, Gayomart. But Angra Mainyu hated this perfection and burst through the great cosmic egg that contained the world and the primal sea. This breakthrough caused such a disturbance that the sun began to rotate rather than standing still. Thus day and night began and mountains and valleys were formed. The interference of evil in the perfect world led to death, work, and pain for humankind.

In short, as in Genesis, a perfect world, created for humans, was polluted by Angra Mainyu, and Ahura Mazda had to place his opposite in Hell.

CHINA: Cosmic Egg and Yin and Yang   *creation from MENTECS*

There are many early Chinese creation myths. Most can be found in popular legend and in the third-century text the *San-wu li-chi*. The first myth told here is a creation from chaos cosmic egg and world parent narrative involving the primal being, a Chinese Purusha called Phan Ku, and the concept of yin and yang. The second myth is somewhat more philosophical and is also focused on yin and yang.

> In the beginning was a huge egg containing chaos, a mixture of yin-yang—female-male, passive-active, cold-heat, dark-light, and wet-dry. Within this yin-yang was Phan Ku, that which was not yet anything but which broke forth from the egg as the giant who separated chaos into the many opposites, including earth and sky. Each day for 18,000 years Phan Ku grew ten feet between the sky, which was raised ten feet, and the earth, which grew by ten feet. So it is that heaven and earth are now separated by 90,000 li or 30,000 miles.

Phan Ku was covered with hair; horns sprang from his head and tusks from his mouth. With a great chisel and a huge mallet, he carved out the mountains, valleys, rivers, and oceans. During his 18,000 years he also made the sun, moon, and stars. He taught the people what they know. All was suffused by the great primal principles of the original chaos, yin and yang.

When Phan Ku finally died, his skull became the top of the sky, his breath the wind, his voice thunder, his legs and arms the four directions, his flesh the soil, his blood the rivers, and so forth. The people say that the fleas in his hair became human beings. Everything that is is Phan Ku, and everything that Phan Ku is is yin-yang. With Phan Ku's death a vacuum was created, and within this vacuum pain and sin were able to flourish.

In the beginning was chaos, from which light became the sky and darkness formed the earth. Yang and yin are contained in light and darkness, and everything is made of these principles.

When yang and yin became one and the five elements were separated, humankind was born. As the first man watched the patterns of the sun, moon, and stars, a gold being came down and stood before him. The Gold One taught the man—now named the Old Yellow One—how to stay alive and how to read the sky.

He explained the beginning of things to the Old Yellow One. He explained how the life force that flows through us was created by earth and heaven, how the relative power of yin and yang at any given time results in heat or cold. He explained how the sun and moon trade light, how this act causes the passing of time, and how it creates the four directions and the midpoint. He said that the sky and earth together produced man and that the yang principle gave and the yin principle received.

The Gold One told the Old Yellow One about a great stone in earth's center and about the poles that support the earth. He told how the waters of earth surround it the way the flesh of fruit surrounds the seed. It is in this way that all things correspond—the fruit, the egg, the earth, the body—all things.

[David A. Leeming, *A Dictionary of Creation Myths* (Oxford University Press, 1994), pp. 49–50.]

GREECE: Hesiod's *Theogony*

Hesiod probably lived in the eighth century B.C.E. His *Theogony* contains the pre-classical Greek view of the founding of the universe. Essentially, Hesiod gave voice to an early Greek understanding of the myths of Homer and the mythic lore of the ancient Near East in general. Not surprisingly, then, we find in Hesiod's cosmogony a number of familiar themes: creation out of chaos, a war in heaven, and the establishment of an organized monarchy in heaven. The reader of the Greek myth of creation and the subsequent struggles between divine fathers and their mother-supporting sons will inevitably see the stories through the filter of the more modern Freudian version, which stresses the psychological struggle between father and son for possession of the mother and of power. The myth of the defeat of the Titans, the "sons of Gaia," by Zeus and the other sky gods is also, of course, a metaphor for the establishment of a patriarchal hierarchy in place of an older, earth-oriented society, originally springing from the Earth Mother, Gaia, that was perhaps more matriarchal in its outlook.

First came the Chasm; and then broad-breasted Earth, secure seat for ever of all the immortals who occupy the peak of snowy Olympus; the misty Tartara in a remote recess of the broad-pathed earth; and Eros, the most handsome among the immortal gods, dissolver of flesh, who overcomes the reason and purpose in the breasts of all gods and all men.

Out of the Chasm came Erebos and dark Night, and from Night in turn came Bright Air and Day, whom she bore in shared intimacy with Erebos. Earth bore first of all one equal to herself, starry Heaven, so that he should cover her all about, to be a secure seat for ever for the blessed gods; and she bore the long Mountains, pleasant haunts of the goddesses, the Nymphs who dwell in mountain glens; and she bore also the undraining Sea and its furious swell, not in union of love. But then, bedded with Heaven, she bore deep-swirling Oceanus,

Koios and Kreios and Hyperion and Iapetos,
Thea and Rhea and Themis and Memory,
Phoebe of gold diadem, and lovely Tethys.

After them the youngest was born, crooked-schemer Kronos, most fearsome of children, who loathed his lusty father.

And again she bore the proud-hearted Cyclops,
Thunderer, Lightner, and Whitebolt stern of spirit,

who gave Zeus his thunder and forged his thunderbolt. In other respects they were like the gods, but a single eye lay in the middle of their forehead; they had the surname of Circle-eyes because of this one circular eye that lay on their forehead. And strength and force and resource were upon their works.

And again there were born of Earth and Heaven three more sons, mighty and stern, not to be spoken of, Kottos, Briareos, and Gyges, overbearing children. A hundred arms sprang from their shoulders—unshapen hulks—and fifty heads grew from the shoulders of each of them upon their stalwart bodies. And strength boundless and powerful was upon their mighty form.

For all those that were born of Earth and Heaven were the most fearsome of children, and their own father loathed them from the beginning. As soon as each of them was born, he hid them all away in a cavern of Earth, and would not let them into the light; and he took pleasure in the wicked work, did Heaven, while the huge Earth was tight-pressed inside, and groaned. She thought up a nasty trick. Without delay she created the element of grey adamant, and made a great reaping-hook, and showed it to her dear children, and spoke to give them courage, sore at heart as she was:

"Children of mine and of an evil father, I wonder whether you would like to do as I say? We could get redress for your father's cruelty. After all, he began it by his ugly behaviour."

So she spoke; but they were all seized by fear, and none of them uttered a word. But the great crooked-schemer Kronos took courage, and soon replied to his good mother:

"Mother, I would undertake this task and accomplish it—I am not afraid of our unspeakable father. After all, he began it by his ugly behaviour."

So he spoke, and mighty Earth was delighted. She set him hidden in ambush, put the sharp-toothed sickle into his hand, and explained the whole stratagem to him.

Great Heaven came, bringing on the night, and, desirous of love, he spread himself over Earth, stretched out in every direction. His son reached out from the ambush with his left hand; with his right he took the huge sickle with its long row of sharp teeth and quickly cut off his father's genitals, and flung them behind him to fly where they might. They were not released from his hand to no effect, for all the drops of blood that flew off were received by Earth, and as the years went round she bore the powerful Erinyes and the great Giants in gleaming armour with long spears in their hands, and the nymphs whom they call Meliai on the boundless earth.

As for the genitals, just as he first cut them off with his instrument of adamant and threw them from the land into the surging sea,
even so they were carried on the waves for a long time. About them
a white foam grew from the immortal flesh, and in it a girl formed.
First she approached holy Cythera; then from there she came to sea-
girt Cyprus. And out stepped a modest and beautiful goddess, and
the grass began to grow all round beneath her slender feet. Gods
and men call her Aphrodite, because she was formed in foam, and
Cytherea, because she approached Cythera, and Cyprus-born, because she was born in wave-washed Cyprus, and "genial," because
she appeared out of genitals. Eros and fair Desire attended her birth
and accompanied her as she went to join the family of gods. And
this has been her allotted province from the beginning among men
and immortal gods:

> the whisperings of girls; smiles; deceptions;
> sweet pleasure, intimacy, and tenderness.

As for those children of great Heaven, their father who begot
them railed at them and gave them the surname of Titans, saying
that straining tight in wickedness they had done a serious thing,
and that he had a title to revenge for it later. Rhea, surrendering to
Kronos, bore resplendent children:

> Hestia, Demeter, and gold-sandalled Hera,
> mighty Hades who lives under the earth,
> merciless of heart, and the booming Shaker of Earth,
> and Zeus the resourceful, father of gods and men,
> under whose thunder the broad earth is shaken.

The others great Kronos swallowed, as each of them reached their
mother's knees from her holy womb. His purpose was that none
but he of the lordly Celestials should have the royal station among
the immortals. For he learned from Earth and starry Heaven that it
was fated for him to be defeated by his own child, powerful though
he was, through the designs of great Zeus. So he kept no blind
man's watch, but observed and swallowed his children. Rhea suffered terrible grief. But when she was about to give birth to Zeus,
father of gods and men, then she begged her dear parents, Earth
and starry Heaven, to devise a plan so that she could bear her child

in secrecy and make Kronos pay her father's furies and those of the children he had been swallowing, great Kronos the crooked-scheming. And they took heed and did as their dear daughter asked, and told her all that was fated to come to pass concerning Kronos the king and his stern-hearted son. And they told her to go to Lyktos, to the rich Cretan land, when she was due to bear the youngest of her children, great Zeus. Mighty Earth accepted him from her to rear and nurture in broad Crete. There she came carrying him through the swift, dark night, not stopping until she came to Lyktos, and taking him in her arms she hid him in a cave hard of access, down in the secret places of the numinous earth, in the Aegean mountain with its dense woods. Then she wrapped a large stone in babycloth and delivered it to the son of Heaven, the great lord, king of the Former Gods. Seizing it in his hands, he put it away in his belly, the brute, not realizing that thereafter not a stone but his son remained, secure and invincible, who before long was to defeat him by physical strength and drive him from his high station, himself to be king among the immortals.

Rapidly then the lord's courage and resplendent limbs grew; and when the due time came round, the great crooked-schemer Kronos, tricked by the cunning counsel of Earth, defeated by his son's strength and stratagem, brought his brood back up. The first he spewed out was the stone, the last he swallowed. Zeus fixed it in the wide-pathed earth at holy Pytho, in the glens of Parnassus, to be a monument thereafter and a thing of wonder for mortal men.

He set his father's brothers free from their baneful bondage, the sons of Heaven whom their father in his folly had imprisoned; and they returned thanks for his goodness by giving him thunder and lightning and the smoking bolt, which mighty Earth had kept hidden up to then. With these to rely on he is lord of mortals and immortals.

[Oxford's World Classics, *Hesiod, Theogony and Works and Days*, trans. and with an introduction by M. L. West (Oxford University Press, 1988, 1999, 2008), pp. 6–9, 16–18.]

ICELAND (NORSE): The World Parent of the *Eddas*

The Historian Snorri Sturluson (1179–1241) tells the story of the Norse (Icelandic-Viking) creation in his *Prose Edda*, based primarily on a tenth-century poem, the *Voluspa*. In the Ymir story, we find a world parent creation that reminds us of the Babylonian creation from the monstrous Tiamat. And there is the familiar war in Heaven.

Creation occurred between two entities that were at ready in existence—Muspell in the south and Niflheim in the north. Muspell was a place of fire where Black Surt with his flaming sword waited for his chance to destroy the world that would be created. Niflheim was a place of ice and snow, at the center of which was Hvergelmir, the spring from which the Elivagar, the eleven rivers, flowed. Between these two places was Ginnungagap, the great void into which the rivers poured, creating a desolate iciness in the north, which stood in contrast to equally desolate volcanic like moltenness in the south. But in the middle of Ginnungagap, at the meeting of the two conflicting climates, was a mild area where melting ice became the evil frost-giant Ymir. From under the left armpit of the sweating giant came a man and a woman. His legs came together to give birth to a family of frost-giants. From the melting ice of the center a cow called Audumla was born, and Ymir drank the four rivers of milk that poured from her. Audumla licked the ice for three days until a man named Buri appeared. Buri's son Bor married Bestla, the daughter of the frost-giant Bolthor, and Bestla gave birth to the gods Odin, Vili, and Ve.

As they hated Ymir and the savage frost-giants, the three sons of Bor killed Ymir. Then the three gods used Ymir's body to create the world; his flesh became earth, his bones became mountains and stones, his blood served well to make the lakes that dotted the world and the seas that surrounded it, and his skull was used for the sky. A dwarf stood at each of the four corners of the sky. The dwarfs were named East, West, North, and South. The gods made the sun and moon and stars from the sparks of Muspell. To the giants they assigned a place called Jotunheim. The brothers then created a protected and fertile area called Midgard from Ymir's eyebrows, and they created a man from a fallen ash tree and a woman from a fallen elm. Odin gave them life, Vili gave them intelligence and emotions, and Ve gave them senses. Ask was the man and Embla was the woman. These were the parents of the human race.

Odin took Night, the daughter of the giant Narvi, and placed her in a chariot in which to ride across the sky at set intervals. Night had married several times and had given birth to Earth by Annar and Day by Delling. Odin placed the shining Day in another chariot in which to cross the sky.

A man named Mundilfari had two children, a beautiful daughter whom he called Sun and a handsome son he named Moon. Odin did not appreciate this arrogance so he caused the two children to guide the chariots of the actual sun and moon. The gods allowed two wolves, Skoll and Hati, to chase Sun and Moon to keep them moving.

Out of the maggots that had come from Ymir's rotting flesh the gods made dwarfs. These beings were presided over by Modsognir and his assistant, Durin.

As for the sons of Bor, they formed a family of gods and goddesses called the Aesir, led by the father-god Odin. They built a wondrous home over Midgard and called it Asgard. The two zones were linked by the rainbow bridge Bifrost.

Over all of the parts of the universe rose the world tree Yggdrasil, the three roots of which reached to Asgard, Midgard, and the old hot Niflheim which became a kind of hell under the world.

The upper world contained not only Asgard but also Vanaheim, the home of the ancient fertility gods or Vanir, who at first went to war with the Aesir and then agreed to a truce and union with them.

[Christopher R. Fee with David A. Leeming,
Gods, Heroes, and Kings: The Battle for Mythic Britain
(Oxford University Press, 2001), pp. 140–142.]

MESO-AMERICA (AZTEC-MEXICA): Coatlicue the World Mother

Still another world parent creation—this one also with earth diver characteristics—is that of the Aztecs or Mexicas in Mexico, whose stories in great part derived from earlier traditions of the Olmec and Toltec civilizations and the even more ancient culture associated with the great pyramid ruins of Teotihuacan. A central figure in the Mexica creation myth, for instance, is the man god Quetzalcoatl, whose roots reach back to the Feathered Serpent of these earlier cultures.

It is said that Quetzalcoatl and his dark opposite, his mysterious brother Tezcatlipoca, living in Heaven, noticed a giant goddess, Coatlicue, floating in the primeval waters below. The goddess had become a destructive force consuming everything with which she came into contact. So the brothers became giant serpents and dove into the depths and tore the goddess apart. The various pieces of Coatlicue became our universe—half of her the sky, half the earth; her hair became the plants, her eyes the water, her mouth the rivers, her shoulders the mountains.

NATIVE NORTH AMERICA (ONONDAGAN): Star Woman and Earth Divers

The creation myth of the Onandaga, like those of the other Iroquoian tribes of North America, features a woman—Star Woman—who falls from the sky and becomes the creative force in a new world made by earth divers on the back of a turtle.

They say that there were once man-beings who lived in the sky of the world above this one, and that a woman-being went there with a comb and began straightening out the hair of one of the man-beings. Soon she became pregnant and the man-being became the first to experience the mystery of death, for with birth must come death. The man-being was placed by his mother in a coffin.

When the woman-being gave birth to a girl, her mother (the Ancient One) asked the woman-being who would be the child's father, but the woman-being did not answer. The child grew, and one day she began crying and would not stop. It was the Ancient One who told her daughter to take the child to the male-being's coffin. When the child saw the coffin, she was happy. The corpse of the man-being gave her instructions on the right way to be until she married.

When the girl child herself had a baby called Zephyrs, her husband, a chief, became ill. He sang a song, telling the other man-beings to pull the tree called Tooth that grew near his hut. Through the hole left by the tree, he threw his wife and Zephyrs down to the world below—our world.

The woman-being, Star Woman, fell and fell and saw only water beneath her. The animals below saw her falling and decided to make land for her. Many animals tried to dive below the waters to get earth, but only Muskrat succeeded, and he died in the process. With the earth he brought up, however, the animals made land on the Turtle's back. Then the flying creatures formed themselves into a huge net in which they caught the falling woman, and they brought her safely to the new earth.

Star Woman and her daughter brought fire and taught the people the art of hunting. When the daughter had grown, she was visited in the night and she soon became pregnant. Just before she gave birth, she heard two male-beings talking inside her body, arguing about how to be born. One came out by the normal way, the other by an armpit. This armpit child killed his mother and told his grandmother the other son had done the deed. Thus, there are good and evil people. These were the first man-beings on earth.

[David A. Leeming, *A Dictionary of Creation Myths*
(Oxford University Press, 1994), p. 217.]

AFRICA (BOSHONGO-BANTU): Bumba's Creation

The dominant theme in this myth is that of creation out of the male principle. Bumba's vomiting reminds us of the Egyptian High God's creation by spitting and seed spilling. The absence of the female principle here suggests a patrilineal culture. The fact that Bumba is white suggests that this is a late myth, affected, like so much African mythology, by the presence of the white race in colonial Africa.

In the beginning, in the dark, there was nothing but water. And Bumba was alone.

One day Bumba was in terrible pain. He retched and strained and vomited up the sun. After that, light spread over everything. The heat of the sun dried up the water until the black edges of the world began to show. Black sandbanks and reefs could be seen. But there were no living things.

Bumba vomited up the moon and then the stars, and after that the night had its light also.

Still Bumba was in pain. He strained again and nine living creatures came forth; the leopard named Koy Bumba, and Pongo Bumba the crested eagle, the crocodile, Ganda Bumba, and one little fish named Yo; next, old Kono Bumba, the tortoise, and Tsetse, the lightning, swift, deadly, beautiful like the leopard, then the white heron, Nyanyi Bumba, also one beetle, and the goat named Budi.

Last of all came forth men. There were many men, but only one was white like Bumba. His name was Loko Yima.

The creatures themselves then created all the creatures. The heron created all the birds of the air except the kite. He did not make the kite. The crocodile made serpents and the iguana. The goat produced every beast with horns. Yo, the small fish, brought forth all the fish of all the seas and waters. The beetle created insects.

Then the serpents in their turn made grasshoppers, and the iguana made the creatures without horns.

Then the three sons of Bumba said they would finish the world. The first, Nyonye Ngana, made the white ants; but he was not equal to the task, and died of it. The ants, however, thankful for life and being, went searching for black earth in the depths of the world and covered the barren sands to bury and honour their creator.

Chonganda, the second son, brought forth a marvellous living plant from which all the trees and grasses and flowers and plants in the world have sprung. The third son, Chedi Bumba, wanted something different, but for all his trying made only the bird called the kite.

Of all the creatures, Tsetse, lightning, was the only trouble-maker. She stirred up so much trouble that Bumba chased her into the sky. Then mankind was without fire until Bumba showed the people how to draw fire out of trees. "There is fire in every tree," he told them, and showed them how to make the firedrill and liberate it. Sometimes today Tsetse still leaps down and strikes the earth and causes damage.

When at last the work of creation was finished, Bumba walked through the peaceful villages and said to the people, "Behold these wonders. They belong to you." Thus from Bumba, the creator, the First Ancestor, came forth all the wonders that we see and hold and use, and all the brotherhood of beasts and man.

[Mircea Eliade, *Gods, Goddesses, and Myths of Creation*
(New York, 1974), pp. 91–92.]

NATIVE NORTH AMERICA (ACOMA):
Goddesses and the Emergence

The traditional home of the Acoma Indians of New Mexico is a settlement perched on a 600-foot mound, or butte. Like several other southwestern Native American cultures, the Acoma people are matrilineal; ownership is passed down through the female line. It is not surprising, then, that the Acoma creation, like those of many New Mexican Pueblos, is orchestrated primarily by a goddess figure who leads the people in an emergence process out of the universal womb, which is earth itself. A central structure in all Pueblo communities and in the communities of the Pueblo ancestors—the Anasazi or Pre-Pueblans—is the *kiva*, usually a round underground space at the center of which is a small hole, the *sipapu*, which is symbolic of the hole in the earth through which the people, led by a female spirit—for example, Prophesying Woman or Spider Woman—emerged into this world from the world inside the earth. In Acoma the creatrix is Tsichtinako (Thinking Woman).

In the beginning two sister-spirits were born in the underground. Living in constant darkness, they grew slowly and knew one another only by touch. For some time they were fed by a female spirit named Tsichtinako who taught them language.

When the proper time had arrived, the sisters were given baskets containing seeds for all the plants and models of all the animals that would be in the next world. Tsichtinako said they were from their father and that they were to be carried to the light of the upper world. She helped the sisters find the seeds of four trees in the baskets, and these seeds the sisters planted in the dark. After a long time the trees sprouted and one—a pine—grew sufficiently to break a small hole through the earth above and let in some light. With Tsichtinako's help, the spirits found the model of the badger, to whom they gave the gift of life and whom they instructed to dig around the hole so it would become bigger. They cautioned the animal not to enter into the world of light, and he obeyed. As a reward he was promised eventual happiness in the upper world. Next the sisters found the model of the locust in the baskets. After they gave him life, they asked him to smooth the opening above but warned him not to enter the world of light. When he returned after doing his job, he admitted he had indeed passed through the hole. "What was it like up there?" the sisters asked. "Flat," he answered. Locust was told that for having done his work he could accompany the spirits to the upper world but that for his disobedience he would live in the ground and would have to die and be reborn each year.

Then it was time for the sister-spirits to emerge. Instructed by Tsichtinako, they took the baskets, Badger, and Locust, climbed the pine tree to the hole above, and broke through into the world. There they stood waiting until the sun appeared in what Tsichtinako had told them was the east. They had learned the other three directions from her, too, as well as a prayer to the sun, which they now recited, and the song of creation, which they sang for the first time.

Tsichtinako revealed that she had been sent to be their constant guide by the creator, Uchtsiti, who had made the world from a clot of his blood. The sisters were to complete the creation by giving life to the things in the baskets. This they did by planting the seeds and breathing life into the animals, but when the first night came the sisters were afraid and called on Tsichtinako, who explained that the dark time was for sleep and that the sun would return.

The creation was duly completed by the sisters, who took the names Iatiku (Life-Bringer) and Nautsiti (Full Basket). Some say the sisters quarreled and that Nautsiti disobeyed their father by giving birth to two sons fathered by hot rain drops from the rainbow and that, as punishment, the sisters were deserted by Tsichtinako.

It is said that one of the boys was brought up by Iatiku. When he was old enough, he became his aunt's husband. Together they made the people. Some say that Iatiku later created the spirits, or kachinas, who would spend part of the year in the sacred mountains and part of the year with the people dancing for them in a way that would bring rain.

[David A. Leeming, *A Dictionary of Creation Myths* (Oxford University Press, 1994), pp. 3–5.]

DARWIN: Origins

Charles Darwin's theory of evolution stands in opposition to traditional stories of creation. It is considered merely a theory—a myth—by many religious fundamentalists today, but it is generally accepted by the scientific community. According to Darwin's concept of evolution, all of life descended from a common source and developed gradually over time from a simple to a more complex structure based on "natural selection," a natural drive in life forms for survival. In short, natural selection makes it possible for species to compete more efficiently for whatever they need to survive. In common parlance, when we apply this theory to human society, we speak of the "survival of the fittest." Darwin, however, referred to a gradual process by which organisms evolve over long periods of time. Darwin wrote, "Natural selection acts only by taking advantage of slight successive variations; she can never take a great and sudden leap, but must advance by short and sure, though slow steps." In other words, the idea of creation ex nihilo, by emergence, from a primal egg or any other instantaneous means would be impossible in Darwin's conception.

MODERN PHYSICS: The Big Bang

Creation stories are treated as truth by the culture from which they emerge—at least until they are "exposed" as mere myths. One creation story of modern culture is the big bang theory. Like all other creation myths, this one reveals the priorities of a culture; it is a record of our culture's understanding of its own place in the universe and its sense of what the universe is. It is told here by Brian Swimme in the form of an interview between a man called Thomas, whose ideas reflect those of the philosopher Thomas Berry, and a youth who is simultaneously the author and the collective voice of our curiosity.

YOUTH: Where should we start?

THOMAS: At the beginning. We need to start with the story of the universe as a whole. Our emergent cosmos is the fundamental context for all discussions of value, meaning, purpose, or ultimacy of any sort. To speak of the universe's origin is to bring to mind the great silent fire at the beginning of time.

Imagine that furnace out of which everything came forth. This was a fire that filled the universe—that *was* the universe. There was no place in the universe free from it. Every point of the cosmos was a point of this explosion of light. And all the particles of the universe churned in extremes of heat and pressure, all that we see about us, all that now exists was there at the beginning, in that great burning explosion of light.

YOUTH: How do we know about it?

THOMAS: We can see it! We can see the light from the primeval fireball. Or at least the light from its edge, for it burned for nearly a million years. We can see the dawn of the universe because the light from its edge reaches us only now, after traveling twenty billion years to get here.

YOUTH: We can see the actual light from the fireball?

THOMAS: When you see a candle's flame, you see the light from the candle. In that sense, we see the fireball. We are able to interact physically with photons from the beginning of time.

YOUTH: So we're in direct contact with the origin of the universe?

THOMAS: That's right.

YOUTH: I can't believe I didn't know this.

THOMAS: Scientists have only just learned to see the fireball. The light has always been there, but the ability to respond to it required a tremendous development of the human senses. Just as an artist learns to see a lakeshore's subtle shades and contours, the human race learns to develop its sensitivities to what is present. It took millions of years to develop, but humans can now interact with the cosmic radiation from the origin of the universe. We can now see the beginnings of time—a stupendous achievement.

YOUTH: It's amazing.

THOMAS: Most amazing is this realization that every thing that exists in the universe came from a common origin. The material of your body and the material of my body are intrinsically related because they emerged from and are caught up in a single energetic event. Our ancestry stretches back through the life forms and into the stars, back to the beginnings of the primeval fireball. This universe is a single multiform energetic unfolding of matter, mind, intelligence, and life. And all of this is new. None of the great figures of human history were aware of this. Not Plato, or Aristotle, or the Hebrew Prophets, or Confucius, or Thomas Aquinas, or Leibniz, or Newton, or any other worldmaker. We are the first generation to live with an empirical view of the origin of the universe. We are the first humans to look into the night sky and see the birth of stars, the birth of galaxies, the birth of the cosmos as a whole. Our future as a species will be forged within this new story of the world....

[Brian Swimme, *The Universe Is a Green Dragon: A Cosmic Creation Story* (Santa Fe, NM, 1984), pp. 27–29.]

BIBLIOGRAPHY

✦

An important contribution to the study of cosmogonic myths has been made by Mircea Eliade, who sees the creation story as the basis for all myth. See especially *Cosmos and History: The Myth of the Eternal Return* (New York, 1954); *Gods, Goddesses, and Myths of Creation* (New York, 1974); *Myth and Reality* (New York, 1963); and *Patterns in Comparative Religion* (New York, 1958). Charles H. Long's *Alpha: The Myths of Creation* (New York, 1963) is a comprehensive collection of creation myths. Also useful is Long's overview entitled "Cosmogony" in *The Encyclopedia of Religion*, ed. Mircea Eliade (New York, 1987), vol. 4, pp. 94–100. Barbara C. Sproul's *Primal Myths: Creation Myths Around the World* (San Francisco, 1991) is a valuable source for the myths themselves. David and Margaret Leeming's *A Dictionary of Creation Myths* (Oxford University Press, 1994) is another useful source. An excellent feminist approach to creation is Marta Weigle's *Creation and Procreation: Feminist Reflections on Mythologies of Cosmogony and Parturition* (Philadelphia: University of Pennsylvania Press, 1989). The most extensive collection of creation myths and analyses of them is David Leeming's two-volume *Creation Myths of the World: An Encyclopedia* (Santa Barbara, CA: ABC-CLIO, 2010).

THE FLOOD

The flood myth is common to many cultures, partly because floods, like great earthquakes and other natural disasters, are distinctly memorable. Floods do occur, and when they do, the destruction and loss are frequently so total as to suggest a cosmic conspiracy of some sort and, necessarily, the hope of a new beginning. The flood myths that emerge from the human psyche, therefore, tend to be dual in nature. The pattern behind the many forms that the flood myth takes is the archetype of the productive sacrifice. Thus, Jung could write of the "Noah's Ark that crosses the waters of death and leads to a rebirth of all life" (*The Archetypes and the Collective Unconscious,* p. 353). The Deluge cleanses and gives birth to new forms even as it destroys the old. It is the breaking of the eternal waters of the Great Mother—the destructive mother who, whether her name is Kali or Demeter, sweeps away the old life but preserves the germ of a new beginning. The Noah or the Utnapishtim or the Manu who is spared is the hero of new life who is born of the cosmic waters of the womb of the Great Mother. The flood myth, like the myths of the Destroyer-Mother herself, reminds us that life depends on death, that without death there can be no cycle, no birth.

That the new creation is preceded by a flood is appropriate, since the first life itself emerged from the waters. The flood myth, like the original creation myth, is what Mircea Eliade calls a "festival" of productive chaos, a "restoration of primordial chaos, and the repetition of the cosmogonic act" (*The Myth of the Eternal Return,* pp. 57–59).

The flood myth has personal as well as universal ramifications. Rituals of purification by water are microcosmic versions of the Deluge. In Christianity, for example, the baptized "sinner" immersed in the waters of the font-womb dies to the old life and on emerging is born into the new. Just as the hero descends into the underworld to confront death itself, the baptized individual symbolically overcomes the destructive powers of chaos. J. Danielou writes,

> The flood . . . was an image which baptism comes to fulfill. . . . Just as Noah had confronted the Sea of Death in which sinful humanity had been destroyed, and had emerged from it, so the newly baptized man descends into the baptismal piscina to confront the water Dragon in a supreme combat from which he emerges victorious. (*Sacramentum futuri,* p. 65)

Finally, in psychological terms, the flood myth, like the story of the hero's descent into the underworld, can be seen as a metaphor for the individual's necessary time in the dark world of the unconscious before the rebirth that is the achievement of individuation.

MESOPOTAMIA (SUMER-BABYLON): Utnapishtim (Ziusudra)

In the eleventh tablet of the Semitic Babylonian epic of the legendary king Gilgamesh, we find a flood story that is clearly the source for the Old Testament Noah story. The Gilgamesh story itself is based on an earlier, third-millennium B.C.E. myth of the Sumerians. In the Sumerian myth, the gods decide to destroy humankind with a flood. The god Enki, disagreeing with this decision, instructs a worthy man named Ziusudra, who narrates the tale, to build a great boat in which to save himself, his family, and a few other people, as well as animals. In the later second-millennium B.C.E. Babylonian version, Ziusudra has become Utnapishtim, and Enki has become Ea.

> Ut-napishtim spoke to him, to Gilgamesh,
> "Let me reveal to you a closely guarded matter,
>   Gilgamesh,
> And let me tell you the secret of the gods.
> Shuruppak is a city that you yourself know,
> Situated [on the bank of] the Euphrates.
> That city was already old when the gods within it
> Decided that the great gods should make a flood.
> There was Anu their father,
> Warrior Ellil their counsellor,
> Ninurta was their chamberlain,
> Ennugi their canal-controller.
> Far-sighted Ea swore the oath (of secrecy) with them,
> So he repeated their speech to a reed hut,
> 'Reed hut, reed hut, brick wall, brick wall,
> Listen, reed hut, and pay attention, brick wall:
> (This is the message:)
> Man of Shuruppak, son of Ubara-Tutu,
> Dismantle your house, build a boat.
> Leave possessions, search out living things.
> Reject chattels and save lives!
> Put aboard the seed of all living things, into the boat.
> The boat that you are to build
> Shall have her dimensions in proportion,
> Her width and length shall be in harmony,

Roof her like the Apsu.'
I realized and spoke to my master Ea,
'I have paid attention to the words that you spoke in this way,
My master, and I shall act upon them.
But how can I explain myself to the city, the men and the elders?'
Ea made his voice heard and spoke,
He said to me, his servant,
'You shall speak to them thus:
"I think that Ellil has rejected me,
And so I cannot stay in your city,
And I cannot set foot on Ellil's land again.
I must go down to the Apsu and stay with my master Ea.
Then he will shower abundance upon you,
A wealth of fowl, a treasure of fish.
[   ] prosperity, a harvest,
In the morning cakes/ "darkness,"
In the evening a rain of wheat/ "heaviness" he
    will shower upon you.
When the first light of dawn appeared
The country gathered about me.
The carpenter brought his axe,
The reed-worker brought his stone,
The young men [. . .]
[   ]
Children carried the bitumen,
The poor fetched what was needed [ ].
ii On the fifth day I laid down her form.
    One acre was her circumference, ten poles each the height of her walls,
    Her top edge was likewise ten poles all round.
    I laid down her structure, drew it out,
    Gave her six decks,
    Divided her into seven.
    Her middle I divided into nine,
    Drove the water pegs into her middle.
    I saw to the paddles and put down what was needed:
    Three *sar* of bitumen I poured into the kiln,
    Three *sar* of pitch I poured into the inside.
    Three *sar* of oil they fetched, the workmen who
        carried the baskets.

Not counting the *sar* of oil which the dust (?) soaked up,
The boatman stowed away two more *sar* of oil.
[. . .] I slaughtered oxen.
I sacrificed sheep every day.
I gave the workmen ale and beer to drink,
Oil and wine as if they were river water
They made a feast, like the New Year's Day festival.
When the sun [rose (?)] I provided hand oil.
[When] the sun went down the boat was complete.
[The launching was (?)] very difficult;
Launching rollers had to be fetched (from) above
     (to) below.
Two-thirds of it [stood clear of the water
     line (?)].
I loaded her with everything there was,
Loaded her with all the silver,
Loaded her with all the gold
Loaded her with all the seed of living things, all
     of them.
I put on board the boat all my kith and kin.
Put on board cattle from open country, wild
     beasts from open country, all kinds of
          craftsmen.
Shamash had fixed the hour:
'In the morning cakes/ "darkness,"
In the evening a rain of wheat/ "heaviness"
(I) shall shower down:
Enter into the boat and shut your door!'
That hour arrived;
In the morning cakes/ "darkness," in the evening
     a rain of wheat/ "heaviness" showered down.
I saw the shape of the storm,
The storm was terrifying to see.
I went aboard the boat and closed the door.
To seal the boat I handed over the (floating)
     palace with her cargo to Puzur-Amurru the
          boatman.
When the first light of dawn appeared,
A black cloud came up from the base of the sky.
Adad kept rumbling inside it.

Shullat and Hanish were marching ahead,
Marched as chamberlains (over) (?) mountain and
    country.
Erakal pulled out the mooring (?) poles,
Ninurta marched on and made the weir(s)
    overflow.
The Anunnaki had to carry torches,
They lit up the land with their brightness.
The calm before the Storm-god came over the
    sky,
Everything light turned to darkness.
[   ]

iii On the first day the tempest [rose up],
Blew swiftly and [brought (?) the flood-weapon],
Like a battle force [the destructive *kašūšu*-
    weapon] passed over [the people]
No man could see his fellow,
Nor could people be distinguished from the
    sky.
Even the gods were afraid of the flood-weapon.
They withdrew; they went up to the heaven of
    Anu.
The gods cowered, like dogs crouched by an
    outside wall.
Ishtar screamed like a woman giving birth;
The Mistress of the Gods, sweet of voice, was
    wailing,
'Has that time really returned to clay,
Because I spoke evil in the gods' assembly?
How could I have spoken such evil in the gods'
    assembly?
I should have (?) ordered a battle to destroy my
    people;
I myself gave birth (to them), they are my own
    people,
Yet they fill the sea like fish spawn!'
The gods of the Anunnaki were weeping with
    her.
The gods, humbled, sat there weeping.
Their lips were closed and covered with scab.

For six days and (seven (?)] nights
The wind blew, flood and tempest overwhelmed
    the land;
When the seventh day arrived the tempest, flood
    and onslaught
Which had struggled like a woman in labour,
    blew themselves out (?).
The sea became calm, the *imhullu*-wind grew
    quiet, the flood held back.
I looked at the weather; silence reigned,
For all mankind had returned to clay.
The flood-plain was flat as a roof.
I opened a porthole and light fell on my cheeks.
I bent down, then sat. I wept.
My tears ran down my cheeks.
I looked for banks, for limits to the sea.
Areas of land were emerging everywhere (?).
The boat had come to rest on Mount Nimush.
The mountain Nimush held the boat fast and did
    not let it budge.
The first and second day the mountain Nimush
    held the boat fast and did not let it budge.
The third and fourth day the mountain Nimush
    held the boat fast and did not let it budge.
The fifth and sixth day the mountain Nimush
    held the boat fast and did not let it budge.
When the seventh day arrived,
I put out and released a dove.
The dove went; it came back,
For no perching place was visible to it, and it
    turned round.
I put out and released a swallow.
The swallow went; it came back,
For no perching place was visible to it, and it
    turned round.
I put out and released a raven.
The raven went, and saw the waters receding.
And it ate, preened (?), lifted its tail and did not
    turn round.

Then I put (everything ?) out to the four winds,
    and I made a sacrifice,
Set out a *Surqinnu*-offering upon the mountain
    peak,
Arranged the jars seven and seven;
Into the bottom of them I poured (essences of ?)
    reeds, pine, and myrtle.
The gods smelt the fragrance,
The gods smelt the pleasant fragrance,
The gods like flies gathered over the sacrifice.
As soon as the Mistress of the Gods arrived

iv She raised the great flies which Anu had made to
    please her:
'Behold, O gods, I shall never forget (the
    significance of) my lapis lazuli necklace,
I shall remember these times, and I shall never
    forget.
Let other gods come to the *surqinnu*-offering
But let Ellil not come to the *surqinnu*-offering,
Because he did not consult before imposing the
    flood,
And consigned my people to destruction!'
As soon as Ellil arrived
He saw the boat. Ellil was furious,
Filled with anger at the Igigi gods.
'What sort of life survived? No man should have
    lived through the destruction!'
Ninurta made his voice heard and spoke,
He said to the warrior Ellil,
'Who other than Ea would have done such a
    thing?
For Ea can do everything!'
Ea made his voice heard and spoke,
He said to the warrior Ellil,
'You are the sage of the gods, warrior,
So how, O how, could you fail to consult, and
    impose the flood?
Punish the sinner for his sin, punish the criminal
    for his crime,

But ease off, let work not cease; be patient, . . .
Instead of your imposing a flood, let a lion come up
        and diminish the people.
Instead of your imposing a flood, let a wolf come
        up and diminish the people.
Instead of your imposing a flood, let famine be
        imposed and [lessen] the land.
Instead of your imposing a flood, let Erra rise up
        and savage the people.
I did not disclose the secret of the great gods,
I just showed Atrahasis a dream, and thus he
        heard the secret of the gods.'
Now the advice (that prevailed) was his advice.
Ellil came up into the boat,
And seized my hand and led me up.
He led up my woman and made her kneel down
        at my side.
He touched our foreheads, stood between us,
        blessed us:
'Until now Ut-napishtim was mortal,
But henceforth Ut-napishtim and his woman shall
        be as we gods are.
Ut-napishtim shall dwell far off at the mouth of
        the rivers.'
They took me and made me dwell far off, at the
        mouth of the rivers.

[Stephanie Dalley, trans., *Myths from Mesopotamia*
(Oxford University Press, revised 2000), pp. 109–116.]

ISRAEL: Noah

The Hebrew story in the Bible's Book of Genesis, although clearly based on the older Babylonian one, emphasizes the idea of humanity's sinfulness. The Flood is a punishment, and Noah is saved so that humankind can be reborn in a cleansed state. Whereas the Babylonian flood is the result of a whim of the gods, the Hebrew flood is harsh but constructive.

Chapter 6

... God saw that the wickedness of man was great in the earth, and that every imagination of the thoughts of his heart was only evil continually.

6 And it repented the Lord that he had made man on the earth, and it grieved him at his heart.

7 And the Lord said, I will destroy man whom I have created from the face of the earth; both man, and beast, and the creeping thing, and the fowls of the air; for it repenteth me that I have made them.

8 But Noah found grace in the eyes of the Lord.

9 These are the generations of Noah: Noah was a just man and perfect in his generations, and Noah walked with God.

10 And Noah begat three sons, Shem, Ham, and Jā´-phĕth.

11 The earth also was corrupt before God, and the earth was filled with violence.

12 And God looked upon the earth, and, behold, it was corrupt; for all flesh had corrupted his way upon the earth.

13 And God said unto Noah, The end of all flesh is come before me; for the earth is filled with violence through them; and, behold, I will destroy them with the earth.

14 Make thee an ark of gopher wood; rooms shalt thou make in the ark, and shalt pitch it within and without with pitch.

15 And this is the fashion which thou shalt make it of: The length of the ark shall be three hundred cubits, the breadth of it fifty cubits, and the height of it thirty cubits.

16 A window shalt thou make to the ark, and in a cubit shalt thou finish it above; and the door of the ark shalt thou set in the side thereof; with lower, second, and third stories shalt thou make it.

17 And, behold, I, even I, do bring a flood of waters upon the earth, to destroy all flesh, wherein is the breath of life, from under heaven; and every thing that is in the earth shall die.

18 But with thee will I establish my covenant; and thou shalt come into the ark, thou, and thy sons, and thy wife, and thy sons' wives with thee.

19 And of every living thing of all flesh, two of every sort shalt thou bring into the ark, to keep them alive with thee; they shall be male and female.

20 Of fowls after their kind, and of cattle after their kind, of every creeping thing of the earth after his kind, two of every sort shall come unto thee, to keep them alive.

21 And take thou unto thee of all food that is eaten, and thou shalt gather it to thee; and it shall be for food for thee, and for them.

22 Thus did Noah; according to all that God commanded him, so did he.

Chapter 7

And the Lord said unto Noah, Come thou and all thy house into the ark; for thee have I seen righteous before me in this generation.

2 Of every clean beast thou shalt take to thee by sevens, the male and his female: and of beasts that are not clean by two, the male and his female.

3 Of fowls also of the air by sevens, the male and the female; to keep seed alive upon the face of all the earth.

4 For yet seven days, and I will cause it to rain upon the earth forty days and forty nights; and every living substance that I have made will I destroy from off the face of the earth.

5 And Noah did according unto all that the Lord commanded him.

6 And Noah was six hundred years old when the flood of waters was upon the earth.

7 And Noah went in, and his sons, and his wife, and his sons' wives with him, into the ark, because of the waters of the flood.

8 Of clean beasts, and of beasts that are not clean, and of fowls, and of every thing that creepeth upon the earth.

9 There went in two and two unto Noah into the ark, the male and the female, as God had commanded Noah.

10 And it came to pass after seven days, that the waters of the flood were upon the earth.

11 In the six hundredth year of Noah's life, in the second month, the seventeenth day of the month, the same day were all the fountains of the great deep broken up, and the windows of heaven were opened.

12 And the rain was upon the earth forty days and forty nights.

13 In the selfsame day entered Noah, and Shem, and Ham, and Jā´-phĕth, the sons of Noah, and Noah's wife, and the three wives of his sons with them, into the ark;

14 They, and every beast after his kind, and all the cattle after their kind, and every creeping thing that creepeth upon the earth after his kind, and every fowl after his kind, every bird of every sort.

15 And they went in unto Noah into the ark, two and two of all flesh, wherein *is* the breath of life.

16 And they that went in, went in male and female of all flesh, as God had commanded him: and the Lord shut him in.

17 And the flood was forty days upon the earth; and the waters increased, and bare up the ark, and it was lift up above the earth.

18 And the waters prevailed, and were increased greatly upon the earth; and the ark went upon the face of the waters.

19 And the waters prevailed exceedingly upon the earth; and all the high hills, that *were* under the whole heaven, were covered.

20 Fifteen cubits upward did the waters prevail; and the mountains were covered.

21 And all flesh died that moved upon the earth, both of fowl, and of cattle, and of beast, and of every creeping thing that creepeth upon the earth, and every man:

22 All in whose nostrils was the breath of life, of all that was in the dry land, died.

23 And every living substance was destroyed which was upon the face of the ground, both man, and cattle, and the creeping things, and the fowl of the heaven; and they were destroyed from the earth: and Noah only remained alive, and they that were with him in the ark.

24 And the waters prevailed upon the earth an hundred and fifty days.

Chapter 8

And God remembered Noah, and every living thing, and all the cattle that was with him in the ark: and God made a wind to pass over the earth, and the waters assuaged;

2 The fountains also of the deep and the windows of heaven were stopped, and the rain from heaven was restrained;

3 And the waters returned from off the earth continually: and after the end of the hundred and fifty days the waters were abated.

4 And the ark rested in the seventh month, on the seventeenth day of the month, upon the mountains of Ararat.

5 And the waters decreased continually until the tenth month: in the tenth month, on the first day of the month, were the tops of the mountains seen.

6 And it came to pass at the end of forty days, that Noah opened the window of the ark which he had made:

7 And he sent forth a raven, which went forth to and fro, until the waters were dried up from off the earth.

8 Also he sent forth a dove from him, to see if the waters were abated from off the face of the ground;

9 But the dove found no rest for the sole of her foot, and she returned unto him into the ark, for the waters were on the face of the whole earth: then he put forth his hand, and took her, and pulled her in unto him into the ark.

10 And he stayed yet other seven days; and again he sent forth the dove out of the ark;

11 And the dove came in to him in the evening; and, lo, in her mouth was an olive leaf plucked off: so Noah knew that the waters were abated from off the earth.

12 And he stayed yet other seven days; and sent forth the dove; which returned not again unto him any more.

13 And it came to pass in the six hundredth and first year, in the first month, the first day of the month, the waters were dried up from off the earth: and Noah removed the covering of the ark, and looked, and, behold, the face of the ground was dry.

14 And in the second month, on the seven and twentieth day of the month, was the earth dried.

15 And God spake unto Noah, saying,

16 Go forth of the ark, thou, and thy wife, and thy sons, and thy sons' wives with thee.

17 Bring forth with thee every living thing that is with thee, of all flesh, both of fowl, and of cattle, and of every creeping thing that creepeth upon the earth; that they may breed abundantly in the earth, and be fruitful, and multiply upon the earth.

18 And Noah went forth, and his sons, and his wife, and his sons' wives with him:

19 Every beast, every creeping thing, and every fowl, and whatsoever creepeth upon the earth, after their kinds, went forth out of the ark.

20 And Noah builded an altar unto the Lord; and took of every clean beast, and of every clean fowl, and offered burnt offerings on the altar.

21 And the Lord smelled a sweet savour; and the Lord said in his heart, I will not again curse the ground any more for man's sake; for the imagination of man's heart is evil from his youth; neither will I again smite any more every thing living, as I have done.

22 While the earth remaineth, seedtime and harvest, and cold and heat, and summer and winter, and day and night shall not cease.

Chapter 9

And God blessed Noah and his sons, and said unto them, Be fruitful, and multiply, and replenish the earth.

2 And the fear of you and the dread of you shall be upon every beast of the earth, and upon every fowl of the air, upon all that moveth upon the earth, and upon all the fishes of the sea; into your hand are they delivered.

3 Every moving thing that liveth shall be meat for you; even as the green herb have I given you all things.

4 But flesh with the life thereof, which is the blood thereof, shall ye not eat.

5 And surely your blood of your lives will I require; at the hand of every beast will I require it, and at the hand of man; at the hand of every man's brother will I require the life of man.

6 Whoso sheddeth man's blood, by man shall his blood be shed: for in the image of God made he man.

7 And you, be ye fruitful, and multiply; bring forth abundantly in the earth, and multiply therein.

8 And God spake unto Noah, and to his sons with him, saying,

9 And I, behold, I establish my covenant with you, and with your seed after you;

10 And with every living creature that is with you, of the fowl, of the cattle, and of every beast of the earth with you; from all that go out of the ark, to every beast of the earth.

11 And I will establish my covenant with you; neither shall all flesh be cut off any more by the waters of a flood; neither shall there any more be a flood to destroy the earth.

12 And God said, This is the token of the covenant which I make between me and you and every living creature that is with you, for perpetual generations:

13 I do set my bow in the cloud, and it shall be for a token of a covenant between me and the earth.

14 And it shall come to pass, when I bring a cloud over the earth, that the bow shall be seen in the cloud:

15 And I will remember my covenant, which is between me and you and every living creature of all flesh; and the waters shall no more become a flood to destroy all flesh.

16 And the bow shall be in the cloud; and I will look upon it, that I may remember the everlasting covenant between God and every living creature of all flesh that is upon the earth.

17 And God said unto Noah, This is the token of the covenant, which I have established between me and all flesh that *is* upon the earth.

18 And the sons of Noah, that went forth of the ark, were Shem, and Ham, and Jā´-phĕth: and Ham is the father of Cā´-nă-ăn.

19 These are the three sons of Noah: and of them was the whole earth overspread.

20 And Noah began to be a husbandman, and he planted a vineyard:

21 And he drank of the wine, and was drunken; and he was uncovered within his tent.

22 And Ham, the father of Cā´-nă-ăn, saw the nakedness of his father, and told his two brethren without.

23 And Shem and Jā´-phĕth took a garment, and laid it upon both their shoulders, and went backward, and covered the nakedness of their father; and their faces were backward, and they saw not their father's nakedness.

24 And Noah awoke from his wine, and knew what his younger son had done unto him.

25 And he said, Cursed be Cā´-nă-ăn; a servant of servants shall he be unto his brethren.

26 And he said, Blessed be the Lord God of Shem; and Cā´-nă-ăn shall be his servant.

27 God shall enlarge Jā´-phĕth, and he shall dwell in the tents of Shem; and Cā´-nă-ăn shall be his servant.

28 And Noah lived after the flood three hundred and fifty years.

29 And all the days of Noah were nine hundred and fifty years: and he died.

[Genesis 6:5–9.]

IRAN (ZOROASTRIAN): Yima

In the Zoroastrian tradition, the Noah figure is Yima, and the high god is Ahura Mazda.

> When the world had become overwhelmed by the constant multiplication of its immortal beings, Ahura Mazda decided that the earth must be enlarged and a new beginning made. He warned the faithful king Yima that a great flood was coming to cleanse the world and that Yima had to protect himself and two of each species in his castle on top of the highest mountain. The flood came, and the world, except for Yima's castle and its inhabitants, was destroyed. When the flood passed, Yima opened his doors and the world was inhabited again.
>
> [David A. Leeming, *A Dictionary of Asian Mythology*
> (Oxford University Press, 2001), p. 211.]

FLOODS CLEAR FAILURES

EGYPT: Hathor, Blood and Beer

In an ancient text known as *The Book of the Heavenly Cow*, a copy of which was found in the tomb of King Tutankhamun, one of the strangest of the world's many flood myths features the great goddess Hathor, the Eye of the supreme god Ra. As the Eye of Ra, Hathor is "the Eye of Heaven," the sun itself. This myth, like the flood myth in Genesis and the Mayan *Popol Vuh* story, for instance, tells of a flood sent by the gods in reaction to what they perceive as a failure in the creation of humans.

> After Ra had become the ruler of both gods and men, Humanity plotted against him, while his majesty, may he live, may he prosper, may he be healthy, had grown old. His bones became silver, his flesh became gold, his hair true lapis-lazuli. When his majesty saw how humanity was plotting against him, his majesty said to his followers, "Summon for me, my Eye, Shu, Tefnut, Geb, Nut and the father and mothers who were with me when I was in the primeval waters, as well as the god Nun. Let him bring his followers with him, but bring them secretly in case the humans see and their hearts escape."

The gods and goddesses all came and asked Ra to speak. He told them, "Humanity, which came into being from my Eye, is plotting against me. Advise me what you would do about it." Nun and the other deities advise Ra to send his Eye against the rebels. "No Eye is more able to smite them. Let it go down as Hathor."

The guilty ones among humanity flee into the desert through fear of Ra, but Hathor slaughters them and wades in their blood. When she returns to Ra, she tells him that she has "overpowered humanity and it was sweet to my heart." Ra replies, "I shall have power over them as king by culling them." Thus, says the text, "the Powerful One came into being."

The goddess intends to continue her slaughter the next day, but for reasons that are not explained, Ra has changed his mind. He summons messengers who can travel as fast as shadows and sends them to fetch a large quantity of a red mineral. Then he orders the Side-Lock Wearer in Heliopolis, a title of the high priest of Ra, to grind up the mineral while his maid servants mash barley to make beer. They make 7,000 jars of beer and add the red mineral to it to make the beer look like blood. Ra has the beer taken to the place where the goddess plans to destroy humanity. Before dawn Ra pours the red beer out until the fields are flooded to a depth of "three palms." When the goddess arrives at dawn, she sees her own beautiful reflection in the flood. "She drank and it delighted her heart. She came back drunk without having noticed humanity." Ra welcomed her back and from that day on alcohol was drunk during the festivals of Hathor.

[Geraldine Pinch, *Egyptian Mythology*
(Oxford University Press, 2002), pp. 74–75.]

CHINA: Yü   OVERCOMING FEARS

The flood theme is one of the very oldest in Chinese mythology. A flood myth from the *Shu ching* in the Chou dynasty—perhaps from as early as 1000 B.C.E.—reveals a distinctly nonmystical sense of the gods and is clearly earth oriented. The emphasis is on a very practical matter, the channeling of unruly water in such a way as to make cultivation of the land possible. We are told that tremendous flood waters were spreading everywhere, even up to Heaven. Answering the desperate appeals of the people, the high god Ti called on Kun to stop the flood. Kun labored against the flood for nine years without success and was executed. Kun's son Yu was ordered to take up the task.

The greatest deed that Yu performed was that he stopped the world flood. A version tells that Yu was commanded by the Supreme Divinity to spread Xirang to control the floodwaters and stabilize the world. In another popular version, Yu was recommended to King Yao by Shun to fight against the flood. However it is recounted, being born of Gun's indomitable spirit, Yu continued his father's unfinished work as he grew.

It is said that in dealing with this difficult task, Yu suffered and struggled for thirteen years. He devoted himself thoroughly to the mission of stopping the flood, so that he did not visit his home even once during this long term. According to a famous story, even when he had three opportunities to pass by his home, he did not go into his house. This virtue of selflessness and strong-mindedness won him great respect from people in later times.

As a wise and astute hero, he sought assistance from different mythical helpers and performed many miracles in battling the flood. Differing from the method of only barricading against the overflowing water with soil his father had used, Yu mainly applied a strategy to channel the floodwater into the sea together with building barricades. Evidence for this can be found in an account in "Tianwen." It states in a questioning style, "The whirlpool was so deep, how could Yu fill it in with mud? How did Yinglong (Responding Dragon) drag on the earth with his tail so that the flood was channeled into the sea?" A similar depiction may be found in another text from *Shiyiji* (*Researches into Lost Records*, ca. fourth century). It mentions that when Yu was on his mission of stopping the flood, Yinglong dragged its tail to channel the water in front of him, while a huge black turtle carrying green mud followed him.

Many stories mention Yu getting help from different gods. One of the popular versions is that he was given a detailed map for controlling the flood by He Bo, the god of the Yellow River (*he* literally means "river," and *bo* means "master" or "god"). It was said that He Bo used to be a human being named Fengyi (sometimes Pingyi or Bingyi; names differ in some versions). He was drowned while ferrying the Yellow River. The Supreme Divinity had compassion for him, so that he appointed Fengyi to be the god of the river. When Yu started his mission of flood control with an investigation of the situation at the Yellow River, a god with a white human face and a fish trunk emerged from the water. He told Yu that he was He Bo, and he gave a map of the locations of rivers to Yu. Then he dove into the river again. With this map, Yu got the big picture concerning the situation of world flooding and made reasonable methods to deal with it, which helped him greatly in stopping the flood.

In order to control the flood, Yu defeated and controlled many different monsters that brought disasters to men. One example is that he executed Xiangliu, a nine-headed monster that, wherever it passed, turned land into marshes and gullies in which no animals could survive. Another example is that he controlled Wuzhiqi, the monster in the Huai River. When Yu traveled to Tongbai Mountain on his mission of flood control, several times he encountered gales and thunder made by the monster Wuzhiqi and its mythical followers, which prevented him from starting his work here. Yu became angry. He assembled all the gods and ordered Kui to clear all of the evils. Cods from Tongbai and other mountains who used to follow Wuzhiqi were scared, lo they yielded to Yu. Yu put some of them into jail and hence enticed Wuzhiqi, spirit of the Huai River, to appear. It appeared as a monkey with a green trunk, white head, yellow eyes, and white paws. Its neck reached nearly 100 feet when stretched, and its strength was as powerful as that of nine elephants. The monster was good at talking, very smart, and quick to act. After failing several times in choosing a person among his subordinate gods to control the monster, Yu finally found that Gengchen was the right choice, capable of controlling Wuzhiqi. Gengchen drove away all kinds of demons that came to disturb his work. He tied Wuzhiqi's neck with a thick and sturdy chain, pierced its nose with a golden bell, and kept it at the foot of Gui Mountain. From then on the Huai River was under control.

Because he could not only defeat and execute demons or gods who disobeyed his orders but also govern all the gods, Yu was identified by some scholars as the Supreme Divinity. This assumption might be supported by the stories about his banishing Gonggong, the water god, and killing Fangfeng, a god and giant who arrived late to his assembly of gods.

Among the Yu myths, stories about Yu and his wife, a lady from Tushan, are very rich in detail. It is said that Yu did not marry until he was thirty years old, when he passed by Tushan on his travels to control the flood. According to an account from early texts, Yu was afraid that he would transgress the moral rite of passage that required a man to marry by the age of thirty; he therefore prayed for an omen to signify his marriage. Immediately after this, a white fox with nine tails appeared to him. Yu explained this as an omen that he would marry a girl from the Tushan clan. He thus made his marriage with Tushanshi, the girl from Tushan (*shi* here is an address for a married woman).

Some versions tell that on the fifth day after he got married, Yu left his wife and continued his work of controlling the flood. Nevertheless, a lot of stories mention that Yu was working with his wife's help. The most well-known is that about Yu changing into a bear. When Yu was starting to excavate through a mountain in order to channel the flood to the sea, he told Tushanshi, "Please send me food whenever you hear the drum." Then he went to the mountain and changed into a bear to cut off the mountains and rocks. While working, he stepped on the drum by error. Hearing the drum, Tushanshi brought food to her husband. Yu was unaware of his wife's presence, and he continued to work as a bear. Tushanshi was ashamed of seeing that her husband had changed into a beast, so she fled. At the foot of the mountain, she began to change into a stone. This happened right at the time when she was going to give birth to a baby. When Yu finally found his wife, she had already become a rock. He asked the transformation of his wife to give him back the baby. The rock then split at the side facing the north. From the opening Yu's son, Qi, was born (*qi* literally means "open"). Qi later inherited his father's throne and became the first emperor of Xia, the first civilized state in China.

By working hard for thirteen years, Yu eventually stopped the flood. As a result, the world became dry, and people became settled again. Because of his great contribution to the world and because of his virtues, Yu was chosen by King Shun as the successor to his crown.

[Lihui Yang and Deming An, *Handbook of Chinese Mythology* (Oxford University Press, 2005), pp. 237–239, 239–240.]

INDIA: Manu   *GOD COMING TO THE RESCUE*

The story of Manu, who alone is saved from the great flood, must remind us of the Utnapishtim and Noah stories. Like the other flood heroes, Manu receives supernatural help and is saved by remaining in a ship until he is able to tie up on an Indian version of Mount Ararat. The story is told in the *Shatapatha-Brahmana*.

1. In the morning they brought to Manu water for washing, just as now also they (are wont to) bring (water) for washing the hands. When he was washing himself, a fish came into his hands.

2. It spake to him the word, "Rear me, I will save thee!" "Wherefrom wilt thou save me?" "A flood will carry away all these creatures: from that I will save thee!" "How am I to rear thee?"

3. It said, "As long as we are small, there is great destruction for us: fish devours fish. Thou wilt first keep me in a jar. When I outgrow that, thou wilt dig a pit and keep me in it. When I outgrow that, thou wilt take me down to the sea, for then I shall be beyond destruction."

4. It soon became a *ghasha* (a great fish); for that grows largest (of all fish). There-upon it said, "In such and such a year that flood will come. Thou shalt then attend to me (i.e., to my advice) by preparing a ship; and when the flood has risen thou shalt enter into the ship, and I will save thee from it."

5. After he had reared it in this way, he took it down to the sea. And in the same year which the fish had indicated to him, he attended to (the advice of the fish) by preparing a ship; and when the flood had risen, he entered into the ship. The fish then swam up to him, and to its horn he tied the rope of the ship, and by that means he passed swiftly up to yonder northern mountain.

6. It then said, "I have saved thee. Fasten the ship to a tree; but let not the water cut thee off whilst thou art on the mountain. As the water subsides, thou mayest gradually descend!" Accordingly he gradually descended and hence that (slope) of the northern mountain is called "Manu's descent." The flood then swept away all these creatures, and Manu alone remained here.

[Mircea Eliade, *Gods, Goddesses, and Myths of Creation*
(New York, 1974), p. 151.]

GREECE-ROME: Deucalion and Pyrrha

Ovid tells the story of Jupiter's decision to punish humanity for its sins by means of a great cleansing flood. Only one righteous couple, Deucalion and Pyrrha, are saved. Their boat eventually lands on Mount Parnassus, a mountain sacred to the ancient Greeks. It seems likely that this story was directly influenced by those of the Hebrews and Babylonians.

THE FLOOD

Swiftly within the Wind-god's cave he locked
The north wind and the gales that drive away
The gathered clouds, and sent the south wind forth;
And out on soaking wings the south wind flew,
His ghastly features veiled in deepest gloom.
His beard was sodden with rain, his white hair drenched;
Mists wreathed his brow and streaming water fell

From wings and chest; and when in giant hands
He crushed the hanging clouds, the thunder crashed
And storms of blinding rain poured down from heaven.
Iris, great Juno's envoy, rainbow-clad,
Gathered the waters and refilled the clouds.
The crops lay flat; the farmer mourned his hopes;
The long year's labour died, vain labour lost.
      Nor was Jove's wrath content with heaven above;
His sea-blue brother brings his waters' aid,
And summons all the rivers to attend
Their master's palace. "Now time will not wait
For many words," he says; "pour out your strength—
The need is great! Unbar your doors! Away
With dykes and dams and give your floods free rein!"
The streams returned and freed their fountains' flow
And rolled in course unbridled to the sea.
Then with his trident Neptune struck the earth,
Which quaked and moved to give the waters way.
In vast expanse across the open plains
The rivers spread and swept away together
Crops, orchards, vineyards, cattle, houses, men,
Temples and shrines with all their holy things.
If any home is left and, undestroyed,
Resists the huge disaster, over its roof,
The waters meet and in their whirling flood
High towers sink from sight; now land and sea
Had no distinction; over the whole earth
All things were sea, a sea without a shore.
Some gained the hilltops, others took to boats
And rowed where late they ploughed; some steered a course
Above the cornfields and the farmhouse roofs,
And some caught fishes in the lofty elms.
Perchance in the green meads an anchor dropped
And curving keels brushed through the rows of vines,
And where but now the graceful goats had browsed
Gross clumsy seals hauled their ungainly bulk.
The Nereids see with awe beneath the waves
Cities and homes and groves, and in the woods
The dolphins live and high among the branches
Dash to and fro and shake the oaks in play.

Wolves swim among the sheep, and on the waters
Tigers are borne along and tawny lions.
No more his lightning stroke avails the boar
Nor his swift legs the stag—both borne away.
The wandering birds long seek a resting place
And drop with weary wings into the sea.
The waters' boundless licence overwhelmed
The hills, and strange waves lashed the mountain peaks.
The world was drowned; those few the deluge spared
For dearth of food in lingering famine died.

DEUCALION AND PYRRHA

Between Boeotia and the Oetean hills
The land of Phocis lies, a fertile land
When land it was, but now part of the sea,
A spreading wilderness of sudden waters.
There a great mountain aims towards the stars
Its double peak, Parnassus, soaring high
Above the clouds; and there Deucalion,
Borne on a raft, with his dear wife beside,
Had grounded; all elsewhere the deluge whelmed.
Praise and thanksgiving to the mountain's gods
And nymphs they gave, and to the prophetess,
Themis, then guardian of the oracle;
No man was better, none loved goodness more
Than he, no woman more devout than she.
And when Jove saw the world a waste of waters,
And of so many millions but one man,
And of so many millions but one woman
Alive, both innocent, both worshippers,
He bade the clouds disperse, the north wind drive
The storms away, and to the earth revealed
The heavens again and to the sky the earth.
Spent was the anger of the sea; the Lord
Who rules the main laid by his three-pronged spear
And calmed the waves and, calling from the deep
Triton, sea-hued, his shoulders barnacled
With sea-shells, bade him blow his echoing conch
To bid the rivers, waves and floods retire.

He raised his horn, his hollow spiralled whorl,
The horn that, sounded in mid ocean, fills
The shores of dawn and sunset round the world;
And when it touched the god's wet-bearded lips
And took his breath and sounded the retreat,
All the wide waters of the land and sea
Heard it, and all, hearing its voice, obeyed,
The sea has shores again, the rivers run
Brimming between their banks, the floods subside,
The hills emerge, the swelling contours rise;
As the floods lessen, larger grows the land,
And after many days the woods reveal
Their tree-tops bare and branches lined with mud.
    Earth was restored; but when Deucalion
Saw the deep silence of the desolate lands
And the wide empty wastes, in tears he said:
"Pyrrha, my dearest cousin, dearest wife,
Sole woman left alive, whom ties of blood
And family, then marriage, joined to me,
And now our perils join, in all the lands
The sun beholds from dawn to eve we two
Remain, their peoples—the sea has claimed the rest.
Yet even now our lives are scarce assured,
And still the clouds strike terror in my heart.
Suppose, poor soul, the Fates had rescued you
Alone, what would you feel, how could you face
Your fear without me? Who would staunch your grief?
Be sure that, if the sea had held you too,
I'd follow you; the sea would hold me too.
O for my father's magic to restore
Mankind again and in the moulded clay
Breathe life and so repopulate the world!
Now on us two the human race depends—
So Heaven wills—us, patterns of mankind."
They wept together; then resolved to pray
To Powers above and heavenly guidance seek
In oracles; and quickly, hand in hand,
Went to Cephisus' stream, whose current ran
Not limpid yet but in his wonted course,
And there, in ritual due with holy water

Sprinkling their heads and clothes, they turned their steps
Towards the holy shrine (a pale scum fouled
Its roofs; the altars stood without a flame).
They reached the temple steps and then, prostrate,
With timid lips both kissed the cold wet stone
And said: "If righteous prayers may move and soften
The Powers divine, may turn their wrath away,
Tell, holy Themis, by what art our race,
Now lost, may be restored: in thy great mercy
Hear and grant succour to a world submerged."
The goddess, pitying, gave her answer: "Leave
My temple, veil your heads, loosen your robes,
And cast behind you your great mother's bones."
Long did they wait bewildered, until Pyrrha,
Breaking the silence first, refused assent
And asked in trembling tones the goddess's pardon,
Not daring to offend her mother's ghost
By violence to her bones. In vain they sought
The hidden meaning, searching to and fro
The baffling words' blind coverts. Then at last
Prometheus' son calmed Epimetheus' daughter
With words of cheer: "Either my reasoning
Misleads me or in truth (since oracles
Are holy and will never counsel crime)
The earth is our great mother and the stones
Within earth's body surely are the bones
The oracle intends. These we must throw
Over our shoulders as Themis directs."
So he interpreted, and Pyrrha's heart
Was warmed, but still hope wavered, such distrust
Oppressed them both; and yet what harm to try?
They leave the temple, veil their heads, ungird
Their robes and, as the oracle commanded,
Behind them, past their footprints, throw the stones.
Those stones (who would believe did ancient lore
Not testify the truth?) gave up their hardness;
Their rigidness grew slowly soft and, softened,
Assumed a shape, and as they grew and felt
A gentler nature's touch, a semblance seemed
To appear, still indistinct, of human form,

Like the first rough-hewn marble of a statue,
Scarce modelled, or old uncouth images.
The earthy part, damp with some trace of moisture,
Was turned to flesh; what was inflexible
And solid changed to bone; what in the stones
Had been the veins retained the name of veins.
In a brief while, by Heaven's mysterious power,
The stones the man had thrown were formed as men,
Those from the woman's hand reshaped as women.
Hence we are hard, we children of the earth,
And in our lives of toil we prove our birth.

　　All other forms of life the earth brought forth,
In diverse species, of her own accord,
When the sun's radiance warmed the pristine moisture
And slime and oozy marshlands swelled with heat,
And in that pregnant soil the seeds of things,
Nourished as in a mother's womb, gained life
And grew and gradually assumed a shape.
So when the seven-mouthed Nile has left at last
The sodden acres and withdrawn its flow
Back to its ancient bed, and the fresh mud
Is warmed by the bright sunshine, farmers find,
Turning the clods, so many forms of life,
Some just begun, still in the stage of birth,
Others unfinished, short of proper parts,
And often, in one creature, part alive,
Part still raw soil. Because when heat and moisture
Blend in due balance, they conceive; these two,
These, are the origin of everything.
Though fire and water fight, humidity
And warmth create all things; that harmony,
So inharmonious, suits the springs of life.
Thus when the earth, deep-coated with the slime
Of the late deluge, glowed again beneath
The warm caresses of the shining sun,
She brought forth countless species, some restored
In ancient forms, some fashioned weird and new.

[Ovid, *Metamorphoses*, trans. A. D. Melville
(Oxford University Press, 1986), pp. 9–14.]

MESO-AMERICA (MAYAN): The *Popol-Vuh*

The *Popol-Vuh,* the sacred book of the Mayas, contains this strange creation story, which includes the destruction of an early, experimental form of humanity. The Flood here is used to erase a mistake rather than to punish sins. The mistake in question was in the creation of humanity. After various attempts at human creation, God created wooden men.

Then He made men out of wood. . . .; they could walk and talk. They built houses and had children, and there were very many of them. But they were dry and yellow, and their faces had no expression, because they had no minds nor souls nor hearts. They beat their dogs and they burned the bottoms of their cooking pots. They had forgotten how they were made, and could not remember any of the names of God. So He said: "These men will not do either. I must destroy them also."

And He sent a great flood, and the houses of the wooden men fell down. The wooden men wanted to escape, but the animals they had starved and beaten, and cooking pots they had burned, and the trees whose branches they had chopped off, all turned against them and wouldn't help them. Only a few of them escaped from the flood, and it is said that their descendants are the monkeys.

And still it hadn't dawned; and God wanted to make real men when the dawn came and the sun rose.

He thought about it, and He saw that the earth and the sky were not yet ready and that there were things that had to be done before the sun could move and make light and man could be made. He saw that He had to send two parts of Himself to put things in order. These two needed two sons of their own to help them, but at last all was ready, and the two sons entered the sun and moon to make them move.

Then God said: "It is time. I need men on the earth who will know My names, who will obey Me and love Me; and that will nourish and sustain Me."

He pondered deeply and discovered the way to make man.

He found a beautiful valley full of many plants and fruits, and He took ears of yellow corn and of white corn and ground them into meal. With the corn meal He made nine kinds of liquor, and these became man's strength and energies. With the dough of the meal He shaped the body. And He made four men, very strong and handsome.

While the men slept, he made four women very carefully, and when the men woke, each found at his side a beautiful wife. And they were very happy when they saw their wives.

The Creator said to the four men:

"You are alive. What do you think about it? You can see, and hear, and move, and speak. Do you like it? Look at the world! Try to see!"

The men looked and they were able to see the whole world and everything that was in it. They could see the whole sky. They could see everything. They began to give thanks to the Creator.

"Thank you for our life!" they said. "We can see, we can hear, we can move and think and speak, we feel and know everything, we can see everything in the earth and in the sky. Thank you for having made us, O our Father!"

Then the Creator was troubled, for He realized that these men could see too much and too far, so that they would not really be men, but gods. He saw that He had to change them so that they could be what He needed. So He leaned down and blew mist in their eyes and clouded their vision, like breathing on a mirror, and from then on nothing was clear to their sight except what was close to them.

The four men and their wives went up on a mountain and waited for the dawn. First, they saw the shining face of the great star, the Morning Star which comes ahead of the sun, and they burned incense and unwrapped three gifts to offer the sun.

And then the sun came up.

Then the puma and the jaguar roared, and all the birds stretched their wings and sang, and the men and their wives danced with joy because the sun had risen.

[Paul Jordan Smith, "In the Very Beginning," *Parabola* 2, no. 2 (Spring 1977), pp. 41–43.]

SOUTH AMERICA (INCAN): Viracocha and the Giants

Several Incan creation stories contain versions of a flood myth. In South American flood myths, like those of many parts of the rest of the world, a creator god destroys his own creation, which has somehow been corrupted.

In ancient times, after he made the world, Viracocha became angry at the giants he had created to live there. Because the giants were lazy and ungrateful and ill-natured, he decided to destroy them and their world. He sent a flood, which rose up to cover even the Andes themselves, and almost everything in the world perished. Only one human couple survived by floating in a box. When the flood subsided, the creator told the couple to settle in Tiahuanacu, where their box had drifted. Then, with the surviving couple, the creator made new people in Tiahuanacu. From the waters of the flood only the lakes of Titicaca and Poopo remained. Viracocha brought out the sun and the moon from the depths of Titicaca. Now his postflood new creation had light and warmth, and life could begin again.

BIBLIOGRAPHY

✦

For an overview of the flood myth, see Jean Rudhardt's article on the Flood in *The Encyclopedia of Religion*, ed. Mircea Eliade (New York, 1987, vol. 5, pp. 353–357). An important work on the relationship between the Babylonian and Hebrew floods is Alexander Heidel's *The Gilgamesh Epic and Old Testament Parallels* (Chicago, 1949, 1967). For an account of the development of the Gilgamesh flood story itself, see Jeffrey H. Tigay, *The Evolution of the Gilgamesh Epic* (Philadelphia, 1982). Samuel Noah Kramer's *Mythologies of the Ancient World* (New York, 1961) and his *Sumerian Mythology* (New York, 1961) are also useful on the Babylonian flood, as is Robert Best's *Noah's Ark and the Ziusudran Epic: Sumerian Origins of the Flood Myth* (Winona Lake, IN: Eisenbanus, 1999). A basic collection of flood myths is *The Flood Myth*, edited by Alan Dundes (Berkeley: University of California Press, 1988). An interesting political and social analysis of the flood myth in China is Mark Edward Lewis's *The Flood Myths of Early China* (Albany: State University of New York Press, 2006). For the significance of the Flood and its connection with baptism, see Alan Watts, *Myth and Ritual in Christianity* (Boston, 1968). Carl Jung provides a psychological perspective in *Symbols of Transformation* (Princeton, NJ, 1956, 1976) and in *The Archetypes and the Collective Unconscious* (Princeton, NJ, 1959, 1976). Mircea Eliade has perceptive comments on aquatic symbolism and the paradigmatic history of baptism in *The Sacred and the Profane* (New York, 1959) and on the Flood and cosmic rhythm in *The Myth of the Eternal Return* (Princeton, NJ, 1954, 1974). Eliade's *Patterns in Comparative Religion* (New York, 1958, 1974) contains a thorough discussion of water symbolism and of deluge symbolism in particular.

THE APOCALYPSE

An apocalypse, strictly speaking, is a revelation (from the Greek *apocalypsis*, a revealing), a prophetic vision. In common usage it has come to mean a vision of the catastrophic end of the world. Apocalypse myths, then, are eschatological (Greek *eschatos*, last, and *eschata*, the last things), and the study of the end of things is called eschatology.

The idea of a catastrophic end to the world is common in human culture. In most cases the apocalypse marks the end of an old world and the emergence of a new. But the emphasis is on the end of the current order of things: "The sun will be turned to darkness, and the moon to blood, before the great and terrible day of the Lord comes" (Joel 2:31).

Through their myths of the apocalypse human societies express a sense that the higher powers of the universe must intervene definitively to put an end to the failure of humanity. In some cases the righteous will be allowed to survive, but usually in a nonworldly state.

Apocalyptic writers tend to make heavy use of symbol and fantasy. Their writings are, above all, visionary and prophetic. Apocalypses contain strange beasts and a resurrection of the dead.

The apocalypse motif must be seen as closely related to the flood archetype. The apocalypse is a ritual cleansing of cosmic proportions, a large-scale expression of the human fascination with the death and resurrection process. Psychologically, it speaks to a need to confront reality, to make ultimate decisions. In our culture the literary archetype for this aspect of the apocalyptic process is Armageddon (Hebrew Haer Megiddon, the famous battlefield of ancient Israel in Judges and Kings). In the Book of Revelation (16:16) Armaggedon becomes the symbolic battlefield where good and evil must finally fight it out at the time of the Last Judgment. We speak metaphorically of Armaggedon in reference to great moments of decision or confrontation. Much of the Christian view of the apocalypse is related to the Persian Zoroastrian Day of Judgment, on which the forces of light confront those of darkness and the dead arise to be judged. A still more important influence is that of the apocalyptic visions of the Old Testament prophets.

If the apocalypse of the Western world stresses the end of things and a final establishment of the Kingdom of God, if the Western view is essentially millennial, the Eastern view is more cyclical, placing less emphasis on human failings justly punished and more on the rhythm of the universe itself. Existence for the Hindu, for instance, is a cosmic breathing, with creation and apocalypse endlessly repeating themselves.

Apocalyptic imagery is very much a part of the way we see reality today. The recent experience of genocidal holocaust and the ever-present threat of a nuclear one bring the myth all too close to home, and science itself teaches an eventual descent into "heat death," before Earth returns, as all systems eventually must, to a natural state of entropic equilibrium or no-thing-ness.

ISRAEL: The Day of Yahweh

The apocalyptic mode is common in the Old Testament. Daniel (7–12), Isaiah (24–27), Ezekiel (37), and Joel (3) all contain apocalyptic moments, as does the Zechariah selection (14) included here. The Hebrew prophets, when berating the Hebrews for their failure to follow their God, speak in dire terms of the Day of Yahweh, when the dead will return to be judged and the enemies of God will be destroyed before the true Kingdom is established. The Old Testament prophets establish the motifs of which John will make full use in the New Testament Book of Revelation.

Behold, the day of the Lord cometh, and thy spoil shall be divided in the midst of thee.

2   For I will gather all nations against Jerusalem to battle; and the city shall be taken, and the houses rifled, and the women ravished; and half of the city shall go forth into captivity, and the residue of the people shall not be cut off from the city.

3   Then shall the Lord go forth, and fight against those nations, as when he fought in the day of battle.

4   And his feet shall stand in that day upon the mount of Olives, which is before Jerusalem on the east, and the mount of Olives shall cleave in the midst thereof toward the east and toward the west, and there shall be a very great valley; and half of the mountain shall remove toward the north, and half of it toward the south.

5   And ye shall flee to the valley of the mountains; for the valley of the mountains shall reach unto Azal: yea, ye shall flee, like as ye fled from before the earthquake in the days of Ŭz-zī-ăh king of Judah: and the Lord my God shall come, and all the saints with thee.

6   And it shall come to pass in that day, that the light shall not be clear, nor dark.

7   But it shall be one day which shall be known to the Lord, not day, nor night: but it shall come to pass, that at evening time it shall be light.

8   And it shall be in that day, that living waters shall go out from Jerusalem; half of them toward the former sea, and half of them toward the hinder sea: in summer and in winter shall it be.

9   And the Lord shall be king over all the earth: in that day shall there be one Lord, and his name one.

10 All the land shall be turned as a plain from Geba to Rimmon south of Jerusalem: and it shall be lifted up, and inhabited in her place, from Benjamin's gate unto the place of the first gate, unto the corner gate, and from the tower of Hăn´-ă-neel unto the king's winepresses.

11 And men shall dwell in it, and there shall be no more utter destruction; but Jerusalem shall be safely inhabited.

12 And this shall be the plague wherewith the Lord will smite all the people that have fought against Jerusalem; their flesh shall consume away while they stand upon their feet, and their eyes shall consume away in their holes, and their tongue shall consume away in their mouth.

13 And it shall come to pass in that day, that a great tumult from the Lord shall be among them; and they shall lay hold every one on the hand of his neighbour, and his hand shall rise up against the hand of his neighbour.

14 And Judah also shall fight at Jerusalem; and the wealth of all the heathen round about shall be gathered together, gold, and silver, and apparel, in great abundance.

15 And so shall be the plague of the horse, of the mule, of the camel, and of the ass, and of all the beasts that shall be in these tents, as this plague.

16 And it shall come to pass, that every one that is left of all the nations which came against Jerusalem shall even go up from year to year to worship the King, the Lord of hosts, and to keep the feast of tabernacles.

17 And it shall be, that whoso will not come up of all the families of the earth unto Jerusalem to worship the King, the Lord of hosts, even upon them shall be no rain.

18 And if the family of Egypt go not up, and come not, that have no rain; there shall be the plague, wherewith the Lord will smite the heathen that come not up to keep the feast of tabernacles.

19 This shall be the punishment of Egypt, and the punishment of all nations that come not up to keep the feast of tabernacles.

20 In that day shall there be upon the bells of the horses, HOLINESS UNTO THE LORD; and the pots in the Lord's house shall be like the bowls before the altar.

21 Yea, every pot in Jerusalem and in Judah shall be holiness unto the Lord of hosts: and all they that sacrifice shall come and take of them, and seethe therein: and in that day there shall be no more the Cā´nă-ăn-īte in the house of the Lord of hosts.

[Zechariah 14.]

ASIA MINOR (CHRISTIAN): The Book of Revelation

The last book of the New Testament, the Book of Revelation of the Apocalypse of St. John the Divine, was probably composed at Ephesus in about 95 C.E. It is contemporaneous with such late Hebrew apocalypses as those in Esdras (2) and Baruch (2), and it owes much to Old Testament symbology and tone in general. Like most apocalypses, it predicts the coming of the Kingdom, the raising of the dead, and a final judgment. It is from John's mysterious work that our literature takes such terms as the "Antichrist" and "the hour of fulfillment is near." John establishes for the early Christians what the four Gospels had only suggested, that the Kingdom of God is at hand, that the Second Coming of Christ is imminent. John's vision was to color Western culture from the first century on. Through John, the millennial outlook of the Hebrews took precedence over the less historically oriented and less visionary Greek attitude in the Christian worldview. The effects remain with us today, even in the atheistic but millennial and visionary philosophy of Marxism.

Chapter 15

And I saw another sign in heaven, great and marvellous, seven angels having the seven last plagues; for in them is filled up the wrath of God.

2   And I saw as it were a sea of glass mingled with fire: and them that had gotten the victory over the beast, and over his image, and over his mark, and over the number of his name, stand on the sea of glass, having the harps of God.

3   And they sing the song of Moses the servant of God, and the song of the Lamb, saying, Great and marvellous are thy works, Lord God Almighty; just and true are thy ways, thou King of saints.

4   Who shall not fear thee, O Lord, and glorify thy name? for thou only art holy: for all nations shall come and worship before thee; for thy judgments are made manifest.

5   And after that I looked, and, behold, the temple of the tabernacle of the testimony in heaven was opened:

6   And the seven angels came out of the temple, having the seven plagues, clothed in pure and white linen, and having their breasts girded with golden girdles.

7   And one of the four beasts gave unto the seven angels seven golden vials full of the wrath of God, who liveth for ever and ever.

8   And the temple was filled with smoke from the glory of God, and from his power; and no man was able to enter into the temple, till the seven plagues of the seven angels were fulfilled.

Chapter 16

And I heard a great voice out of the temple saying to the seven angels, Go your ways, and pour out the vials of the wrath of God upon the earth.

2   And the first went, and poured out his vial upon the earth; and there fell a noisome and grievous sore upon the men which had the mark of the beast, and upon them which worshipped his image.

3   And the second angel poured out his vial upon the sea; and it became as the blood of a dead man; and every living soul died in the sea.

4   And the third angel poured out his vial upon the rivers and fountains of waters; and they became blood.

5   And I heard the angel of the waters say, Thou art righteous, O Lord, which art, and wast, and shalt be, because thou hast judged thus.

6   For they have shed the blood of saints and prophets, and thou hast given them blood to drink; for they are worthy.

7   And I heard another out of the altar say, Even so, Lord God Almighty, true and righteous are thy judgments.

8   And the fourth angel poured out his vial upon the sun; and power was given unto him to scorch men with fire.

9   And men were scorched with great heat, and blasphemed the name of God, which hath power over these plagues: and they repented not to give him glory.

10   And the fifth angel poured out his vial upon the seat of the beast; and his kingdom was full of darkness; and they gnawed their tongues for pain,

11   And blasphemed the God of heaven because of their pains and their sores, and repented not of their deeds.

12   And the sixth angel poured out his vial upon the great river Eûphrā́-tēṡ; and the water thereof was dried up, that the way of the kings of the east might be prepared.

13   And I saw three unclean spirits like frogs come out of the mouth of the dragon, and out of the mouth of the beast, and out of the mouth of the false prophet.

14   For they are the spirits of devils, working miracles, which go forth unto the kings of the earth and of the whole world, to gather them to the battle of that great day of God Almighty.

15   Behold, I come as a thief. Blessed is he that watcheth, and keepeth his garments, lest he walk naked, and they see his shame.

16   And he gathered them together into a place called in the Hebrew tongue Är-mă-gĕd́-dŏn.

17   And the seventh angel poured out his vial into the air; and there came a great voice out of the temple of heaven, from the throne, saying, It is done.

18 And there were voices, and thunders, and lightnings; and there was a great earthquake, such as was not since men were upon the earth, so mighty an earthquake, and so great.

19 And the great city was divided into three parts, and the cities of the nations fell: and great Babylon came in remembrance before God, to give unto her the cup of the wine of the fierceness of his wrath.

20 And every island fled away, and the mountains were not found.

21 And there fell upon men a great hail out of heaven, every stone about the weight of a talent: and men blasphemed God because of the plague of the hail; for the plague thereof was exceeding great.

[Revelation 15–16.]

IRAN (ZOROASTRIAN): The Savior Saoshyant

Zoroastrians believe that those who follow the path of evil, the path of the evil lord Angra Mainyu, outnumber those who follow the path of good, represented by the wise lord Ahura Mazda and Zoroaster. They also believe that after an apocalypse a new age will arise.

Fire, the son of Ahura Mazda, will flow like a river over the universe, as an ultimate sacrifice, destroying all before it—including even Hell—and separating the good from the evil at a "Last Judgment." Then, through ceremonies presided over by the savior, Saoshyant, the resurrection of the bodies of the good will take place and a new Golden Age will follow. In some stories it is said that the castle of the primal man, flood survivor, and sacred king Yima is Paradise and that at the Great Renewal, Yima's dominion will encompass the earth itself as the basis of a new Golden Age.

[David A. Leeming, *Dictionary of Asian Mythology*
(Oxford University Press, 2001), p. 210.]

ARABIA (MUSLIM): End of the World

The holy book of Islam, the *Qur'an,* tells of an end of the world time when, as in the traditions of other faiths, the good will be separated from the bad. What follows here is an apocalyptic depiction attributed to the Prophet Muhammad himself in the collection of oral traditions known as the *Hadith*.

The companion of the holy prophet Muhammad asked him what the signs would be of the end of the world. The prophet told him of this terrible time, about which much is written in the Holy Koran:

People will no longer study the Koran but will spend all of their time seeking material wealth, pleasure, and worldly power. There will be an epidemic in Jedda, a famine in Medina, and a plague in the holy city of Mecca. There will be earthquakes, unlike any ever seen before, throughout the entire Maghreb [North Africa]; lethal thunderstorms will strike throughout Turkey and Iran; Iraq will be the domain of murderous bandits. The peoples of the Far East will be wiped out through a succession of floods. The morality that binds societies together will be completely loosened—it will be every man for himself. At that time, the Dajjal—the Antichrist—will appear, riding on a donkey and subjecting all the peoples of the earth to his rule.

Dajjal will rule but forty days through terror and force. Then God will send Jesus from heaven on a white horse, with a lance in his hand, to subdue Dajjal. The remnant of faithful believers will form a powerful army of God to assist Jesus in the defeat of the Dajjal. Dajjal will be defeated but not killed, until God causes the feet of Dajjal to be fixed firmly to the earth; then Jesus will administer the fatal blow.

A throne will come down from heaven and Jesus will reign over the earth for forty years of perfect peace and justice. Each of three forty years will be twenty-six months in length, rather than the usual twelve—so they will actually be like eighty-seven of our present years.

At the end of his reign, Jesus will go to Jerusalem and pray at the Mosque of the Dome of the Rock, where God will take Jesus into heaven. Seven days after the arrival of the soul of Jesus in heaven, the monstrous Gog and Magog, monsters who had been imprisoned by Alexander [Iskandar] the Great, will break free, ruining civilization.

At this point God will call two angels into service. The first of these is Azrail, the angel of death. For believers, Azrail will appear as a beautiful star that calls them to their rest in a sweet, gentle voice. To the wicked, in contrast, Azrail will appear as a monster that rips their souls out of their bodies.

Another angel, Israfil, has the duty of blowing the trumpet of the last day. As all of the righteous will have been killed by the wicked at this point, all those left on earth will deserve the doom that begins with this trumpet call. Tired of the wickedness, God will tell Israfil to blow the horn and the mountains will crumble into dust. At the end of this destruction, forty years of terrible earthquakes and storms, the trumpet will sound again. At this sound, the souls of the faithful dead will search for their bodies to be reunited for the resurrection. Then, when souls and bodies are joined, the faithful will spend forty years praising Allah.

At the third blast of the trumpet, the holy prophet Muhammad will return to earth on his horse, Burak, led by a rope held by the angel Gabriel. All will then see the great scales of judgment descend from heaven. The throne of God will then be visible to all. There will be no secrets: The secret sins of everyone, believer and unbeliever, will be known to all. These secret sins will be weighed on the left side of the scale, and all good deeds, no matter how small, will be weighed on the right. If the right outweighs the left, then the soul is saved; if the opposite is true, the soul will be damned.

But what of those whose good deeds and evil deeds balance equally? These souls may be saved on that terrible day by crying out in God for mercy. If the soul cries in sincerity, honestly sorry for its sins, a note written in God's own hand will fall onto the right side of the scale and paradise will be opened for that soul.

The Judgment will last only one hour.

Then the righteous and wicked alike will cross the bridge into Paradise, which is as thin as a hair. The righteous will cross it with ease, even as the wicked fall down into the chasm of hell. Some will be able, with much difficulty and a heart of sincere repentence, to crawl up out of hell. These and all faithful ones will drink of the sweet waters of Muhammad's lake and never know sorrow, thirst, hunger, or any suffering.

[J. F. Bierlein, *Parallel Myths*
(New York: Ballantine, 1994), pp. 243–245.]

INDIA: The End of the Kali Age *End Evil by Destroying Earth*

As seen in the series of sacred texts called the *purānas* (meaning "stories of the old days"), apocalypse for the Hindu is the natural ending of the world in the fourth age, the Kali Age. It is but one of a series of apocalypses, each of which marks the end of one cycle and the beginning of another creation. The central figure in the story is Vishnu, the preserver god, into whose self the world is absorbed before being born again.

The Kali Age

All kings occupying the earth in the Kali Age will be wanting in tranquillity, strong in anger, taking pleasure at all times in lying and dishonesty, inflicting death on women, children and cows, prone to take the paltry possessions of others, with character that is mostly *tamas*, rising to power and soon falling. They will be short-lived, ambitious, of little virtue and greedy. People will follow the customs of others and be adulterated with them; peculiar, undisciplined barbarians will be vigorously supported by the rulers. Because they go on living with perversion, they will be ruined. The destruction of the world will occur because of the departure from virtue and profit, little by little, day by day. Money alone will confer nobility. Power will be the sole definition of virtue. Pleasure will be the only reason for marriage. Lust will be the only reason for womanhood. Falsehood will win out in disputes. Being dry of water will be the only definition of land. The sacred thread alone will distinguish brahmins. Praiseworthiness will be measured by accumulated wealth. Wearing the *linga* will be sufficient cause for religious retreat. Impropriety will be considered good conduct, and only feebleness will be the reason for unemployment. Boldness and arrogance will become equivalent to scholarship. Only those without wealth will show honesty. Just a bath will amount to purification, and charity will be the only virtue. Abduction will be marriage. Simply to be well-dressed will signify propriety. And any water hard to reach will be deemed a pilgrimage site. The pretense of greatness will be the proof of it, and powerful men with many severe faults will rule over all the classes on earth. Oppressed by their excessively greedy rulers, people will hide in valleys between mountains where they will gather honey, vegetables, roots, fruits, birds, flowers and so forth. Suffering from cold, wind, heat and rain, they will put on clothes made of treebark and leaves. And no one will live as long as twenty-three years. Thus in the Kali Age humankind will be utterly destroyed.

The Dissolution of the World in Viṣṇu

At the end of a thousand periods of four Ages, when the earth's surface is for the most part wasted, there arises a dreadful drought that lasts for a hundred years. Then all these earthly beings whose strength has declined perish completely through oppression. And so the imperishable lord Viṣṇu, who abides in himself, adopts the form of Rudra, and exerts himself to act in order to destroy all creatures. Permeating the seven rays of the sun, the lord Viṣṇu then drinks up all the waters, O excellent sage. When he has consumed all the waters that had gone to the world of creatures, he dries up the earth's surface. Oceans, rivers and flowing mountain streams as well as whatever water lies in the Pātālas[1]—all this he leads to dissolution. Then due to his power, those same seven rays become seven suns, invigorated by the absorption of water. These seven blazing suns ignite all three worlds, above and below, along with the surface of the Netherworld, O twice-born. The three worlds, O twice-born one, consumed by these fiery suns, complete with mountains, rivers and the expanse of the ocean, become arid. Then the whole triple world whose water and trees are burned away, and this earth as well, become as bare as a turtle's back. Likewise, when the monstrous fire has burned up these Pātālas, it rises to the earth and utterly devours its surface. And a frightful tornado of flame rolls through the entire Bhuvarloka and Svarloka. The three worlds then blaze like a frying-pan; all things moving and unmoving are consumed by the surrounding flames. The inhabitants of these two worlds, overcome by heat, their duties done, retreat to Maharloka, O great seer. Still seared by the heat they flee again; seeking safety in a different place, they hurry thence to Janaloka. So when Janārdana in Rudra's form has consumed all creation, he produces clouds from the breath of his mouth that look like a herd of elephants, emitting lightning, roaring loudly. Thus do dreadful clouds arise in the sky. Some are dark like the blossom of the blue lotus; some look like the white water-lily; some are the color of smoke; and others are yellow. Some resemble a donkey's hue; others are like red lacquer; some have the appearance of a cat's-eye gem; and some are like sapphire. Still others are white as a conch shell or jasmine, or similar to collyrium; some are like fireflies, while others resemble peacocks. Huge clouds arise resembling red or yellow arsenic, and others look like a blue-jay's wing. Some of these clouds are like fine towns, and some like mountains; others resemble houses, and still others, mounds of earth. These dense, elephantine clouds fill up the surface of the sky, roaring loudly. Pouring down rain they completely extinguish this dreadful fire which has overtaken the three worlds. And when the fire is thoroughly quenched, the clouds raining day and night overwhelm the entire world with water, O excellent seer. When they have completely inundated the atmosphere with copious streams of water, then, O twice-born, they flood Bhuvarloka on high. When everything movable and immovable in the world has perished in the

---

[1] Netherworlds.

watery darkness, these vast clouds pour down rain for another one hundred years. So is it as the end of every Eon, O excellent seer, by the majesty of the eternal Vāsudeva, the supreme lord.

When the waters come to rest, having reached the realm of the seven seers, then this single ocean completely covers the three worlds. Wind blown out of Visnu's mouth makes the clouds disappear in a hundred years. When the eternal lord, fashioner of all creatures, inconceivable, the condition of creation, the beginning of everything who has no beginning himself, has entirely consumed the wind, then, reposing on Śesha in the single ocean, the lord, first creator, rests in the form of Brahmā, praised by Sanaka and others, the seers who went to Janaloka, and also meditated upon by those who went to Brahmaloka seeking freedom. Resting in meditative sleep, in the divine form of his own illusive power, Visnu, destroyer of Madhu, concentrates on the form of himself called Vāsudeva. This is the dissolution called occasional, O Maitreya[2]; the occasion is that Hari rests in the form of Brahmā. When the soul of all awakens, then the world stirs; when the imperishable one has gone to his bed of illusion, it falls completely asleep. A day of Brahmā, born of from the lotus, lasts a thousand periods of four Ages; a night, when the world is destroyed and made into a vast ocean, is of the same length. At the end of the night, Visnu, unborn, having awakened, takes the form of Brahmā in order to create, as it has already been told to you.
[Cornelia Dimmitt and J. A. B. van Buitenen, eds. and trans., *Classical Hindu Mythology* (Philadelphia, 1978), pp. 41–43.]

NATIVE NORTH AMERICA (HOPI): Emergence to the Fifth World

This Hopi prophecy, one of many versions, resembles other millennial visions of the destruction of the world before the establishment of a new order. It sees the ancient Hopi village of Oraibi as the center of the world and Hopi ceremonies as the repository of life's remaining spiritualism. The Hopis, like the ancient Hebrews, see themselves as surrounded by a world lost in spiritual darkness.

The end of all Hopi ceremonialism will come when a *kachina* removes his mask during a dance in the plaza before uninitiated children. For a while there will be no more ceremonies, no more faith. Then Oraibi will be rejuvenated with its faith and ceremonies, marking the start of a new cycle of Hopi life.

---

[2] Sage to whom this text is narrated.

World War III will be started by those peoples who first received the light [the divine wisdom or intelligence] in the other old countries [India, China, Egypt, Palestine, Africa].

The United States will be destroyed, land and people, by atomic bombs and radioactivity. Only the Hopis and their homeland will be preserved as an oasis to which refugees will flee. Bomb shelters are a fallacy. "It is only materialistic people who seek to make shelters. Those who are at peace in their hearts already are in the great shelter of life. There is no shelter for evil. Those who take no part in the making of world division by ideology are ready to resume life in another world, be they of the Black, White, Red, or Yellow race. They are all one, brothers."

The war will be "a spiritual conflict with material matters. Material matters will be destroyed by spiritual beings who will remain to create one world and one nation under one power, that of the Creator."

That time is not far off. It will come when the Saquasohuh [Blue Star] Kachina dances in the plaza. He represents a blue star, far off and yet invisible, which will make its appearance soon. The time is also foretold by a song sung during the Wúwuchim ceremony. It was sung in 1914 just before World War I, and again in 1940 before World War II, describing the disunity, corruption, and hatred contaminating Hopi rituals, which were followed by the same evils spreading over the world. This same song was sung in 1961 during the Wúwuchim ceremony.

The Emergence to the future Fifth World has begun. It is being made by the humble people of the little nations, tribes, and racial minorities. "You can read this in the earth itself. Plant forms from previous worlds are beginning to spring up as seeds. This could start a new study of botany if people were wise enough to read them. The same kinds of seeds are being planted in the sky as stars. The same kinds of seeds are being planted in our hearts. All these are the same, depending how you look at them. That is what makes the Emergence to the next, Fifth World.

"These comprise the nine most important prophecies of the Hopis, connected with the creation of the nine worlds: the three previous worlds on which we have lived, the present Fourth World, the future three worlds we have yet to experience, and the world of Taiowa, the Creator, and his nephew, Sótuknang."

[Frank Waters, *Book of the Hopi*
(New York, 1963), pp. 408–409.]

ICELAND (NORSE): Ragnarök   *Overturn — Betrayal*

One of the best known of the apocalyptic stories is the Norse myth of Ragnarök. The gods themselves are doomed in this myth of the end of the world (from the ancient *Voluspa*, the soothsaying of the *volva*, or seeress), movingly retold by the thirteenth-century Icelandic writer Snorri Sturluson in his *Prose Edda*.

Many recognizable events are present here: the earthquakes, the darkening of the sun, the rising of monsters, Armaggedon, the destroying fire followed by the renewal of life.

At last the doom of the gods will fall upon them; Gullinkambi, the golden cock of Asgard, will waken Odin's hosts. His cousins in Hel and Jotunheim will crow likewise. The strife of man against man and brother against brother will increase and not abate. The Great Winter will fall, three years long, and the snows will bury life, the winds will quench it, and the sun will give no respite. The wolf Skoll will swallow the sun, and Hati will devour the moon: their gore will splatter earth and heavens. The stars will flicker and die. The earth will shake and quake, and all Yggdrasill will tremble. The old bonds will be no more. Loki the Trickster and Fenrir the Wolf will burst free, and the seas will overlap their shores with a violent tide as Jormungand—the great Midgard Serpent—makes his way to shore. Naglfar—the ghastly ship made of the nails of dead men—will sail to battle. Loki will captain the ship of the dead from Hel, and Hrim will command a bursting load of giants. Fenrir's wide jaws will scrape both heaven and earth, and Jormungand will spew venom and poison throughout creation. Surt will lead the fire demons of Muspell across Bifrost the Rainbow Bridge, and it will shatter and fall beneath them; Fire will encompass them, and Surt's sword will take the place of the sun. The enemies of the gods will gather on the plain of Vigrid, and they will be terrible to behold.

The gods will be no less prepared. Heimdalr will call a blast on his mighty Gjallarhorn, and the gods will rush to assemble. Odin will leap upon Sleipnir and hasten to consult Mimir, while the Aesir and the Einherjar arm themselves: they will don helm and mailcoat, and grasp sword, shield, and spear. Eight hundred strong will march shoulder-to-shoulder through each of Valhalla's five hundred and forty doors; they will be led to Vigrid by Odin, resplendent in golden helm and shining mail. He will grip Gungnir grimly. Odin will greet Fenrir with cold cheer, and Thor beside him will look to settle his old score with Jormungand. The Serpent will prove a match for the

Thunderer: Odin may expect to have no help from that quarter. Freyr will grapple with Surt, and well might he rue the day he pledged his mighty blade to Skirnir. After a great struggle, Freyr falls to the fiery sword of Surt. Tyr and Garm the Hound each will prove the death of the other, and Loki and Heimdalr likewise will even ancient enmity. Thor will best Jormungand in the end, but will live to step back only nine paces before he succumbs to the poison the Serpent spewed upon him. Fenrir will swallow the One-eyed God at the last, but his victory will be cut short by Vidar, who will avenge his father and vanquish the wolf by stepping on its lower jaw and stretching the other up until he rips it asunder. Vidar's shoe that day will take all of time to cobble; it will be made of all of the scraps of leather ever snipped off of shoe leather and cast away, and it will prove too thick and tough even for the fangs of Fenrir. Then Surt will cast his fire through the three levels and nine worlds of creation, and all will die: men and gods, dwarfs and elves, birds and beasts, all manner of creatures and monsters. The sun will be extinguished, the stars drowned, and the earth will sink beneath the waves.

The earth will rise from the deeps again one day, green and blossoming, and crops will flourish where none were planted. A new sun will take the place of her mother, and a number of gods will return to the ancient ruins of Asgard, led now by Baldr. Lif and Lifthrasir will survive to renew the race of men: they will have hidden themselves securely in Yggdrasill's embrace, and the fire of Surt will not scorch them: they will survive on the morning dew, and keep watch through the branches above them for the new sun rising. And thus, through its death, the world will be born again.

[Christopher Fee and David A. Leeming, *Gods, Heroes, and Kings* (Oxford University Press, 2001), p. 144.]

MODERN PHYSICS: Entropy and Heat Death

Modern science provides us with the following picture of the end of the world. This "myth" might best be read in conjunction with the Hindu myths of the destruction of the world at the end of each eon.

Whenever scientists begin speculating about the second law, the question ultimately arises as to how broadly it can be applied. For example, does the Entropy Law apply to the macroworld of stars and galaxies that make up the universe? In fact, the Entropy Law is the basis of most cosmological theories. Scientist Benjamin Thompson became the first to draw the cosmological implications of the second law back in 1854. According to Thompson, the Entropy Law tells us that within a finite period of time past, the earth must have been, and within a finite period of time to come the earth must again be, unfit for the habitation of man as at present constituted, unless operations have been, or are to be performed, which are impossible under the laws to which the known operations going on at present in the material world are subject.

Two years later Helmholtz formulated what has become the standard cosmological theory based on the Entropy Law. His theory of "heat death" stated that the universe is gradually running down and eventually will reach the point of maximum entropy or heat death where all available energy will have been expended and no more activity will occur. The heat death of the universe corresponds to a state of eternal rest.

Today the most widely accepted theory about the origin and development of the universe is the big bang theory. First conceptualized by Canon Georges Lemaître, the big bang theory postulates that the universe began with the explosion of a tremendously dense energy source. As this dense energy expanded outward, it began to slow down, forming galaxies, stars, and planets. As the energy continues to expand and become more diffused, it loses more and more of its order and will eventually reach a point of maximum entropy, or the final equilibrium state of heat death. The big bang theory coincides with the first and second laws. It states that the universe started with complete order and has been moving toward a more and more disordered state ever since. If this theory appears familiar, it should. Both the ancient Greek and the medieval Christian view of history share much in common with the cosmologists' notion of the history of the universe.

[Jeremy Rifkin, *Entropy: A New World View*
(New York, 1980), pp. 44–45.]

BIBLIOGRAPHY

✦

The best overall discussion of the end-of-the-world motif is found in Mircea Eliade's *Myth and Reality* (New York, 1963)—especially the fourth chapter ("Eschatology and Cosmogony")—and his *The Myth of the Eternal Return or, Cosmos and History* (New York, 1954). Useful books on the apocalypse in the Old Testament version include Paul D. Hanson's *The Dawn of the Apocalyptic* (Philadelphia, 1975) and D. S. Russell's *Apocalyptic, Ancient and Modern* (Philadelphia, 1978). A great deal has been written about the Book of Revelation in the New Testament. One of the better works, containing a clear interpretation, is Hans Lilje's *The Last Book of the Bible* (Philadelphia, 1975). Another useful work is Bernard McGinn's *Visions of the End: Apocalyptic Traditions in the Middle Ages* (New York, 1979). A more general work, touching on the apocalyptic tradition in many cultures, is a collection of essays called *Apocalypse: The Morphology of a Genre,* published in the journal *Semia* (vol. 14, 1979). Kurt Spellmeyer, in his *Buddha at the Apocalypse: Awakening from a Culture of Destruction* (Somerville, MA: Wisdom Publishers, 2010), presents a Buddhist-inspired response to the apocalypse traditions and myths. J. F. Bierlein in his *Parallel Myths* (New York: Ballantine Books, 1994) provides a variety of apocalypse myths.

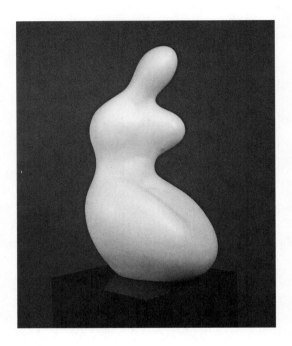

✦ Demeter by Jean (Hans) Arp

PART 2

MYTHS OF THE GODS

Worrld mythology is dominated by a concept to which we apply the terms "god" and "goddess." Virtually no version of the universal dream that is myth is without the concept of the gods. Whether God or Allah or Brahman or the Great Mother or their many relatives, the gods are seen as immortal; they are personified projections of the human mythmaker's dream of overcoming the inevitable effects of the physical laws that require death and disintegration. Gods are also what Mircea Eliade has called "fecundators" (*Patterns in Comparative Religion*, p. 288) of the universe. They represent the creative force that struggles against the tendency toward the equilibrium of nothingness, the force that works to fill the world with life. Furthermore, the gods and goddesses are metaphors for elements of human society. Zeus is a patriarch—a father and a husband, sometimes a philandering one. Hera is a mother and a wife, often a jealous one. Their relationship is a human relationship, their family is a reflection of our families, their hierarchies mirror ours. The gods are also personifications of aspects of nature and of human nature—the sun, the winds, impatience, love.

The existence of the deity fulfills a still more important human need. Gods are symbols of ultimate reality. Their existence provides us with a sense of significance in an otherwise random universe. To say that there are gods or a God is to say that we have meaning, a reason for being. We are made "in the image of God," we are "namers," we are the "guardians" of nature. We are the voice of a meaningful creation. Deity is humankind's metaphor for what Raimundo Pannikar has called "man's effort to discover his identity in confrontation with the limits of his universe" (*The Encyclopedia of Religion*, vol. 4, p. 264). The God archetype in our universal dream is a symbol of the relationship between a meaningful or significant cosmos and our innermost being. Again quoting Pannikar, "Deity is the immanence and transcendence inserted in the heart of every being" (p. 269).

THE PANTHEONS

The officially recognized gods of a culture—its pantheon (Greek *pan-theon,* all gods)—reflect that culture's value system and view of itself. The Egyptian pantheon speaks directly to that culture's obsession with death and resurrection, which may have arisen from its constant confrontation with the processes and effects of the passage of the sun and the flooding of the Nile. The Hebrew development of a single patriarchal god concerned with the actions of a "chosen people" suggests a culture with a sense of exclusive identity and mission. The Greek immortal family on Mount Olympus, a family preoccupied with both its own pleasures and the actions of mortals, personifies a realistic if somewhat skeptical view of human nature and the dilemma of a species that revels in life even as it is defined by death.

All pantheons are ontological and teleological; that is, they are metaphors for the human attempt to make sense of existence itself and to assign ultimate cause. To "read" a pantheon is to read a culture's sense of itself and of the nature of the cosmos.

MESOPOTAMIA (SUMER): Gods of the Elements

The oldest pantheon known to scholars is that of ancient Sumer in Mesopotamia (now Iraq). The Sumerian pantheon is fully representative of the elements of nature and the universe and creation itself. The goddess Ki (Ninsurhag, Urash, Earth) mates with An (Sky). An also mates with Nammu (the primal waters). From the An-Ki union comes Ninlil, the air goddess, and Enlil, the air god. From the An-Nammu relationship comes the trickster god Enki. Enki's union with his sister Ningikuga, the goddess of the reeds, results in the moon goddess Ningal. Ningal joins with Nanna, the moon god son of Ninlil and Enlil, and produces the sun god Utu and the "Queen of Heaven and Earth," the great goddess of love, Inanna (Ishtar). Inanna's sister is Ereshkigal, Queen of the Underworld. Inanna's husband is the shepherd Dumuzi, the son of Enki and the sheep goddess Sirtur (Ninsun). Ereshkigal's mate is Gugalanna, the Bull of Heaven.

It was the Sumerians who invented writing, and one of the world's earliest recorded myths, that of the conception of the moon god Nanna, a patron of the city of Ur, is found in cuneiform script on a clay tablet dating from the second millennium B.C.E.

Ninlil, the air goddess, loves Enlil, the air god, the greatest of the Sumerian deities, the source of order in the universe. Ninlil's mother, Ki, the earth goddess, tells her daughter how to attract her beloved's attention.

> In those days the mother, her begetter, gave advice to the maid,
> Nunbarshegunu gave advice to Ninlil:

"At the pure river, O maid, at the pure river wash thyself,
O Ninlil, walk along the bank of the Idnunbirdu,
The bright-eyed, the lord, the bright-eyed,
The 'great mountain,' father Enlil, the bright-eyed, will see thee,
The shepherd . . . who decrees the fates, the bright-eyed, will see
    thee,
He will . . ., he will kiss thee."

[Samuel Noah Kramer, *Sumerian Mythology*
(New York: Harper, 1961), p. 45.]

Ki's instructions work. Enlil notices Ninlil and impregnates her, and the moon god Nanna comes into the world.

EGYPT   Death & Ressurection

The Egyptian pantheon is marked by a struggle for supremacy among various gods, a struggle that mirrors conflicts among ruling religious and political factions in various parts of Egypt beginning as early as 4000 B.C.E. At one moment in Egyptian history the pantheon of Heliopolis, led by Atum or Re, predominates. At another time Amun in Thebes reigns supreme. The pharaoh Akhenaton even introduced a form of sun god monotheism in the fourteenth century B.C.E. Because of this struggle for religious supremacy and because of the existence of distinct cultural centers, the Egyptian pantheon is marked by inconsistency. The few consistent themes reflect the culture's emphasis on the sun and on death and renewal (probably associated with the passage of the sun and with the seasonal flooding of the Nile). In another consistent motif, the Egyptian immortals are typically depicted as having human bodies and animal heads. If one god emerges as the central figure in the overall Egyptian pantheon, it is Osiris, whose myth, with that of his son Horus, is intricately related to questions of pharoanic legitimacy and the afterlife. A pharaoh dies as Osiris; his successor reigns as Horus.

The Gods of Heliopolis

Summarized below is the Ennead, essentially the pantheon of Heliopolis, which is usually considered to be the most orthodox of Egyptian religious centers. This pantheon was formed by the twenty-eighth century B.C.E. and is found in the Pyramid Texts.

Atum is the sun god. He is at various times and places Ra or Re or Khepri or Amun. As Amun, or Amen-Ra, the sun god of Upper Egypt, He is the great eye of the heavens and of creation.

Shu and his sister Tefnut are the result of Atum's act of masturbation or expectoration. The god embraces his children, bestowing on them his divine essence, or Ka. Shu is the life spirit, while Tefnut is world order or cosmos. Shu and Tefnut produce Geb and Nut.

Geb is the spirit of life; Nut, an Egyptian Great Mother goddess, is the spirit of order. One of the great images of Egyptian mythology is that of Geb and Nut being separated by their father, Shu; Nut becomes the star-filled heavens and Geb becomes Earth, with his erect penis (perhaps represented in Egypt by the ubiquitous obelisk) reaching for his consort.

The children of Geb and Nut complete this most important of Egyptian pantheons:

Osiris is the god of the underworld and of grain. He was the most popular of Egyptian gods, equivalent in spirit to Attis in Phrygia, Adonis in Babylonia, and Dionysos in Greece. He is a god who dies and in one sense or another is revived. Isis, like Demeter in Greece, is a goddess of mysteries. Her cult spread as far as Rome. Isis is the goddess of earth and moon. She is the sister-wife of Osiris and plays the most significant role in his resurrection.

Seth (sometimes spelled Set) is the brother of Osiris and Isis and is their nemesis, a force of evil and darkness in the world. He murders his brother and is married to their sister Nephtys.

Nephthys is a goddess of death and dusk. She assists her sister, Isis, in the reviving of the dead Osiris.

Horus, conceived miraculously by Isis and her dead husband, Osiris, has aspects of the sun god; he is the light that defeats the darkness associated with Seth. Horus is the *puer aeternus*, or divine child, of the Egyptian pantheon. He is the spiritual force behind the reigning pharaoh.

The Separation of Geb and Nut

Reprinted here is a portion of the Pyramid Text story of the Egyptian pantheon. By implication, it concerns the separation of Geb and Nut.

(Priest speaks):
    O Nut, spread yourself over your son Osiris, and hide him from Seth.
        Protect him, O Nut!
    Have you come to hide your son? . . .
(Words to be spoken by Geb):
    O Nut! You became a spirit,
    you waxed mighty in the belly of your mother Tefnut
    before you were born.

How mighty is your heart!
You stirred in the belly of your mother in your name of
Nut,
you are indeed a daughter more powerful than her mother . . .
O Great One who has become the sky!
You have the mastery, you have filled every place with your beauty.
the whole earth lies beneath you, you have taken possession thereof,
you have enclosed the whole earth and everything therein within your
        arms. . . .
As Geb shall I impregnate you in your name of sky,
I shall join the whole earth to you in every place.
O high above the earth! You are supported upon your father Shu,
but you have power over him,
he so loved you that he placed himself—and all things
beside—beneath you
so that you took up into you every god with his heavenly barque,
and as "a thousand souls is she" did you teach them
that they should not leave you—as the stars.

> [R. T. Rundle Clark, *Myth and Symbol in Ancient Egypt*
> (London, 1959), pp. 48–49.]

INDIA: The Triad

The Indian-Hindu pantheon develops over time. In the early pre-Hindu Vedic mythology, Dyaus and Prithivi, the sky father and earth mother, were central. They were followed later by the triad of Surya the sun god, Indra the king of the gods, and Agni the fire god. In the Vedas the creator was Prajapati. Eventually, there was the concept of the all-encompassing Brahman, the single essence of all reality—something less tangible than but comparable to the God of monotheistic religions. In classical Hinduism the primary embodiments of Brahman are the triad of Shiva the ascetic lord of the dance of life, Vishnu the preserver, and Brahma the creator, although the great goddess Devi in her various forms has long been a more important figure than Brahma.

Most Hindus worship one of the three gods of the triad as the supreme deity, and connected with each of the three are stories of marriages. Shiva's wife was Parvati, goddess of the mountain Himalaya. Parvati was the mother of the much-loved Ganesha, who had been born as Vighneshvara.

> Pârvatî's companions, Jayâ and Vijayâ, tried to convince her that she
> needed her own servant. And when Śiva intruded into her bath, she

decided to create a gate-keeper (*dvârapâlaka*) from a little dirt from her skin. In so doing, she created a formidable being, Vighneshvara. The next time that Śiva attempted to burst in upon his wife, Vighneshvara prevented him—even driving him away with a cane that left a few cuts on Śiva. Furious, Śiva sent his *Bhuta-ganas* (demons), who were also promptly defeated. The gods, including Vishnu, tried to gain Śiva's favor by defeating this upstart. Pârvatî saw the gods ganging up on her son and sent two fierce goddesses to help with magic. They protected Vighneshvara from injury by using *mâyâ* ("magic," "illusion") to misdirect the aim of the god's weapons. Then Vishnu, lord of mâyâ, confused the goddesses, and they returned to Pârvatî. At that moment Śiva attacked Vighneshvara and easily cut off his head. Of course, the meddling sage Nârada appeared to tell Pârvatî about the death of her son, and Pârvatî created a thousand fighting goddesses to punish the slayers. The gods were suffering pitifully, so Nârada and other sages raced to Pârvatî and begged that she end her revenge. This she did as soon as her son was brought back to life.

In all versions of this myth, Śiva sent attendants to find a head, and one of a dead elephant was brought back. That head had only one tusk (*eka-danta*) and would make Vighneshvara into the elephant-faced god (*gajânana*), Ganeśa. When Pârvatî saw her restored son, she took him before the assemblage of gods, presided over by her husband Śiva, and presented her son. Śiva promptly apologized to all and gave Ganeśa command of his demon forces (*ganas*), acquiring a role that gained him the title Ganapati.

[George M. Williams, *Handbook of Hindu Mythology* (Oxford University Press, 2003), p. 133.]

Vishnu's wife is Sri or Lakshmi, who represents, among many other qualities, prosperity and good fortune. Lakshmi was born from the supreme being's left side. Vishnu had many earthly incarnations, or avatars, of whom the most famous are Krishna and Rama, who play major roles in the epics known as the *Mahabharata* and the *Ramayana*. Lakshmi was incarnated as the wives of the avatars: Rukmini, for instance, as Krishna's feminine counterpart and Sita as the heroic wife of Rama.

The most famous of the Vishnu myths takes place in the context of a war in heaven between the gods (*devas*) and the demons (*asuras*).

In the sixth *manvantara* (world cycle) of the current *kalpa* (eon), the *devas* were losing in their battles with the *asuras*. One account said that the god Indra had slighted a *brâhmin* sage named Durvâsa and from that day on the power of the gods declined. So the *devas* went to Brahmâ, who immediately—as was usually the case in the Vaishnava myth cycle—counseled them to go to Vishnu.

Vishnu told the gods to follow his instructions exactly. They would have to work with the demons, but in the end Vishnu would enhance their glory. So the *devas* convinced the *asuras* that they must work together in order to obtain the drink of immortality. They would need to churn it up from the Milky Ocean (*kshîra-sâgara*). First, herbs were thrown in the clear waters. Mount Manthara was used as a churning staff, and the giant snake Vâsuki became the churning rope. The *devas* took Vâsuki's tail, while the *asuras* grabbed his head with its fiery breath. Vishnu became the support for the mountain as the turtle *avatâra* (Kûrma) and simultaneously took an invisible form and pressed down on the mountain from above. The gods and demons pulled back and forth with Vâsuki, stirring the ocean and bringing all manner of things into being: Kâmadhenu (the wish-granting cow), Vârunîdevî, Pârijâtam, the *apsaras*, Chandra-Soma (the moon), venom (*halâhala*), which was absorbed by the serpents (*nâgas*), Dhanvantari with the pot of amrita, and Mahâlakshmî. The avatâra Kûrma raised Mount Mandara when it started to sink. The demons grabbed the pot of amrita from the sage Dhanvantari and would have become immortal had they drunk it. But the demons were tricked out of their share when Vishnu appeared as Môhinî and mesmerized them with her feminine charm and beauty. She told the *asuras* that she was lonely and looking for a mate. Môhinî said that they should close their eyes and the one who opened them last would be the one she would marry. But Môhinî went immediately to Devaloka (heaven) and gave the amrita to the *devas*. And even though the *asuras* attacked, the *devas* were strengthened by the divine drink and won dominion over the three worlds.

[Geroge M. Williams, *Handbook of Hindu Mythology* (Oxford University Press, 2003) pp. 189–190.]

Devi is Mahadevi—the great goddess. She is also embodied in the wives of Shiva, Brahma, and Vishnu and in various other beings such as the terrifying monster slayer Durga or Kali, the Black One, the goddess of destruction, the manifestation of the anger of Shiva's wife Parvati. Kali demands blood sacrifice. Devi is also Shakti, the energizing force without which Shiva, or perhaps anyone, is not real.

GREECE: Originators and Olympians

Like the Egyptian pantheon and the Indian one, the Greek pantheon, as we saw in our discussion of creation myths, emerges in stages. Two dynasties must be overcome violently before Zeus and his family can rule the universe. Hesiod's *Theogony*, the epics of Homer, and the *Homeric Hymns* are among our major sources for the theogonic Greek myths as they emerged in the ninth through seventh centuries B.C.E.

More than any other pantheon, the Greek hierarchy of gods and goddesses, which emerged from the ancient wars in heaven, is modeled on human families. The official Olympian gods, the family of Mount Olympus, headed by Zeus, is simply the most powerful of Greek families. Like other members of the rich and powerful classes, the Olympian family is marred by instances of immorality, arrogance, and stubbornness. In the Greek view, the gods were to be approached warily rather than in a familiar or loving manner. They were not to be trusted and could not be counted on for mercy. They were an exaggerated version of what a human family might become if endowed with infinite power. They were a mirror of human nature itself. Furthermore, they represented the irrational forces of physical nature.

Other aspects of Greek religion were not so deeply rooted in hierarchy and in the existing social structure. The cults of Dionysos and Demeter, for example, have been called earth religions, as opposed to the sky religion of the Olympians. Their cults were associated with fertility, with deep emotion, and even with mystery or mysticism and had a wide following among the people. The earth religions were probably well established in the land we now call Greece or in the lands to the east of Greece long before the emergence there of the religion of Zeus, which very likely results from a merging of the religions of various Mediterranean and northern peoples.

The Greek pantheon, as it had developed by the time of Homer and Hesiod, was made up officially of twelve gods and goddesses, although there is disagreement as to the exact composition of the group.

The Children of Kronos and Rhea

Zeus is the Greek version of the Indo-European chief sky god. He is the patriarch of the Greek pantheon, a pantheon that gives cosmic significance to a patriarchal social system. As a sky god concerned particularly with weather—his standard is the thunderbolt—and as a lover of many, Zeus has links to the older fertility gods. He is the father of Herakles and Helen of Troy by mortal women (Alcmene and Leda). He produces Athena out of his own head. And he is the father of Dionysos by Semele, who herself has earth goddess antecedents.

It is generally assumed now that Zeus was himself originally an earth god of ancient Crete.

In one myth, Zeus, in the form of a swan, takes advantage of the mortal Leda. The latter subsequently lays an egg, from which Helen and possibly also Clytemnestra or Castor and Pollux are hatched. Leda was later deified as the goddess Nemesis. This is William Butler Yeats's version of the rape of Leda:

> A sudden blow: the great wings beating still
> Above the staggering girl, her thighs caressed
> By the dark webs, her nape caught in his bill,
> He holds her helpless breast upon his breast.
> How can those terrified vague fingers push
> The feathered glory from her loosening thighs?
> And how can body, laid in that white rush,
> But feel the strange heart beating where it lies?
> A shudder in the loins engenders there
> The broken wall, the burning roof and tower
> And Agamemnon dead.
> Being so caught up,
> So mastered by the brute blood of the air,
> Did she put on his knowledge with his power
> Before the indifferent beak could let her drop?
>
> [W. B. Yeats, "Leda and the Swan," in
> *The Collected Poems of W. B. Yeats* (New York, 1957), p. 211.]

Hera was Zeus's sister. She was also his constantly cross wife, unhappy with his extramarital affairs. Poseidon was Zeus' brother and after the defeat of the Titans was made lord of the seas, a role reflected in his tempestuous and often quarrelsome nature. These characteristics would also seem to be appropriate to his role as god of earthquakes, although it is possible that this role refers to an earlier stage of the god's existence when he was associated, as he was at Athens and Troezen even in classical times, with powers of fertility that came from within the earth. Poseidon was also the god of horses and was the father by Medusa of the winged horse Pegasus. Among his other children, by many women—immortal and mortal—were the great Athenian hero Theseus and the cyclops Polyphemus, the one-eyed monster blinded by Odysseus in the *Odyssey*. Poseidon's revenge on Odysseus for having thus insulted him is the reason for Odysseus' difficulties as described in the Homeric epic. Poseidon's symbol was the trident. Traditionally, bulls were sacrificed to him.

Hestia was the first-born of Kronos and Rhea, a virgin goddess whose name was well known to all Greeks as goddess of the home—specifically, of the hearth or sacred fire. Few stories are told of her, but she was important as a figure to be honored in rituals of sacrifice.

One of the most famous of the Greek myths involves three important members of the Olympian family: Demeter, Persephone, and Hades. Demeter, the sister of Zeus and the mother by him of Persephone (or Kore), spent more time in the world than on Mount Olympus. This is appropriate, as she is the goddess of agriculture, the Olympian version of the Great Goddess. Her daughter is identified with young crops and, as the wife of Hades, with death. Demeter's cult, most fully developed in the mysteries of Eleusis, was, with that of Dionysos, pervasive in Greece. The Eleusinian Mysteries grew out of a popular cult that had been strongly influenced by a similar cult centered on the Egyptian goddess Isis. The Eleusinian version was eventually recognized officially in Athens. It was a cult concerned with the earth and with fertility and, like the cult of Dionysos, with the connection between fertility and death—with the burying of the seed in order that it might generate new life. Given this connection, it is not surprising that Demeter came to be associated with the idea of the human soul's immortality.

Hades was, with Zeus and Poseidon, among the most powerful of the gods. When Zeus divided up responsibility for his dominions, he gave Hades control over the underworld, which was also called Hades. Hades is the dark god, the god who carries the two-pronged staff with which to goad people into the lower world. He also carries the keys of Hades and is accompanied by the three-headed dog Cerberus. Like his brother Poseidon, he is associated with horses.

The myth of Demeter, Persephone (Kore), and Hades, originally told in the *Homeric Hymns* and later recounted by Ovid, is retold here by William Hansen.

> Persephonê is the daughter of Zeus and Demeter. According to the *Homeric Hymn to Demeter,* Zeus gave his unmarried brother Hades permission to seize Persephonê, saying nothing of this arrangement to the girl or her mother. One day as Persephonê gathered flowers in a meadow with a number of Oceanids, the earth in the Nysian Plain gaped open and Hades burst forth on his golden chariot, seized her, and carried her away against her will to his gloomy kingdom. She cried out, but by the time her mother heard her voice, the girl had disappeared. While Persephonê dwelled with Hades in Erebos, Demeter in grief searched the earth for her, and when she learned what had happened, she was furious. She kept herself apart from the other gods in her grief and anger, keeping the seeds concealed in the

ground, so that agriculture came entirely to a halt. Had not Zeus intervened, the human race would have perished and the gods would have been deprived of their sacrifices.

Since Demeter angrily refused to return to Olympus or to allow the seeds to emerge until she should see her daughter, Zeus dispatched Hermes to the House of Hades to persuade the god to bring Persephonê back. Hermes went beneath the earth to Hades's mansions, where he found the lord and his consort sitting on a couch. Persephonê was longing for her mother. Hades said Persephonê was free to visit her mother, but he also pointed out that he was no unsuitable husband for her, since he was a brother of her own father, Zeus, and since as Hades's spouse she would become mistress of everything that lived and would acquire great honors among the gods. But secretly he gave Persephonê a pomegranate seed to eat before her departure so that she would not remain forever with her mother. Demeter and Persephonê were joyously reunited, but when Demeter discovered that Persephonê had eaten in Erebos, she perceived that Persephonê would have to live a third of the year with her spouse and two-thirds of the year with her mother and the other immortals. Zeus gave his approval to this plan. After Demeter caused the fields once again to luxuriate in produce, she and her daughter went to Olympus to join the other gods, where they dwell beside Zeus.

[William Hansen, *Classical Mythology*
(Oxford University Press, 2004), p. 259.]

The Children of Zeus

Athena, or Pallas Athena, the patroness of Athens, was the goddess of wisdom, and she was concerned with the arts, especially weaving and spinning. She created the olive tree, which was sacred to her. Athena was also associated with war and was depicted carrying a spear and shield and wearing a helmet decorated with griffins. She was one of the great virgin goddesses; the Parthenon (Greek *parthenos*, virgin) on the Acropolis was her temple. Athena was the particular patron of the wily Odysseus in Homer's epic, and she cast the deciding vote in favor of Orestes in his trial for the revenge killing of his mother Clytemnestra and her lover Aighistos.

This ancient goddess in all probability originated as a fertility-oriented patroness of the pre-Greek Mycenean and Minoan rulers and gained her virginal aspect only after the establishment of the patriarchal sky religion during classical times.

Her paradoxical nature is reflected in the story of her remarkable birth. In the classical version of her story, as told by Hesiod, Pindar, and Apollodorus, Athena sprang fully armed from the head of her father Zeus. Thus stripped of her feminine origins and nature, she reflects the patriarchal value system. Athena stands in direct contrast to her sister Aphrodite, whose exaggerated sexuality and stereotypical femininity is equally revealing of that system.

Zeus had four children by his wife Hera. Of these, Hebe, the cupbearer for the gods, goddess of youth, and wife of Herakles after he is immortalized on Mount Olympus, and Eileithyia, goddess of childbirth, are not made much of in Greek myth. Two other offspring, the gods Ares and Hephaistos, however, are more important. Ares, the god of war, carries a torch and a spear. Hephaistos, the lame god of fire and crafts, carries a smith's hammer and tongs. Ares and Hephaistos are perhaps best known for their relationships with the goddess Aphrodite. Hephaistos is her husband. Ares is her lover and the father by her of Eros, the god specifically associated with the pangs of love.

According to one story, Aphrodite (Greek, "foam-born"), as the meaning of her name suggests, was born of the foam of the sea. The foam was said to have been caused by the semen from the mutilated genitals of the god Uranos. Aphrodite is often depicted emerging from a seashell. She came to land on the island of Cythera but was also attached to Cyprus. In another birth story, Aphrodite is the child of Zeus by the nymph Dione.

As goddess of love and beauty, Aphrodite is, above all, seductive—an immortal version of the femme fatale. Two of her most famous liaisons are with the youth Adonis, who was killed by a wild boar but was restored to her for six months of each year, and with the mortal Anchises, by whom she became the mother of Aeneas, the hero of Virgil's great Roman epic, the *Aeneid*. Representing the dangers of love, she is partly responsible for the Trojan War, because it is she who tempts Paris to award her the golden apple by promising him the most beautiful woman in the world, Helen.

The following tale of a love triangle is told by Homer about Aphrodite, Ares, and Hephaistos.

> The herald arrived with the minstrel's singing lyre. Demodocus advanced into the cleared space. About him grouped boys in their first blush of life and skilful at dancing, who footed it rhythmically on the prepared floor. Odysseus watched their flying, flashing feet and wondered.
>
> Then the lyre-player broke into fluent song, telling of the loves of Ares and coiffed Aphrodite in the house of Hephaestus. How they first came together by stealth and of the many gifts that Ares gave

her, until he was able to defile the bed and marriage of Hephaestus the King: and of the eventual coming of Helios, the Sun, to the King, with word of their loving intercourse as he had witnessed it. When Hephaestus had heard the dismal tale, he hastened to his forge, elaborating evil for them in the depths of his breast. He set the great anvil in its stock and wrought chains which could be neither broken nor loosed, that the guilty pair might be gyved in them for ever and ever. Out of his bitter rage against Ares was born this device. He went then into his marriage chamber, where stood the bed he had cherished, and about its posts he interlaced his toils. Others, many of them, hung down from aloft, from the main roof-tree over the hearth; gossamer chains so fine that no man could see them, not even a blessed God, with such subtlety of craft had they been forged. When Hephaestus had meshed all the bed in his snare, he pretended to set forth for Lemnos, that well-built city which in his eyes is much the dearest land of earth. Nor was it a loose watch that Ares of the golden reins was keeping upon Hephaestus. As soon as he saw the great craftsman leave he took his journey to the famous house, chafing for love of well-crowned Cytherea. She was but newly come from Zeus, her mighty father, and had just sat down when Ares was in the house, grasping her hand and saying: "Come, darling, let us to bed and to our pleasure; for Hephaestus is now abroad, visiting in Lemnos among the barbarous-spoken Sintians."

His word of their lying together gave her joy. They went to their bed and snuggled deep into it, whereupon the springes of artful Hephaestus closed about them and tightened till they were not able to lift a limb nor move it. At last they understood there was no escape. Then the great God of the mighty arms drew near again and re-entered: he had turned back short of Lemnos when Helios, the spying Sun, had given him word. As he made heavily toward his home grief rooted in his heart: but when he stood there in its entry savage passion gripped him so that he roared hideously and de-claimed to all the Gods: —

"Father Zeus and every other Blessed Immortal, hither to me, and see a jest which is unpardonable. Because I am crippled, Aphrodite daughter of Zeus, does me dishonour, preferring Ares the destroyer, Ares being beautiful and straight of limb while I was born crooked. And whose fault is that, if not my parents'? Would they had not brought me into life! Look how these two are clipped together in love's embrace, here, in my very bed. To watch them cuts me to the heart. Yet I think they will not wish to lie thus, not even for a very little while longer, however mad their lust. Soon they will not wish to be together, yet shall my cunning bonds chain them as they are until her father has utterly repaid the marriage fee—every single thing I gave him for this bitch-eyed girl: though indeed his daughter is beautiful, despite her sin."

His mouthing gathered the gods to the house of the brazen floor. Poseidon the Earth-girdler, beneficent Hermes and royal Apollo the far-darting, came: but the Lady Goddesses remained at home, all of them, quite out of countenance. In Hephaestus' forecourt collected the Givers of Weal: and unquenchable was the laughter that arose from the blessed Gods as they studied the tricky device of Hephaestus. One would catch his neighbour's eye and gibe: "Bad deeds breed no merit. The slow outrun the speedy. See how poor crawling Hephaestus, despite that limp, has now overtaken Ares (much the most swift of all divine dwellers upon Olympus) and cleverly caught him. Ares will owe him the adulterer's fine." Words like this one whispered to the other: but of Hermes did Zeus' royal son Apollo loudly ask: "Hermes, son of Zeus, messenger and giver of good things: would you not choose even the bondage of these tough chains, if so you might sleep in the one bed by golden Aphrodite?" And to him the Gods' messenger, Argus-bane, replied: "If only this might be, kingly, far-darting Apollo! If there were chains without end, thrice as many as are here, and all you Gods with all the Goddesses to look on, yet would I be happy beside the Golden One."

At his saying more laughter rose among the Immortals: only Poseidon laughed not but was still entreating lame Hephaestus the craftsman to let Ares go. Now he spoke out, with winged words: "Loose him: and for him I promise whatever you require; as that he shall discharge the penalty he has incurred before the undying Gods." The famous strong-thewed God answered him: "Do not thus constrain me, Poseidon, Earth-girdler. The bonds of a worthless man are worthless bonds. How could I hold you liable before the Immortals, if Ares gets away free of his debt and this snare?" And to him replied the Earth-shaker: "Hephaestus, even if Ares absconds, leaving his debt unpaid, I myself will discharge it to you, wholly." And the lame master said, "I cannot refuse: nor would it be seemly to refuse such surety." So saying great Hephaestus loosed the chain and the couple when they were freed of the trap and its restraint swiftly fled away—he to Thrace and smiling Aphrodite to

Cyprus, to Paphos, her sanctuary with its incense-burning altar. There the Graces bathed her and anointed her with ambrosial oil, such as is set aside for the ever-living Gods. There they put upon her glorious clothing, till she was an enchantment to the eye. Such was the song of the famous minstrel.

[T. E. Lawrence, trans., *The Odyssey of Homer* (Oxford University Press), pp. 111–114.]

Apollo, or Phoibos Apollo, as Homer calls him, is a relative latecomer to Mount Olympus. His origins are unclear, but it is possible that he was originally an Asiatic god. His mother was Leto, thought by some to be the Anatolian goddess Lada from Lycia. The Greeks said that he was born on the island of Delos and that he was a sacred twin, one of many in mythology. His sister was the great virgin huntress Artemis. Regardless of whether he is Asian in origin, Apollo becomes in Greece a metaphor for the very essence of things Greek. He is the god of what has come to be thought of as the peculiarly Greek ideal of moderation—in the arts as well as in style of life. He is the god of law. With Athena, he brings reason to the Greek world in the trial of Orestes, in which the old earth forces are made subservient to Olympian reason.

To think of Apollo is to think of beauty and order. He has often been compared to Dionysos. Thus we speak of the necessary and productive tension between the Apollonian and the Dionysian in the arts—the tension between orderly discipline and deep emotion—as, for instance, in a Shakespearean sonnet, with its Apollonian form (its strict meter and its fourteen lines), which contains and gives particular urgency to the poet's Dionysian passion.

Apollo's home is Delphi (once Pytho), where he wrested control of the famous oracle from the dragon or python that guarded it. Again, Pythian Apollo and all that he represents as the protector of the organized Olympian religion thus takes control of prophecy from the older, more mysterious earth forces. The mystery is not altogether lost, however. If Delphi is the home of Apollo, it is also a favorite haunt of Dionysos in the winter months.

Apollo is the god who reminds us of the necessity of self-control and self-knowledge. "Know thyself" and "Nothing too much" are his primary mottoes. By the fifth century B.C.E., the cult of Apollo had taken precedence over that of Zeus himself. The great Sophoclean tragedies make this abundantly clear. The quest of Oedipus is a quest for self-knowledge on the personal as well as on the general human level.

Finally, in late classical times, Apollo, as a god of light, was associated with the sun—sometimes with the sun god, Helios. His sister, Artemis, was associated with the moon goddess, Selene.

More often than not, Apollo is depicted in art as a handsome youth, usually nude, with a lyre or a bow and a quiver of arrows.

The goddess Artemis, considered by the Greeks to be the twin sister of Apollo, was the virgin goddess of the hunt and the protector of the young (both animal and human). She was almost certainly Asian—specifically Anatolian—in origin. As Ma in Cappadocia or Cybele in Phrygia, she was the greatest of the Great Mothers, anything but a virgin. In Ephesus, where her cult was strongest, she was Artemis of the many breasts, a mother to all life. Much of this aspect of her character probably blended into the Demeter and Persephone cults in Greece, but remnants of the old Artemis remain in the new Greek version. The Greek Artemis is still the goddess of childbirth, and as a huntress, she is still associated with the wild. Her virginity and the masculine aspect of her nature suggest, as in the case of Pallas Athena, a defeminization of the Great Goddess—an undermining of her powerful matriarchal cult—by the patriarchal Homeric/Olympian religion. The Olympian Artemis had no qualms about employing violence. When young Acteon, hunting in the wilds, happened to come upon the naked Artemis bathing, the goddess, made furious by this intrusion on her virginal privacy, set her hunting hounds upon the youth, who paid with his life. As Ovid describes it, Artemis (Diana) turned the youth into a stag and set his own hounds upon him to tear his body to pieces.

✦

Among the most popular of Greek gods was Hermes, the son of Zeus by Maia, daughter of the Titan Atlas, who holds the world on his shoulders. Hermes was probably of Minoan/Mycenean origin. His name in Greek is related to the word for stone cairn. The tradition of Hermes and the cairn took form in the herms— the small posts or pillars with human head and phallus (to represent fertility) that were so prevalent in ancient Greece. The herms had particular functions that were in keeping with qualities associated with the god. They were road markers, and Hermes was the god of the road, of travelers. He was himself a frequent traveler from Mount Olympus, serving as the messenger of Zeus. Herms were often used as grave markers, and Hermes was the god who led people to Hades. Finally, herms were property markers that served to ward off evil from Athenian houses; Hermes was a popular household god.

Hermes was a trickster of sorts, delighting in petty theft and shrewd deals (see stories of him in this book's section on tricksters). Yet Zeus seems to have trusted him above all others with his commands. With his broad hat, his golden caduceus (the staff with writhing snakes later given to the medicine god, Asclepius), and his winged sandals, Hermes is most often depicted skimming the earth on an important mission for his father.

Dionysos is at once the most ambiguous and the most foreign of the Greek gods. His cult became so powerful that the gods and their priests had little choice but to admit him to Mount Olympus. If the theologians and poets of the sixth and fifth centuries B.C.E. were Apollonian by nature, they, like Pentheus in Euripides' the *Bacchae*, were forced to confront the ecstasy that was Dionysos, the ecstasy that complements Apollonian order and discipline and is so necessary to art and religion. So it is that the Greeks recognized this popular Thracian and probably Anatolian god, associated with the strange orgiastic rites of the Phrygian mother goddess Cybele and her son-lover Attis (himself a Dionysos figure), and gave him a respected place with Apollo as a resident of the oracular center at Delphi. Dionysos, in fact, reigned at Delphi in the winter months, when his dances were performed there. Through his association with drama, he was also honored at the great dramatic festivals such as the City Dionysia in Athens. As has been suggested, the reconciliation of Apollo and Dionysos is appropriate to the paradoxical nature of both art and prophecy, in which discipline and possession or inspiration are so closely related.

Dionysos was a god who died and returned to life. His ritual is itself a ritual of death and rebirth in which flesh is consumed and fertility celebrated with drums and dance and the constant presence of ecstatic women or maenads, who may have taken part in mysterious orgies. Dionysos is thus, like Osiris in Egypt, Adonis in Babylonia, Tammuz in Sumer, Attis in Phrygia, and even the early form of Zeus in Crete, associated with crops—specifically, in his case, with the grape (and there-fore with wine) and with sexuality (Dionysos was described by Plutarch as the god of all life-giving fluids). Dionysos is a god very much of the earth and, as such, was always an outsider among the gods. Even his birth was odd. Fathered by Zeus on the mortal Semele, he was delivered from Zeus' thigh, where the Supreme Being had hidden the fetus after it was removed from his mother, who had died after foolishly making Zeus promise to reveal himself to her in his true form.

One of Dionysos' most famous escapades is described in the *Homeric Hymns*.

> What I remember now
> is Dionysus, son of
> glorious Semele, how he appeared
> by the sand of an empty sea,
> how it was far out, on a promontory, how
> he was like a young man,
> an adolescent
> His dark hair
> was beautiful, it
> blew all around him, and

over his shoulders, the strong
shoulders, he held a purple cloak.
Suddenly,
pirates appeared, Tyrrhenians,
they came on the sea wine
sturdily in their ship
and they came fast.
A wicked fate drove them on.
They saw him,
they nodded to each other,
they leaped out
and grabbed him,
they pulled him
into their boat
jumping for joy!
They thought he was
the son of
one of
Zeus' favorite kings:
they wanted to tie him up
hard.
The ropes wouldn't hold.
Willow ropes,
they fell right off him, off arms and legs.
He smiled at them,
motionless,
in his dark eyes.
The helmsman saw this,
he immediately cried out,
he screamed out to his men:
"You fools!
What powerful god is this
whom you've seized,
whom you've tied up?
Not even our ship,
sturdy as it is,
not even our ship
can carry him.
Either this is Zeus,
or it's Apollo, the silver-bow,

or else it's Poseidon!
He doesn't look like
a human person,
he's like the gods
who live on Olympus.
Come on!
Let's unload him, right now,
let's put him
on the dark land.
Don't tie his hands
or he'll be angry, he'll
draw terrible winds to us,
he'll bring us a big storm!"
That's what he said.
The captain, however,
in a bitter voice,
roared back:
"You fool,
look at the wind!
Grab the ropes,
draw the sail.
We men
will take care of him.
I think
He'll make it to Egypt,
or Cyprus,
or the Hyperboreans,
or even further.
In the end
he'll tell
who his friends are,
and his relatives,
and his possessions.
A god sent him to us."
He said this,
then he fixed the mast
and the sail of the ship.
And a wind began to blow
into the sail. And then
they stretched the rigging.

Suddenly,
wonderful things
appeared to them.
First of all,
wine broke out, babbling,
bubbling over their speedy black ship,
it was sweet, it was fragrant,
its odor was divine.
Every sailor who saw it
was terrified.
Suddenly,
a vine sprang up,
on each side,
to the very top of the sail.
And grapes, all over,
clung to it.
And a dark ivy
coiled the mast,
it blossomed with flowers
and yielded
Suddenly,
all the oar-locks
became garlands.
When they saw this
they cried to the helmsman
then and there
to steer their ship
to land.
But
the god became a lion,
an awful lion
high up on the ship,
and he roared at them
terribly.
And then,
in their midst,
he put a bear,
a bear with a furry neck,
and it made gestures.
It threatened,

and the lion,
on the high deck,
scowled down.
Everybody
fled to the stern,
they panicked, they ran
to the helmsman, because
the head of the helmsman was cool.
But
the lion, suddenly,
leaped up, it seized
the captain!
They all wanted to escape
such a doom
when they saw it.
They all jumped ship
into the sea, they jumped
into the divine sea.
They became dolphins.
As for the helmsman,
he was saved:
the god pitied him,
he made him very rich,
and told him this:
"Courage, divine Hecator,
I like you.
I am Dionysus
the ear-splitter.
My mother,
Cadmaean Semele,
had me
when she slept with Zeus."
Farewell,
son of Semele,
who had such a beautiful face.
Without you,
the way to compose a sweet song
is forgotten.

["The Hymn to Dionysos," trans. Charles Boer, in
The Homeric Hymns (Chicago, 1970), pp. 13–17.]

ROME: The Renamed Olympians

The Romans essentially absorbed the Greek gods, primarily through the Etruscans, who were an important presence on the Italian peninsula between 900 and 500 B.C.E. The primary difference between the Greek and the Roman understanding of the gods lay in the Romans' greater emphasis on the gods as personifications of abstractions—love, war, fortune, and so forth. It can also be said that the Roman version was more an official state religion with political ramifications than a religion that spoke to personal or spiritual needs.

In Western literature, the Latin and Greek names for the Olympians have been used almost interchangeably. The list that follows indicates the equivalent names:

Coelus (Heaven) and Terra (Earth) = Uranos and Gaia
Saturn[1] and Ops (or the Phrygian Cybele) = Kronos and Rhea
Jupiter or Jove = Zeus
Juno = Hera
Neptune = Poseidon
Pluto = Hades
Ceres = Demeter
Proserpina = Persephone
Vesta[2] = Hestia
Apollo = Apollo
Diana = Artemis
Minerva = Athena
Venus = Aphrodite
Cupid = Eros
Mars = Ares
Mercury = Hermes
Vulcan = Hephaistos
Bacchus = Dionysos

ICELAND (NORSE): The Aesir and the Vanir

As in the case of the creation story, our source for the Norse myths are Icelandic works, the *Elder* or *Poetic Edda* of the tenth century C.E. and the *Younger* or *Prose Edda* written by Snorri Sturluson in about 1220 C.E.

---

[1] Saturn is associated with the Roman tradition of the Saturnalia, a festival of renewal and fertility marked at times by licentiousness.

[2] Thus, vestal virgins were priestesses of Vesta.

The Norse gods and goddesses, known as the Aesir, lived in a place called Asgard. As in the case of the Greeks, these gods had gained predominance only at the cost of warfare with another group of gods, called the Vanir. The Aesir were led by Odin and Frigg, the Vanir by Freyr and Freya, who were children of the god Njord and were associated, like the Vanir in general and the Greek Titans, with forces of the earth. Freyr and Freya, as brother and sister, remind us of Osiris and Isis as well. Like the Egyptians, they are, above all, representative of fertility. Eventually the Aesir and the Vanir were reconciled. The end of the gods would come at the apocalyptic Ragnarök.

Odin was the father god. He was also—like Dionysos, Attis, Osiris, and so many others, including Christ—a god who in some sense experiences death. Odin (Wodan or Wotan, as worshipped by the Germanic peoples) was married to Frigg, who possessed knowledge of the future. But Odin was the father of the thunder god, Thor, by Earth herself. Another son of Odin was Baldr, the most beautiful and best of the gods. Baldr was killed by Hoder with the help of the trickster god Loki, whose offspring were the wolf Fenrir and the World Serpent (who would fight against the Aesir at the end of the world), and Hel, the ruler of the underworld. The death of Baldr was the occasion of the Norse version of the descent to the underworld. This is the story of the Norse war in Heaven.

> In the early days there were two sets of gods, the Vanir, led by Njordr and his children Freyr and Freya, and the Aesir, led by Odin, Tyr, and Thor. These tribes went to war, perhaps owing to an insult by the Aesir to a member of the Vanir. At first the Vanir took the advantage, pressing their attack on Asgard, the home of the Aesir, and destroying the protective walls around it. The Vanir were skilled in *seidr* and other forms of magic unknown to the Aesir and feared and loathed by them, and this magic may have been the secret to the early success of the Vanir. Eventually the Aesir seem to have proved to be the greater warriors, however, and battled the Vanir back to Vanaheim, their home. Neither group was entirely victorious, though, and eventually the two tribes sought peace.
>
> According to some accounts, the gods determined to seal their truce with an exchange of hostages. Njordr and his offspring left the Vanir to live among the Aesir, while Honir and Mimir went from Asgard to Vanaheim. At first the exchange seemed an equitable one: Njordr and Freyr soon held high rank as priests among the Aesir, while Freya taught those who would learn the forbidden magic of *seidr.* For their part, Honir was honored as a powerful leader, while Mimir's advice was held to be peerless in its wisdom. It soon became

apparent to the Vanir, however, that they had fared rather poorly in the exchange. While Hoenir was an able leader as long as Mimir was present to advise him, he was indecisive and ineffectual without his counselor. As it appeared that they had been duped, the Vanir decided to take their revenge upon Mimir: they cut off his head and sent it to Odin as a token of their displeasure.

Odin, however, always one to see the profit to be made from adversity, was far from discomfited by this grisly gift. Instead, he smeared the head with herbs and balms to preserve it, and whispered magic charms to give it speech. Henceforth Odin was never without the wise counsel of Mimir, and increased his own power, prescience, and wisdom through his acquisition of the bodiless head.

[Christopher R. Fee and David A. Leeming, *Gods, Heroes, and Kings* (Oxford University Press, 2001), p. 16.]

IRELAND AND WALES: The Family of Don and the Tuatha de Danann

THE FAMILY OF DON

In the Welsh tales collectively known as *The Mabinogi* or *Mabinogion*, we learn of the family of Don. In Ireland we have the equivalent Tuatha De Danann, the people of Danu. Danu/Don is the great goddess whose reign stretches far back into pre-Celtic Britain and beyond that to Indo-European roots in ancient India, where Danu—the mother of the demon Vrtra—mourns the death of her offspring at the hands of the patriarchal god Indra.

In Wales, Don is a daughter of Mathonwy, the ancient founder of the House of Don and is sometimes said to be the wife of the god of death, Beli. Another child of Mathonwy is Math, the god of wealth who requires that his feet rest on a virgin's lap unless he is at battle. When his virgin/footstool is corrupted by his nephews—Gilfaethwy and the storyteller Gwydion—Math turns the young men into wild animals for a year. Gwydion apparently fathered the great Lleu with his sister, the dawn-goddess Aranrhod, whose loss of virginity was revealed when she was brought to Math as a replacement for his corrupted footstool. As she stepped over Math's magic wand to test her supposed virginity, two boys, Dylan and Lleu, emerged from her. Dylan escaped to the sea, and Lleu was protected and reared by Gwydion.

Besides Gofannon, Gwydion, Gilfaethwy, and Aranrhod, the children of Don include, among lesser figures, the god Lludd, described above, and Penar-dun, who with her husband Llyr (the ocean-god Lir in Ireland and probably the source for *King Lear*) parented Manawydan, the sea-god. By another marriage Penardun was the mother of the peacemaker Nisien and the strife-maker Efnisien. Llyr fathered the famous Bran and Branwen by another wife.

Bran, whose Irish equivalent is also Bran, a god of the otherworld, leads an army into Ireland to protect his sister Branwen, wife of the Irish king Matholwch. Branwen's safety had been threatened by the malicious behavior of her half-brother Efnisien. After a terrible battle, only five pregnant women remained in Ireland to form a new population, and only seven Britons—including the great poet-warrior Taliesen—returned home, led by the head of the dead Bran, which remained magically alive and talking.

THE TUATHA DE DANANN, THE FIRBOLG, THE FOMORIANS, AND THE INVASIONS OF IRELAND

The Irish version of Don is Danu (Dana), the great-mother of the Tuatha De Danann. It was said that the Tuatha De Danann had come to Ireland originally from Greece or from a hole in the sky, that they had been protected by a magical mist, that they had once lived in the ancient cities of Findias, Gorias, Murias, and Falias, and that they were expert at magic and enchantment. It was they who brought druidry to Ireland.

The Tuatha De Danann had to fight for the control of Ireland with the terrible sea-born demonic giants called the Fomorians (Fomorii, Fomors, or Fomhoire) in the north and the dark Firbolg (Fir Bholg) in the south. The Fomorians are traditionally associated, like the ancient Greek Titans and the Vedic Asuras, with forces of nature that stand against order; in the Germanic traditions this role is played by the giants. The Fomorians are often depicted as misshapen, with one eye or one foot. The Firbolg were said by some to be descendants of the Nemedians, who had preceded the Firbolg and the other early peoples in Ireland and were led by Nemed (Nemhedh), son of the king of Scythia in Greece. They had come to Ireland in search of the gold of the Fomorian king Conann. Most of the invaders were drowned, but Nemed was able to establish a foothold, and he built forts and cleared land. The Nemedians were known as great artisans.

In their craftsmanship the Nemedians resembled the Partholonians, who, under their king Partholon, had come to Ireland before them, had fought the Fomorians—led then by the footless Cichol Grinchenghos—and had been destroyed by a plague. Partholon had murdered his father and mother in an unsuccessful attempt to take power in his original homeland. As in the case of King Arthur, Partholon's history was marred by the story of his wife Dealgnaid's affair with one of his servants, Togda. The Partholonians them-selves, according to the twelfth-century Christian writers, had been the second invaders of Ireland, the first being pre-Flood followers of Noah's granddaughter Cesair or, according to others, the Irish Banbha. Of this group, only Fintan (the "Old White One"), sur-vived to live for many centuries and to bear witness to the past.

As for the Nemedians, much of their energy was spent in wars with the Fomorians, and eventually Nemed and 3,000 of his people died of a plague. After Nemed's death, the Nemedians were con-trolled by the Fomorians, who demanded excessive tribute of them. But with the help of Greek allies, the Nemedians, led by Nemed's son Fergus, were able to defeat their enemy. It was Fergus who killed the Fomorian king Conann. But few Nemedians survived an attack from the sea by another Fomorian king, More, son of Dele. After this battle, the Nemedians scattered in three groups. One group went to mainland Greece where they were enslaved and made to transport bags of soil on their backs from fertile land to rocky ter-races in the hills. Thus the name Firbolg, or "bag men."

Along with other early peoples, the Gailioin and the Fir Dhomh-nann, the Firbolg would eventually, upon their return, institute in Ireland the idea of the association of the sacred kingship and the fertility of the land. It was they who divided Ireland into provinces or "fifths." Another group of Nemedians, led by Fergus's son, escaped to Britain. The final group, led by Beotac, went to the north-ern Greek Islands. This group set about learning the mysteries of creation, including magic and druidry. According to some, a few of these people became so knowledgeable that they were deified as the Tuatha De Danann.

The rulers of the Tuatha De Danann when they came to Ireland were King Nuada (Nuadhu) and his warrior queen, Macha. They established their court at Tara. Nuada Argetlamhor is known as Nuada of the Silver Hand, whose Welsh counterpart in this aspect is the Lludd cognate, Nudd of the Silver Hand. Nuada was so named because after he lost his hand in a defeat of the Firbolg at the First Battle of Magh Tuireadh, the medicine god, Dian Ceeht, replaced the lost limb with a silver version. It was the loss of the hand that led Nuada to transfer his crown to Bres, the handsome son of a Tuatha De Danann woman and the Fomorian king Elatha, and the husband of the fertility-goddess Brigid. When Bres's tyrannical ways led to his dethronement, he turned to the Fomorians for help.

Nuada was restored to the throne, but he gave up power to Lugh, who used his slingshot at the Second Battle of Magh Tuireadh to kill the much feared Balor, a glance from whose "evil eye" could destroy armies. As Balor's eye was opened, Lugh cast his missile with such force that the eye was driven back through the skull of Balor, and thus its destructive power was unleashed upon the Fomorians. By that time, however, Balor already had killed Nuada as well as Macha, the warrior-goddess queen. With the defeat of the Fomorians the Tuatha De Danann could afford to spare Bres in return for his teaching them the arts of agriculture. That Bres was so clearly related to fertility suggests that the myth of this war might have been derived from the same Indo-European theme of divine conflict as was the Norse myth of the battle between the Vanir and the Aesir. Hence the Fomorians seem to constitute at one time both the productive powers of fertility and the fearsome forces of destruction that exist side by side in nature.

The relationship between the one-handed Nuada and the battle-god Lugh calls to mind a similar one between the Norse Tyr and Odin, and this relationship seems to have very old roots. Further, several similarities between Odin and Lugh imply that both have some common Indo-European ancestor: Lugh was part Fomorian, just as Odin was part giant, and the name *Lugh* itself may well come from a Gaulish word for "raven," an animal explicitly linked to Odin. Finally, the association between Nuada and Lugh also may be the genesis of the Arthurian story of the fisher king; *Nuada* may be derived from a word meaning "fisher," and the original myth seems to have had to do with a powerful war figure who comes to the aid of a maimed king.

Two other deities stand as particularly important figures in the Irish pantheon, figures of whom other tribal gods and goddesses were in some sense emanations. These primary deities are the Dagda as the tribal father and the Morrigan as the earth-mother/war-goddess, who was associated in triple form with Macha—a figure descended from the Gaulish horse-goddess Epona and one related to the British mare-goddess Rhiannon—and Bodb. The Dagda, father of Brigid, was a primary leader of the Tuatha De Danann; he was the protector of a magic cauldron of prosperity that had been brought from the city of Murias. The Dagda was known as "the Good." As the story goes, before a great battle the gods held a council of war during which each god announced his particular powers and intentions. When the Dagda's turn came he said, "I will do on my own all that you promise to do." In short, he is "the Good" because he was good at everything, assimilating the positive qualities of all the gods.

As for the Morrigan, she brings together the fruitful elements of a fertility goddess and the fear associated with a battle-goddess. Like her ancient Indian ancestor the goddess Devi, she is at once mother and destroyer, goddess of life and of war. Celtic goddesses often exhibit voracious sexual appetites, and the Morrigan combines such amorous lust with bloodlust. The story is told of how Morrigan made sexual advances toward the Irish hero Cuchu-lainn, advances to which he did not respond; at his death she took vengeance for this insult by perching on his shoulder as his life blood flowed from him. This story resembles the incident in the ancient Sumerian epic of *Gilgamesh*, in which the advances of the great goddess Inanna or Ishtar are refused by the mortal hero Gilgamesh. The combination of fertility and destructive power manifested in the Morrigan is associated with the identification of goddess and "sovranty" in Irish mythology; cropfields and battlefields both do their part to make up the country, and the Morrigan has power over both.

[Christopher R. Fee and David A. Leeming, *Gods, Heroes, and Kings* (Oxford University Press, 2001), pp. 69–73.]

BIBLIOGRAPHY

✦

Good, general discussions of the god concept are to be found in *The Encyclopedia of Religion*, ed. Mircea Eliade (New York, 1987). See especially the entries under "God" and "Deity" (vol. 4, pp. 264–276; vol. 6, pp. 1–66). For a valuable discussion of the concept of divinity and the question of sky gods versus earth gods, see Eliade's *Patterns in Comparative Religion* (New York, 1958). Northrop Frye, in *The Great Code: The Bible and Literature* (New York, 1982), presents a useful analysis of the metaphorical aspect of God. William Hansen's *Classical Mythology* (Oxford University Press, 2004) provides a good overview of the Greek concept of deity. An important work on the Egyptian concept of the divine is contained in Geraldine Pinch's *Egyptian Mythology: A Guide to the Gods, Goddesses, and Traditions of Ancient Egypt* (Oxford University Press, 2002). George M. Williams's *Handbook of Hindu Mythology* (New York: Oxford University Press, 2003) is a trusty guide through the complexities of Indian mythology. John Lindow's *Norse Mythology: A Guide to the Gods, Heroes, Rituals, and Beliefs* (Oxford University Press, 2001) is a good source for the study of the Norse gods. For a history of the deity of the Abrahamic religions, see Karen Armstrong's lively *A History of God: The 4000 Year Quest of Judaism, Christianity, and Islam* (Ballantine, 1994). A case for many gods is Jordan Paper's *The Deities Are Many: A Polytheistic Theology* (State University of New York Press, 2005). For a provocative denial of deity, see physicist Richard Hawkins's *The God Delusion* (Mariner Books, 2008).

THE GOD AS ARCHETYPE

In our depictions of divinity, we humans have given form to our sense of the ultimate source of our own significance. When we give form to divinity, we derive that form from our own experience. We make our gods in our own image because our own image marks the physical limits of our being. We cannot know the gods; we can know only our experience of them. Not surprisingly, since the essence of whatever it is to be human is as present in the Indonesian or Nigerian as it is in the Irishman or the Indian, these depictions when seen as a whole—as world mythology—reveal a pattern of archetypal motifs that are as universal as the physical characteristics we humans share. As we study the gods of world mythology, we will encounter, below the surfaces of the many cultural masks they inevitably wear, the constant, universal shadows that we call the Father-Creator, the Great Mother, the trickster, the dying god, the destroyer god, the helper god, the primordial sky-earth, male-female pair, the gods who visit the earth and are shunned, and many other familiar figures.

For the student of mythology, it is important to recognize in any god or goddess both the mask, or metaphor, that is worshipped by the culture that created it and the spiritual or psychological source for that mask, the archetype, which is either an aspect of ultimate reality or a creation of what Jung called the collective unconscious—the collective human mind. In either case, the archetypal image is part of our common human heritage. It contains information about our experience as human beings. It is, therefore, of great metaphorical value to the artist, whether he or she be painter, sculptor, or writer. When a Faulkner character called Lena Grove, a product of a particular class of the American South, is depicted in imagery that associates her with the universal Mother Goddess archetype, we recognize her significance whether we are from Atlanta or Madras or Oslo. The same could be said of Hamlet and his association, by way of the tragic hero, with the dying god of myth. The myths presented here will serve to illustrate both the cultural diversity and the universality of our gods.

THE SUPREME BEING

The Supreme Being who emerges from the many world myths about the chief god is one who embodies the prevalent patriarchal arrangement of society. He is, in short, the embodiment of kingship, of male power, of the paterfamilias. Frequently a sun god, he is the giver of life, heat, and light and, at the same time, an unapproachable being. Semele dies when confronted by the revealed Zeus; Dante is nearly overwhelmed by the "light eternal" in the *Paradiso*.

The word *dios* (god)—and the name Zeus itself—is derived from the Sanskrit *div,* meaning shine, light, or day. He is a creator—often, as in the case of the Judeo-Christian-Muslim God, the originator of the universe. And he is a fecundator—often associated with bulls. This is true of Zeus, Indra, Thor, the Sumerian Enlil, and many others.

Sometimes the chief sky god is the husband of the Great Earth Mother, as in the marriage of Gaia and Uranos. This makes sense, as he is of the sky, nearly always revealed by weather—particularly storms that produce moisture—and she is of the earth and is the incarnation of fecundity. There are also cases, especially in matrilineal societies, in which the Supreme Being is the Great Mother.

Perhaps most important, as the concept of the Supreme Being has developed in patriarchal society, a god has emerged whose sky home becomes a metaphor for higher values, higher laws. Thus, the god is more often than not a lawgiver and law preserver, as in the cases of Yahweh, God, Allah, and the Persian Ahura Mazda. The Supreme Being perhaps achieves his highest form in the Hindu concept of Brahman, the Ultimate Reality as idea, of which the great gods Shiva, Vishnu, the Goddess, and Brahma are mere metaphors. Brahman is the absolute reality out of which all forms flow. Brahman is beyond definition and, therefore, not limited or confined by attributes of one gender or the other. As Brahman is never a personality, there are no Brahman myths; yet, as Brahman informs all things, as Brahman is at once immanent and transcendent, all myths are myths of Brahman.

In literature as well as in the other arts, including architecture, the Supreme Being archetype would seem to inform and provide metaphorical support for the tendency toward the patriarchal, the authoritarian, or the monumental. The myth of the Supreme Being is the most universal of archetypes; it is as common as fatherhood and the idea of God. It is realized literally everywhere.

INDIA: Krishna-Vishnu as Brahman

In the *Bhagavad-Gita,* the philosophical center of the great Hindu epic the *Mahabharata,* Krishna-Vishnu reveals himself to the warrior Arjuna as the personal base on which Brahman rests. He is the embodiment of the supreme primal power.

Krishna Gives Arjuna a Celestial Eye

The Blessed Lord said:

5. Son of Prithā, behold my forms in their hundreds and their thousands; how various they are, how divine, how many-hued and multiform. . . .

7. Do you today the whole universe behold centred here in One, with all that it contains of moving and unmoving things; [behold it] in my body, and whatever else you fain would see.

8. But never will you be able to see Me with this your [natural] eye. A celestial eye I'll give you, behold my power as Lord!

Krishna's Transfiguration
Sanjaya said:

9. So saying Hari,[1] the great Lord of power-and-the-skilful-use-of-it, revealed to the son of Prithā his highest sovereign form,—

10. [A form] with many a mouth and eye and countless marvellous aspects; many [indeed] were its divine adornments, many the celestial weapons raised on high.

11. Garlands and robes celestial He wore, fragrance divine was his anointing. [Behold this] God whose every [mark] spells wonder, the Infinite, facing every way!

12. If in [bright] heaven together should arise the shining brilliance of a thousand suns, then would that perhaps resemble the brilliance of that [God] so great of Self.

13. Then did the son of Pāndu see the whole [wide] universe in One converged, there in the body of the God of gods, yet divided out in multiplicity.

Arjuna's Hymn of Praise
Arjuna said:

8. You are the Primal God, Primeval Person, You of this universe the last prop-and-resting-place, You the knower and what is to be known, [You our] highest home, O You whose forms are infinite, by You the whole universe was spun. . . .

40. All hail [to You] when I stand before You, [all hail] when I stand behind You, all hail to You wherever I may be, [all hail to You,] the All! How infinite your strength, how limitless your prowess! All things You bring to their consummation: hence You are All.

[From the *Bhagavad Gita*, trans. R. C. Zaehner
(Oxford University Press, 1969), pp. 304–319.]

---

[1] "Hari": a name of Vishnu.

ISRAEL: Yahweh

The Yahweh of the Book of Job reveals himself to Job "out of the tempest," which is the appropriate element of the sky-storm god, of whom he is a particular embodiment.

Chapter 38

Then the Lord answered Job out of the whirlwind, and said,

2 Who is this that darkeneth counsel by words without knowledge?
3 Gird up now thy loins like a man; for I will demand of thee, and answer thou me.
4 Where wast thou when I laid the foundations of the earth? declare, if thou hast understanding.
5 Who hath laid the measures thereof, if thou knowest? or who hath stretched the line upon it?
6 Whereupon are the foundations thereof fastened? or who laid the corner stone thereof;
7 When the morning stars sang together, and all the sons of God shouted for joy?
8 Or *who* shut up the sea with doors, when it brake forth, *as if* it had issued out of the womb?
9 When I made the cloud the garment thereof, and thick darkness a swaddling-band for it,
10 And brake up for it my decreed *place,* and set bars and doors,
11 And said, Hitherto shalt thou come, but no further: and here shall thy proud waves be stayed?
12 Hast thou commanded the morning since thy days; *and* caused the dayspring to know his place;
13 That it might take hold of the ends of the earth, that the wicked might be shaken out of it?
14 It is turned as clay *to* the seal; and they stand as a garment.
15 And from the wicked their light is withholden, and the high arm shall be broken.
16 Hast thou entered into the springs of the sea? or hast thou walked in the search of the depth?
17 Have the gates of death been opened unto thee? or hast thou seen the doors of the shadow of death?
18 Hast thou perceived the breadth of the earth? declare if thou knowest it all.

19 Where *is* the way *where* light dwelleth? and *as for* darkness, where is the place thereof,

20 That thou shouldest take it to the bound thereof, and that thou shouldest know the paths *to* the house thereof?

21 Knowest thou *it,* because thou wast then born? or *because* the number of thy days *is* great?

22 Hast thou entered into the treasures of the snow? or hast thou seen the treasures of the hail,

23 Which I have reserved against the time of trouble, against the day of battle and war?

24 By what way is the light parted, *which* scattereth the east wind upon the earth?

25 Who hath divided a water-course for the overflowing of waters, or a way for the lightning of thunder;

26 To cause it to rain on the earth, *where* no man *is; on* the wilderness, wherein *there is* no man;

27 To satisfy the desolate and waste *ground;* and to cause the bud of the tender herb to spring forth?

28 Hath the rain a father? or who hath begotten the drops of dew?

29 Out of whose womb came the ice? and the hoary frost of heaven, who hath gendered it?

30 The waters are hid as *with* a stone, and the face of the deep is frozen.

31 Canst thou bind the sweet influences of Plei´-ă-děs̄, or loose the bands of ō-rī̄ō-on?

32 Canst thou bring forth Măzz´-ă-rŏth in his season? or canst thou guide Ärc-tū´-rŭs with his sons?

33 Knowest thou the ordinances of heaven? canst thou set the dominion thereof in the earth?

34 Canst thou lift up thy voice to the clouds, that abundance of waters may cover thee?

35 Canst thou send lightnings, that they may go, and say unto thee, Here we *are?*

36 Who hath put wisdom in the inward parts? or who hath given understanding to the heart?

37 Who can number the clouds in wisdom? or who can stay the bottles of heaven,

38 When the dust groweth into hardness, and the clods cleave fast together?

39 Wilt thou hunt the prey for the lion? or fill the appetite of the young lions,

40 When they couch in *their* dens, *and* abide in the covert to lie in wait?

41 Who provideth for the raven his food? when his young ones cry unto God, they wander for lack of meat.

[Job 38.]

NATIVE SOUTH AMERICA (UITOTO): Nainema

The Uitoto of Colombia in South America tell a strange story of the Supreme Being, who, like many Supreme Beings, is an ex nihilo creator.

> Listen carefully. Put down the tools and the cares of today, and listen carefully for this is how it is. This is where we are.
>
> First there was Nainema, but Nainema was nothing but a vision, an illusion. There wasn't anything else. But the vision which was Nainema affected itself deeply.
>
> So Nainema took this vision which was himself unto himself and meditated. He held the vision by the thread of a dream and looked into it, searching . . . for what?
>
> He found nothing in the vision so he searched within it again, tying the empty vision to the dream-thread with a magical glue. Then he took the vision, this phantasm, and methodically trampled the bottom of it until the earth he dreamed was enough for him to sit upon.
>
> Now, sitting, holding on to the illusion, he spat a stream of saliva and the forests came into being and grew. Nainema then lay down on the earth and envisioned a sky above it, which also came into being.
>
> Then, gazing intently at himself—he, the one who was the story itself—created this story for us to hear.
>
> Now do you understand?
>
> [David A. Leeming and Jake Page, *God: Myths of the Male Divine* (Oxford University Press, 1996), pp. 157–158.]

AFRICA (BUSHMAN): Mantis   — *UNGREATFULNESS / HATE*

A typical theme in African versions of the archetypal supreme creator god is that of his decision to abandon his world. He is the *deus absconditus*, the absent god who is so disgusted by human corruption that he simply leaves and hides.

> The Bushmen, who live in the Kalahari Desert of southwest Africa, believe in an *ex nihilo* creator god who takes the form of the praying mantis and whose name sounds like "kaggen" (sometimes written as Cagn), with the typical clicking sound before it. In fact, the term means praying mantis, and that insect is sacred to the Bushmen.
>
> Mantis, as we can call him, was the creator of almost everything, and in the old days he lived here with humankind. It was the

foolishness of humans that drove him away in disgust and left so many of us hungry.

Many stories are told of the creator in those days long ago. We hear of his wife Coti and two sons who taught the people how to find food in the earth, and of a daughter who married a snake. It is said that Mantis could become any animal he wanted, but most of all he liked becoming an eland bull. The elands are still his favorites, and only they know where he is. People also say that Mantis created the moon by throwing his shoe into the night sky.

[David Leeming and Margaret Leeming, *A Dictionary of Creation Myths* (Oxford University Press, 1994), p. 39.]

NATIVE NORTH AMERICA (CHEROKEE): Sun Goddess

Among many groups of Indians in the American Southwest, the supreme creator god is female. This makes good sense since many of these cultures are matrilineal. In one myth the Cherokee supreme sun goddess resembles the African model in that she hides herself in anger at human transgressions.

The sun's daughter lived in a house in the sky directly above the earth, and every day, when the sun made her journey from the other side of the vault of the sky, she would visit her daughter. Once there, the old woman sun often complained about her grandchildren, the people of the earth. They never would look directly at her, she said; instead, they would only screw up their faces and squint at her briefly.

The moon, though, found the people, his younger brothers, to be handsome, since they often smiled up at him in the night sky. It did not take long before the sun was deeply jealous of the moon and his great popularity, and she decided to kill all the people. Sitting in her daughter's house one day, she refused to leave and, instead, sent down a killing heat. Many people died, and the rest despaired. Desperate, they sought help from some friendly spirits called the Little Men.

The Little Men thought and said that the only way the people could save themselves was to kill the sun herself. They changed two of the people into snakes and sent them up into the sky to wait until the sun went for dinner. Then, it was planned, they would leap out from their hiding place and bite her.

When the time came, one of the snakes—an adder—was blinded by the sun's light and could do nothing but spit out yellow slime. The sun called him a nasty name and flounced back into the house.

At this, the other snake—a copperhead—was so put off that he gave up altogether and crawled away.

Meanwhile, people continued to die from the searing heat of the angry sun, and they pleaded again with the Little Men for help. Again they transformed two of the men—one into a fierce, horned monster, and the other into a rattlesnake. Most people placed their bets on the monster, and the rattlesnake, not to be outdone, raced ahead and coiled himself up on the doorstep of the sun's daughter's house. When the daughter opened the door and called out for her mother, the rattlesnake struck and killed her. So excited was he that he forgot all about the old sun and returned to the people, followed by the disgusted horned monster. The monster continued to be furious, growing so difficult that the people had to banish him to the distant end of the world.

Meanwhile, the sun found her daughter dead and, in grief, shut herself up in the house. The world turned dark, and the people realized they had to coax the sun back out of the house or they would all perish of the cold, not the heat. The Little Men explained that their only hope was to bring the sun's daughter back from the country of the ghosts in the Darkening Land of the west. For this mission, they chose seven men and gave them a box to carry, as well as one wooden rod each, along with some precise instructions.

Before long, the seven men arrived in the Darkening Land and found a huge crowd of ghosts dancing, and there, taking part in the outer circle of dancing ghosts, was the sun's daughter. As she went past, one of the men struck her with his rod. Each man in turn did the same, and after the seventh man struck her, she fell out of the ring and was promptly put in the box, while the other ghosts danced on unnoticing.

As the men headed eastward with the box, the daughter inside repeatedly asked to be let out. She was cramped. She was hungry. She was smothering. As the men neared home, they began to get anxious that she might really be dying in the box, so they opened the lid just a crack and something flitted by them with a fluttering sound. Then, from the bushes nearby, they heard the singing of the redbird. They shut the lid of the box and proceeded, only to discover when they reached home that the box was empty.

(Because they let the daughter of the sun escape—and she now sings for all people in the form of the redbird—it has been impossible since that time to bring back the people who die.)

The sun had been full of hope that she would see her daughter again, but realizing that she would not, she wept and wept, causing a great flood on the earth. Now the people were in danger of drowning. So they sent a number of their most handsome young men and most beautiful young women up into the sky to dance, in hopes of distracting the sun. In her grief, the sun was not to be deterred and wept on. Finally, the dancers told the drummer to play a different song, and they danced to the new one and the sun looked up. The new music and the young people dancing in their circles were so beautiful that the old sun gave up her grieving and once again smiled.

[David A. Leeming and Jake Page, *Goddess: Myths of the Female Divine* (Oxford University Press, 1994), pp. 57–59.]

JAPAN: Amaterasu

The following myth of the Japanese sun goddess Amaterasu is an example of goddess power being threatened by a male force jealous of that power. Like the Cherokee sun goddess she hides herself in anger. In the Shinto tradition Amaterasu is still considered to be the most significant ancestor of Japanese emperors. An important part of an emperor's coronation ceremony takes place at Amaterasu's temple at Ise.

Clap your hands to celebrate Amaterasu's reappearance at dawn while her messengers, the cocks, crow and her visage gleams brightly from the sacred octagonal mirror that enticed her back to her place in the sky so long ago. It was like this.

She is Goddess of the Sun, her full name Amaterasu Omikami, queen of all the *kami*, the forces inherent in nature. She rules in heaven, this Great Woman Who Possesses Noon, and without her rice does not grow. Like the other gods, she has two souls—one gentle, one violent—but true wickedness exists only in the abyssal land of the dead, beneath the world. Amaterasu came into being at a time when the world was young and floated about like a jellyfish.

Amaterasu also had a brother, Susanowo, who ruled the oceans and also erupted as thunder, lightning, and rain. When his gentle soul ruled him, he made things grow; but when he drank too much, his violent soul took command and he brought havoc to the world. One day, he journeyed to heaven to visit his older sister, Amaterasu, and made so much noise on the way, shaking the mountains and the rivers, that Amaterasu suspected him of evil intent and armed herself with a golden bow and a quiver of silver arrows.

But Susanowo pleaded that he had no evil in mind; he merely wished to say goodbye to his sister before going off on a journey. To show his good intentions, he suggested that the two of them create some children. Taking her brother's sword in hand, Amaterasu broke it into three pieces, chewed them, and blew a cloud over them, thus creating three goddesses. In turn, Susanowo asked his sister to hand him her five necklaces of dazzling jewels. He bit them and blew a cloud over them, and they became five gods. Since they had sprung from her jewels, Amaterasu claimed the five gods as her children, too, and as she slept that night, Susanowo drank and fumed, growing more and more belligerent.

Finally, in a drunken stupor and determined to prove himself the most powerful of all deities, Susanowo thundered through the plains of heaven, filling the irrigation ditches with mud and cutting off their flow to the paddies. Under his foot, he crushed all the rice plants and defiantly threw animal excrement into the temples devoted to Amaterasu, the sacred places where the Goddess wove the gods' clothes for the annual festival of the first fruits.

Amaterasu awoke to the terrible sound of the roof buckling and the sight of a piebald horse plummeting through. Susanowo leaped in after it and dispatched the horse with his sword. So terrified were the weavers in the temple that some of them pricked themselves with shuttles and were doomed to the land of the dead. In a fury, Amaterasu ran back into her cave and locked it, depriving heaven and earth of her divine light. In the darkness, the *kami* of rice and other living things began to wilt and die.

The gods and goddesses raced after Susanowo, caught him, and banished him from heaven, but still Amaterasu hid in her cave. The gods and goddesses gathered at the entrance and moaned about the dead and dying. They pleaded with her to return, saying that her brother had been banished and reminding her of the joy that only she could bring. But Amaterasu was unmoved by their lamentations and cajolery, and in the dark that covered the world, wickedness thrived.

Desperate, the gods and goddesses hatched a plan to entice Amaterasu from the cave. They fetched cocks whose crowing announces the dawn; they summoned forth an eight-armed mirror and strings of jewels that were hung on the branches of the Sakaki tree; and they muttered ritual sayings. A voluptuous young goddess, Ama no Uzume, arrayed herself with leaves and, on an upended tub placed outside the cave entrance, began to dance an echoing tattoo with her feet. The more she danced, the more ecstatic she became, finally tearing off her clothes of leaves and gyrating passionately in the shadows. At this sight, the assembled gods all burst forth with uproarious laughter.

In her cave, Amaterasu heard the cocks crow, the sound of Ama no Uzume dancing, and the laughter, and she grew curious. She poked her head through the partly opened door of the cave, and the gods and goddesses rejoiced at the sliver of light.

"What," Amaterasu asked, "is the reason for all this noise?"

The dancing goddess said that there was now a better goddess than Amaterasu, Ama no Uzume herself, and she kept up her ecstatic gyrations to the jubilant approval of the crowd. Ignoring this frivolous challenge, Amaterasu grew curious about the reflection she saw in the octagonal mirror and moved farther out of the cave. Amazed by her own stunning beauty, she came all the way out of the cave, and all the *kami* of the world began to rejoice in her divine warmth and light. Life stirred again, and the world turned green.

Later, the banished Susanowo roamed the earth and rescued the daughter of an old man from an eight-headed snake bent on eating her. He did this by changing the girl into a comb that he put in his hair, at the same time preparing eight bowls of rice wine. The snake approached, and each head smelled the pungent aroma and soon got drunk on the wine, at which point Susanowo cut the serpent into pieces. In the tail he found a sword, named Kusanagi, a wonderful sword that he gave as a peace offering to his sister, Amaterasu.

After many years had passed, she gave the sword Kusanagi, along with her jewels and the mirror that had drawn her from her cave, to her grandson Ninigi. She told him to take these three sacred emblems down to earth, where he and his lineage would rule forever as emperors, which is how it is. Of the mirror, she said, "Adore it as my soul, as you adore me."

[David A. Leeming and Jake Page, *Goddess: Myths of the Female Divine* (Oxford University Press, 1994), pp. 54–57.]

MODERN SCIENCE: Immanent Mind

The modern scientific mind has continued to consider and be fascinated by the idea of a Supreme Being, at least as a metaphor for a transcendent, immanent, and unifying ultimate reality. Gregory Bateson was a philosopher-scientist who postulated a universal Mind of which our individual minds are in some sense the image. Are we, after all, made in the image of God? Is Mind, separate from our individual minds, a reality in itself?

> The individual mind is immanent but not only in the body. It is immanent also in pathways and messages outside the body; and there is a larger Mind of which the individual mind is only a subsystem. This larger Mind is comparable to God and is perhaps what some people mean by "God," but it is still immanent in the total interconnected social system and planetary ecology.
>
> Freudian psychology expanded the concept of mind inwards to include the whole communication system within the body—the autonomic, the habitual, and the vast range of unconscious process. What I am saying expands mind outwards. And both of these changes reduce the scope of the conscious self. A certain humility becomes appropriate, tempered by the dignity or joy of being part of something much bigger. A part—if you will—of God.
>
> [Gregory Bateson, *Steps to an Ecology of Mind*
> (New York, 1972), pp. 461–462.]

THE GREAT MOTHER

In ancient times the archetype that we refer to as the Great Mother seems likely to have been primarily an earth mother—that is, a personification of Earth itself. With the Earth Mother we associate ideas of nourishment and creation. Gaia in Greece existed before any other immortal; it was she who gave birth to her own mate, Uranos. (See the Creation section of this book.) Frequently the Earth Mother is important in connection with an equal or dominant mate, usually a representation of the sky or heaven. Heaven and Earth then become the primal couple, united in the act of creation. This couple is one of the most prevalent motifs in myth: Papa and Rangi among the Maori, Sky Man and Earth Woman among the Navajo, the Sun God and Spider Woman among the Hopi, Izanagi and Izanami among the Japanese, and Geb and Nut among the ancient Egyptians, to mention only a few. The Earth Mother was worshipped as the source of life; out of her body came the necessary nourishment, and she had the capability of giving new birth to objects that had seemed dead. She gave life even as she caused life to wither up and return to her. She was the guardian of the dead and the agent of birth and rebirth. In early societies her importance was rivaled only by that of the sun, the source of heat and light, which was identified with the supreme sky god. In the case of the Cherokee and Japanese sun goddesses discussed earlier, it is the goddess herself who is the supreme source of life.

As agricultural practices began to supersede gathering as a means of obtaining plant food, the Earth Mother gradually lost importance or developed into the Corn Mother, the Great Goddess, whose concern is planting and harvesting. Demeter, who supplanted Gaia in importance in Greece, is the best known of the Great Goddesses, but she has counterparts in such figures as the Roman Ceres, the many-breasted Artemis at Ephesus, Cybele, the Magna Mater of Phrygia, Devi in her various forms in India, Isis in Egypt, and Inanna-Ishtar in Mesopotamia.

The Great Goddess, like the Earth Mother before her, and like nature itself and the mysteries of the unconscious (which she may be said to represent), is often ambiguous, often capable of doing great harm. Her folkloric expressions are at once the wise old woman–fairy godmother and the witch. In her Christian form— that of the Madonna—she has lost the dark side, just as the old Hebrew Yahweh— whose treatment of Job and of Abraham and Isaac, for example, is at least morally questionable—gives way in Christianity to a God who contains no evil.

If the Christian Madonna is a Great Mother unblemished by evil, however, the Great Goddess of the East remains realistically ambiguous. In India, for instance, Devi—the Goddess—is more often worshipped as the fierce Durga or the dark Kali than she is as Lakshmi and Parvati, the more nurturing spouses of Vishnu and Shiva. This is not to say that the positive side of the Goddess is not stressed. The depictions of Shiva in union with his spouse or Vishnu with his—the union with the *shakti*, the animating soul embodied in the female, as in the case of the Greek Psyche or the Byzantine Sophia—represent the same kind of spiritual and psychic wholeness or balance that is represented by the ancient Chinese combination of *yin* and *yang*, masculine and feminine, light and dark, even good and evil. We can think of *yin* as the Great Mother, the *prima materia*, the matrix of forms, the mystery of the unconscious world; and we can think of *yang* as the primal energy that impregnates that matrix and allows forms to be realized, the representative of consciousness and the ego's role in our psychic lives. The Great Mother and that energy are meaningless without each other. Form—life itself—is death defined and is thus the proper province of the ambiguous Great Mother who contains in herself both life and death. For divinity to enter this world, the full mystery of the

Great Mother must be experienced. So it is that the hero—the son-lover—dies and is reunited with the Goddess in her underworld-womb, from which he can, like the flowers of spring, be reborn. Or, to use the psychological "myth" of our own age, so it is that the ego must fully explore the mysteries of the unconscious before it can emerge into wholeness or individuation.

In some stories of the Great Goddess a pattern emerges in which the Goddess figure mourns the loss of a loved one, goes on a search, and in bringing about a form of resurrection—clearly associated with the planting and harvesting of crops—establishes new religious practices or mysteries for her followers. These mysteries are inevitably concerned with the connection between death, planting, sexuality, and resurrection or immortality, on the one hand, and physical as well as spiritual renewal, on the other. The best known of these mystery-fertility cults are the Eleusinian (associated with Demeter), the Egyptian (associated with Isis), and the Phrygian (associated with Cybele). Aspects of these cults also exist in the ritual of Dionysos, whose phallus was carried in procession by the Mother Goddess, and in the story of Jesus, whose rebirth as the Christ or "Son of Man" from the maternal tomb is in a sense presided over by representatives of the two sides of the Great Goddess—the immaculately conceived Virgin Mary, or Madonna, and the worldly Mary Magdalene.

One of the most striking Goddess myths is that of the Hopi creator Spider Woman in which the hero, Tiyo, is placed in a coffinlike object, which is sent by way of various forms of water—the element of birth—to the depths of the Earth, where Spider Woman waits. The symbols of planting, of sexual penetration, and of death and rebirth are all present, corroborated by references to the Hopi *kiva*, the underground sacred space that is itself, like the underworld to which her initiates must often go, representative of the Great Mother's womb and is the place in which the Hopi men weave the sacred stoles used in the Hopi religious ceremonies.

Modern literary embodiments of the Great Goddess are William Faulkner's Lena Grove in *Light in August*, Molly Bloom in James Joyce's *Ulysses*, and Mrs. Ramsay in Virginia Woolf's *To the Lighthouse*.

IRELAND AND WALES: Danu-Don

The Celtic Great Mother perhaps has Indo-European connections with the ancient Vedic goddess Danu, who, in the *Rig Veda*, embodies the primordial waters, the source of life. The waters themselves are representative of the birth waters. It is of interest to note that a group of midwives in New Zealand are called the Danu Midwives.

> The insular Celtic great goddess has already been mentioned. With apparent connections to the ancient Vedic Danu, the Irish Danu (sometimes Anu, Ana, or Dana), who in Wales is Don, is the mother

of all. Danu is the matriarch of the mysterious Tuatha De Danann or children of Don. Little is known of the particular aspects of this goddess. The Welsh Don is married to Beli, god of death, son of Manogan. Her brother is Math, the god of wealth, and her father was the patriarch Mathonwy. The connection with the Vedic Danu or "Heavenly Waters" is indicated by the association of Danu/Don with the northern English river Don and with the continental Danube. The fact that the Irish Danu's husband was perhaps Bile, the god of death, indicates her association with the generative process of which an integral aspect is death. As the apparent mother of the great god the Dagda, she somewhat resembles the ancient Greek goddess Rhea, the mother of Zeus, who, like the still earlier Gaia, is earth itself. In this connection it is notable that there are mountains in Kerry County, Ireland, called the "Paps of Anu." This name suggests the generally animistic aspect of Celtic religion, the essence of animism being the understanding that all aspects of the world are literally alive in some sense—*animated* by the numinous. The cult of the mother-goddess was apparently always important among continental Celts and the tradition of the mother remained strong among the insular Celts as well.

[Christopher R. Fee and David A. Leeming, *Gods, Heroes, and Kings* (Oxford University Press, 2001), p. 80.]

NATIVE NORTH AMERICA (INUIT): Sedna

Sedna, the important sea spirit of the Inuit peoples, is in effect a Great Mother. It is she who provides the animals eaten by the Inuits.

Sedna (Nuliajuk) is the sea spirit of the Inuit people, the other primary spirits being of the air and of the moon. Sedna provides the animals eaten by the people. There are various stories of this spirit, but all have somewhat violent animistic aspects in which parts of Sedna herself become creatures of value to the Inuit. Some say that Sedna was once a girl who lived with her father, Anguta. One day, they say, a great sea bird, a fulmar, enticed the girl and convinced her to follow him to his home over the sea. Once she got to the fulmar's home, however, Sedna was disgusted by its foul condition and by the lack of food, and she called for her father to rescue her. Anguta took his time, arriving with the warm winds of summer a year later. He killed the fulmar and took his daughter to his boat for the trip home. But the fulmar's followers were enraged at the death of their leader and chased down Anguta's boat with violent winds. To lessen the boat's weight and to save himself, the father threw his daughter into the sea, and as she clung desperately to the side of the boat, he cut off her fingers. These became the whales, seals, and fish that the people still eat today. When the storm had passed, Sedna emerged from the depths of the sea and climbed back into the boat. As her father was asleep, she ordered their dogs to eat his hands and feet. This they did, and when Anguta woke up he was furious, causing such a great commotion that the earth swallowed him, Sedna, and the dogs and sent them to Adlivun, where Sedna now rules.

Another myth says that Sedna's father forced her to marry a dog and that after the dissolution of that marriage she married a bird. At that point the story continues in the form of the one above until the point that Sedna loses her fingers and they turn into sea animals. According to this myth, Sedna and her father and Sedna's former dog husband live in the sea.

[David A. Leeming, *Oxford Companion to World Mythology* (Oxford University Press, 2009), p. 349.]

NATIVE NORTH AMERICA (LAKOTA SIOUX):
White Buffalo Woman

Like Spider Woman among the Pueblo and Navajo peoples, White Buffalo Woman is a Great Mother who teaches the people how to live. In short, she is what anthropologists call a culture hero.

White Buffalo Woman is a goddess or goddess-like figure in the Native North American mythology of the Lakota Sioux. It is said that long ago the Sioux called a council to discuss the lack of game for food. A group under Chief Standing Hollow Horn went out to hunt one morning and noticed something approaching them, but the figure was floating rather than walking, so they realized it must be a spirit (*wakan*). Eventually they saw that the spirit was a beautiful woman with two round red dots on her face and powerful shining eyes. She was beautifully clothed in marvelously decorated white buckskin. One strand of the woman's deep black hair was tied with a piece of buffalo fur. She carried a large bundle and some dried sage. The woman was White Buffalo Woman (Ptesan-Wi).

The amazed men stared at her and one reached for her with lust in his heart. He immediately burned up in a flash of lightning. Lust is destructive. White Buffalo Woman instructed another young man to return to his chief and to instruct him to set up a sacred medicine tent with twenty-four poles. She would follow with great gifts.

When the spirit woman arrived, she told the people to set up an altar of red earth within the medicine tent. They were also to place on the altar a buffalo skull and a rack for a sacred object. When all was ready, White Buffalo Woman circled the tent several times and then stopped before the chief and opened her bundle. In it was the sacred pipe (*chanunpa*) that would forever after be the central object of Sioux ritual. She showed the people how to grasp the stem with the left hand and to hold the bowl with the right. This is how the sacred pipe is always held and passed. The chief offered White Buffalo Woman all they had for nourishment, water. They dipped sweet grass into a skin bag full of fresh water and handed it to her. This act, too, is still a part of the Sioux ritual life.

Now White Buffalo Woman showed the people how to fill the pipe with red willow bark tobacco and to walk around the tent four times in the pattern of the great sun. This was the endless circle, what in Asia would have been called a *mandala* and what the Sioux call the Sacred Hoop or the Path of Life. Like a true culture hero, White Buffalo Woman continued her teaching, showing the people how to use the pipe, how to pray, how to sing the proper pipe-filling song, and how to lift the pipe up to "Grandfather Sky" and point it down to "Grandmother Earth" and then to the four directions. "The Sacred Pipe will hold all things together," she said, "the sky, the earth, the world, the people. The ritual of the pipe would please Wakan Tanka, the Great Spirit." She went on to tell them much more about the meaning of the pipe and about the buffalo. Then she got up to leave but promised to come back in every cycle of ages. The ages of creation were within her, she said. She walked off into the bright red sun that was setting. As she went, she rolled over four times. The first time she turned into a black buffalo, the second time into a brown one, the third time into a red one. When she rolled the fourth time, she became a pure white female buffalo calf. So it is that a white buffalo is the most sacred of beings under the sky.

Now the buffalo came and allowed themselves to be killed so that the people would have meat to eat, skins for clothes, and bones for tools. The people always wait for White Buffalo Woman to return.

[David A. Leeming, *Oxford Companion to World Mythology* (Oxford University Press, 2009), pp. 401–402.]

MEXICO: Our Lady of Guadaloupe

For many Christians the Virgin Mary is in effect a Great Mother—even an Earth Goddess, as the popular story of the Virgin of Guadaloupe suggests.

On December 9, 1531, a Christianized Indian peasant of the Mexican village of Tolpetlac heard a beautiful voice singing and saw a golden cloud on a hill in Guadalupe once sacred to the Aztec fertility moon goddess Tonantzin. A voice from the cloud called to Juan Diego, and he climbed the hill to find there a dark-skinned woman who announced that she was the Virgin Mary. She promised to help the Indian people if Juan Diego could persuade the local bishop to build a shrine in her honor on the hill. The peasant went immediately to report these events to the bishop, but the bishop did not believe the story. Juan Diego returned to the woman on the hill and told her what had happened. She insisted that he try again the next day. Again the bishop was skeptical but the lady remained insistent. But the next day, Juan Diego had to take care of his dying uncle and so avoided the hill. But the woman appeared to him on a path and told him that his uncle was cured and that he should climb the hill, where he would find some roses, and bring them back to her. Juan Diego did as he was told and when he returned with the roses, the woman arranged them into a beautiful cloak and told him to take it to the bishop. When Juan Diego presented the cloak to the bishop, a painted depiction of Our Lady of Guadalupe appeared. The amazed bishop agreed to build the shrine. The dark-skinned Virgin of Guadalupe is always pictured standing on a crescent moon. She is one of the world's several Black Madonnas and, as such, is clearly related to the dark earth and moon goddess Tonantzin. It might be noted that in Neolithic Catal Hüyük and other prehistoric sites, goddesses are frequently depicted with the horns of a male counterpart, the bull, its horns forming a crescent moon.

[David A. Leeming, *Oxford Companion to World Mythology* (Oxford University Press, 2009), pp. 396–397.]

MODERN SCIENCE: Gaia as Earth

In recent years the theory of British scientist James Lovelock has suggested that Earth—"a planet-sized entity . . . with properties which could not be predicted from the sum of its parts"—can best be seen as a living organism with the capability of organizing its own biosphere. This theory is now seriously discussed by scientists who study Earth's ecology. Lovelock and others have given their newly discovered giant organism a name, which they have taken from an earlier mythological version of the theory: Mother Earth, or Gaia.

> The concept of Mother Earth or, as the Greeks called her long ago, Gaia, has been widely held throughout history and has been the basis of a belief which still coexists with the great religions. As a result of the accumulation of evidence about the natural environment and the growth of the science of ecology, there have recently been speculations that the biosphere may have been more than just the complete range of all living things within their natural habitat of soil, sea, and air. Ancient belief and modern knowledge have fused emotionally in the awe with which astronauts with their own eyes and we by indirect vision have seen the Earth revealed in all its shining beauty against the deep darkness of space. Yet this feeling, however strong, does not prove that Mother Earth lives. Like a religious belief, it is scientifically untestable and therefore incapable in its own context of further rationalization.
>
> Journeys into space did more than present the Earth in a new perspective. They also sent back information about its atmosphere and its surface which provided a new insight into the interactions between the living and the inorganic parts of the planet. From this has arisen the hypothesis, the model, in which the Earth's living matter, air, oceans, and land surface form a complex system which can be seen as a single organism and which has the capacity to keep our planet a fit place for life. . . .
>
> We have since defined Gaia as a complex entity involving the Earth's biosphere, atmosphere, oceans, and soil; the totality constituting a feedback or cybernetic system which seeks an optimal physical and chemical environment for life on this planet. The maintenance of relatively constant conditions by active control may be conveniently described by the term "homoeostasis."
>
> Gaia has remained a hypothesis but, like other useful hypotheses, she has already proved her theoretical value, if not her existence, by giving rise to experimental questions and answers which were profitable exercises in themselves. If, for example, the atmosphere is, among other things, a device for conveying raw materials to and from the biosphere, it would be reasonable to assume the presence of carrier compounds for elements essential in all biological systems, for example, iodine and sulphur. It was rewarding to find evidence

that both were conveyed from the oceans, where they are abundant, through the air to the land surface, where they are in short supply. The carrier compounds, methyl iodide and dimethyl sulphide, respectively, are directly produced by marine life. Scientific curiosity being unquenchable, the presence of these interesting compounds in the atmosphere would no doubt have been discovered in the end and their importance discussed without the stimulus of the Gaia hypothesis. But they were actively sought as a result of the hypothesis and their presence was consistent with it.

If Gaia exists, the relationship between her and man, a dominant animal species in the complex living system, and the possibly shifting balance of power between them, are questions of obvious importance. . . . The Gaia hypothesis is for those who like to walk or simply stand and stare, to wonder about the Earth and the life it bears, and to speculate about the consequences of our own presence here. It is an alternative to that pessimistic view which sees nature as a primitive force to be subdued and conquered. It is also an alternative to that equally depressing picture of our planet as a demented spaceship, forever travelling, driverless and purposeless, around an inner circle of the sun.

[James E. Lovelock, *Gaia: A New Look at Life on Earth* (Oxford University Press, 1979), pp. ix–x, 11–12.]

THE DYING GOD

As should already be evident, the dying god motif is closely related to the myth of the Great Goddess and to the myth of the dying hero (see the hero section—Part III). In this motif, a god-king dies and is in some sense revived if not actually brought back to the living world. Traditionally, scholars have associated this mythological pattern, so prevalent in the fertile Middle East, with the cycle of vegetation, a cycle also associated with the Great Goddess. The dead god becomes the seed planted in the Mother. Perhaps for this reason, he is sometimes hanged on a tree (Attis, Odin, and Jesus for Christians who believe him to be God as well as man) or in some other way associated with trees (Adonis, Osiris, Dionysos, and Jesus as in the old song, "Were you there when they nailed him to a tree?"). The emphasis on genitals or their loss (Osiris, Dionysos, Attis) is perhaps also suggestive of the god's seed-bearing vegetable role. As has been suggested in connection with the Great Goddess archetype, the descent into death can also be seen as a metaphor for a psychological descent into the unconscious. Any rebirth or resurrection, then, would seem to speak not only to the question of physical fertility but also to the hope of overcoming the brokenness of the ordinary life in favor of the achievement of full individuation.

In *The Golden Bough* (1911–1915), Sir James Frazer first suggested the pattern of the dying god in connection with sacrificial rites in which a sacred king or a surrogate king was sacrificed to ensure the renewed fertility of a given tribe. The mythological evidence supports this theory only partially, in that the myths usually involve a symbolic rather than an actual resurrection. The dead hero-god becomes a flower (Adonis), or he becomes king of the dead (Osiris), or a renewal is only ambiguously hinted at. The dying god model has been most useful to the postmythological writer as a source for metaphors that can suggest psychic, spiritual, or emotional rebirth or the lack of it. Writers of elegies find it especially useful. Milton's *Lycidas* and Eliot's *The Waste Land* are both poems that make concrete use of the dying god archetype.

The rebirth process can also have a social aspect. In both its original ritual and mythic forms as well as in its later metaphorical masks, the dying god or his literary surrogate is often a "scapegoat," one who dies for the good of a society, who somehow takes on the burden of his society's shortcomings or sins: "And the goat shall bear upon him all their iniquities unto a land not inhabited" (Leviticus 16:22). The stories of Jesus, Attis, Osiris, and Dionysos, for instance, all have scapegoat elements. The most obvious literary descendant of the scapegoat gods (and scapegoat heroes) is the tragic hero, be he Oedipus, Lear, Hamlet, or Hedda Gabler. The tragic hero must die before the society that he or she represents can turn from rottenness to normality.

The sources for the metaphorical or literary use of the archetype are evident in the stories that follow.

MESOPOTAMIA (SUMER): Inanna (Ishtar)

In this ancient myth, the Great Goddess herself journeys to the underworld, perhaps to retrieve her lover, the shepherd king Dumuzi-Tammuz, from her sister or dark other half. The myth reminds us of similar journeys undertaken by Isis in search of Osiris and by Demeter in search of Persephone (see the story of Demeter in the Pantheon section). Inanna's descent is clearly a symbolic "dying" to her former self, and her lover Dumuzi also becomes a dying god. In the course of her descent Inanna must give up all that defines her as a living being, including the sacred *me*, the elements of the Sumerian concept of divine, civilized order.

As queen of the above, Inanna, always in search of knowledge, longs to know the below of her sister Ereshkigal, the negative or opposite aspect of the ripe goddess of love. She understands life more fully than anyone, but she knows nothing of death or of the unhealthy, unfruitful sexuality of Ereshkigal. Before leaving for the underworld, Inanna instructs her faithful helper Ninshubur to arrange official mourning for her and to approach Enlil, Nanna, and Enki, in that order, for help if she should fail to return.

Inanna abandons her seven cities and seven temples, thus stripping herself in an official sense for the ritual journey to the dead. But she takes seven of the *me,* wearing them transformed into seven pieces of magnificent clothing and jewelry, and approaches the underworld in personal glory. She knocks on the great gates and demands admittance. When reasons are demanded, she first mentions her relationship to Ereshkigal and then claims to have come for the funeral of Gugalanna, the bull of heaven.

Neti, the guardian of the gates, informs the naked Ereshkigal of the grand visitor decked in the seven *me.* Furious at the intrusion of her opposite, of everything that she can never be—lover, mother— the queen of the underworld instructs her servant to allow Inanna through the seven locked gates of the underworld only if she gives up one of the seven objects (the *me* as ornaments and clothing) at each gate. When Inanna arrives at her sister's throne, then, she is as naked as her host and is thus effectively stripped of her great powers. The significance seems to be that powers that function in life— sexual, familial, political, and priestly powers, for example—are useless in death. Inanna, always in search of new roles, nevertheless tries to usurp her sister's throne and is condemned by the underworld Anunnaki (gods) to death for her efforts. She dies and is hung up on the wall like a piece of meat.

Back in Uruk, three days and nights have passed and the faithful Ninshubur follows her mistress's orders. The temples and cities go into deep mourning and Ninshubur approaches Inanna's paternal grandfather, Enlil, and then her father, Nanna, for help, but both refuse, blaming the goddess for her excessive pride in going to the underworld. But Enki, the wise shamanic god who from his home in the underground waters of the *abzu* has his ear to the underworld, agrees to help. He understands how important his granddaughter's existence is to the welfare of the living world.

Enki creates two creatures from the mud under his fingernails. Apparently lacking sexuality or gender, these beings will not offend the infertile underworld, where Ereshkigal is screaming in pain as she gives negative birth, as it were, perhaps to the stillborn of the earth. To his two creatures Enki gives the plant of life and the water of life and instructs them to comfort the suffering Ereshkigal. In return the underworld queen will offer them gifts, which they will refuse, demanding instead the body of Inanna, which they will revive with the two sacred elements. Everything happens as foreseen by Enki, but the underworld Anunnaki demand a substitute for the revived Inanna. Although she has been reborn in the underworld, she must leave a part of herself there. As Samuel Noah Kramer suggests, from the world of consciousness above she must retain contact with the dark world of the unconscious below: "Inanna must not forget her neglected, abandoned older 'sister'—that part of herself that is Ereshkigal".

As Inanna leaves her sister's land, gathering up her clothing—her old *me* and power—she is accompanied by watchful demons who will ensure the payment of the sacrificial substitute. Entering her own world as once more the glorious queen of heaven, Inanna is greeted by Ninshubur, whose ragged clothes indicate her genuine mourning. When the demons claim the faithful servant as the sacrificial victim, Inanna refuses to give her up. Other faithful mourners—Inanna's two sons—are also spared, but when the great goddess and her underworld demons arrive at Uruk, a cheerful, well-dressed Dumuzi is acting as king, apparently unmindful of the loss of his once beloved wife. An enraged Inanna condemns him to the sacrifice. Terrified, Dumuzi begs his brother-in-law Utu for help, but even when he is turned by the sun god into a snake, he cannot escape. He, too, must experience the dark world of Inanna's other side, Ereshkigal. Thus, Dumuzi is taken away, but his sister Gestinanna arranges to spend six months of the year in the underworld so that he can spend those months back in the world above.

[David A. Leeming, *Jealous Gods and Chosen People* (Oxford University Press, 2004), pp. 48–50.]

EGYPT: Osiris and Isis

The story of Osiris, the god of maize and of the underworld, and his sister-wife Isis is rooted in or closely associated with mummification practices in ancient Egypt. Whether the myth was created to justify the ritual or vice versa is open to question. What is important is the expression the myth gives to the human hope for some kind of permanent existence. In this version of the story, told by Sir James Frazer and based on Plutarch in the early second century C.E., we have an elaboration of the basic story line, which can be found in the much-earlier Pyramid Texts. Present are the tree, the scattering of the god-seed, the loss of genitalia, the return of the god to the Mother (underworld, Earth), the emphasis on immortality, the Earth Goddess as mourner and as midwife for the rebirth. Note the similarity between the story of Demeter's attempt to bestow immortality on the child of which she is a nursemaid (see the Demeter story in the Pantheon section of this book) and the events that take place in this story.

Osiris was the offspring of an intrigue between the earth-god Geb and the sky-goddess Nut. When the sun-god Ra perceived that his wife Nut has been unfaithful to him, he declared with a curse that she should be delivered of the child in no month and no year. But the goddess had another lover, the god Thoth, and he, playing at draughts with the moon, won from her a seventy-second part of every day, and having thus compounded five whole days he added them to the Egyptian year of three hundred and sixty days. On these five days, regarded as outside the year of twelve months— that is, as "epagomenal"—the curse of the sun-god did not rest, and accordingly Osiris was born on the first of them. But he was not the only child of his mother. On the second of the supplementary days she gave birth to the elder Horus, on the third to the god Set, on the fourth to the goddess Isis, and on the fifth to the goddess Nephthys. Afterwards Set married his sister Nephthys, and Osiris his sister Isis.

Reigning as a king on earth, Osiris reclaimed the Egyptians from savagery, gave them laws, and taught them to worship the gods. Before his time the Egyptians had been cannibals. But Isis, the sister and wife of Osiris, discovered wheat and barley growing wild, and Osiris introduced the cultivation of these grains amongst his people, who forthwith took kindly to a corn diet. Moreover, Osiris is said to have been the first to gather fruit from trees, to train the vine to poles, and to tread the grapes. Eager to communicate these beneficent discoveries to all mankind, he committed the whole government of Egypt to his wife Isis, and travelled over the world, diffusing the blessings of civilization and agriculture wherever he went. In countries where a harsh climate or niggardly soil forbade the cultivation of the vine, he taught the inhabitants to console themselves for the want of wine by brewing beer from barley. Loaded with the wealth that had been showered upon him by grateful nations, he returned to Egypt, and on account of the benefits he had conferred on mankind he was unanimously hailed and worshipped as a deity. But his brother Set with seventy-two others plotted against him. Having taken the measure of his good brother's body by stealth, the bad brother fashioned and highly decorated a coffer of the same size, and once when they were all drinking and making merry he brought in the coffer and jestingly promised to give it to the one whom it should fit exactly. They all tried one after the other, but it fitted none of them. Last of all Osiris stepped into it and lay down. On that the conspirators ran and slammed the lid down on him, nailed it fast, soldered it with molten lead, and flung the coffer into the Nile. This happened on the seventeenth day of the month Athyr, when the sun is in the sign of the Scorpion, and in the eight-and-twentieth year of the reign or the life of Osiris. When Isis heard of it, she sheared off a lock of her hair, put on mourning attire, and wandered disconsolately up and down, seeking the body.

By the advice of the god of wisdom she took refuge in the papyrus swamps of the Delta. There she conceived a son while she fluttered in the form of a hawk over the corpse of her dead husband. The infant was the younger Horus, who in his youth bore the name of Harpocrates, that is, the child Horus. Him Buto, the goddess of the north, hid from the wrath of his wicked uncle Set. Yet she could not guard him from all mishap; for one day when Isis came to her little son's hiding-place she found him stretched lifeless and rigid on the ground: a scorpion had stung him. Then Isis prayed to the sun-god Ra for help. The god hearkened to her and staid his bark in the sky, and sent down Thoth to teach her the spell by which she might restore her son to life. She uttered the words of power, and straightway the poison flowed from the body of Horus, air passed into him and he lived. Then Thoth ascended up into the sky and took his place once more in the bark of the sun, and the bright pomp passed onward jubilant.

Meantime the coffer containing the body of Osiris had floated down the river and away out to sea, till at last it drifted ashore at Byblus, on the coast of Syria. Here a fine *erica*-tree shot up suddenly and enclosed the chest in its trunk. The king of the country, admiring the growth of the tree, had it cut down and made into a pillar of his

house; but he did not know that the coffer with the dead Osiris was in
it. Word of this came to Isis and she journeyed to Byblus, and sat
down by the well, in humble guise, her face wet with tears. To none
would she speak till the king's handmaidens came, and them she
greeted kindly, and braided their hair, and breathed on them from her
own divine body a wondrous perfume. When the queen beheld the
braids of her handmaidens' hair and smelt the sweet smell that ema-
nated from them, she sent for the stranger woman and took her into
her house and made her the nurse of her child. Isis gave the babe her
finger instead of her breast to suck, and at night she began to burn all
that was mortal of him away, while she herself in the likeness of a
swallow fluttered round the pillar that contained her dead brother,
twittering mournfully. The queen spied what she was doing and
shrieked out when she saw her child in flames, and thereby she hin-
dered him from becoming immortal. Then the goddess revealed herself and begged for the pillar of the roof, and they gave it her, and she
cut the coffer out of it, and fell upon it and embraced it and lamented
so loud that the younger of the king's children died of fright on the
spot. But the trunk of the tree she wrapped in fine linen, and poured
ointment on it, and gave it to the king and queen, and the wood stands
in a temple of Isis and is worshipped by the people of Byblus to this
day. And Isis put the coffer in a boat and took the eldest of the king's
children with her and sailed away. As soon as they were alone, she
opened the chest, and laying her face on the face of her brother she
kissed him and wept. But the child came behind her softly and saw
what she was about, and she turned and looked at him in anger, and
the child could not bear her look and died; but some say that it was
not so, but that he fell into the sea and was drowned. It is he whom
the Egyptians sing of at their banquets under the name of Maneros.

But Isis put the coffer by and went to see her son Horus at the city
of Buto, and Set found the coffer as he was hunting a boar one night
by the light of a full moon. And he knew the body, and rent it into
fourteen pieces, and scattered them abroad. But Isis sailed up and
down the marshes in a shallop made of papyrus, looking for the
pieces; and that is why when people sail in shallops made of papyrus,
the crocodiles do not hurt them, for they fear or respect the goddess.
And that is the reason, too, why there are many graves of Osiris in
Egypt, for she buried each limb as she found it. But others will have
it that she buried an image of him in every city, pretending it was his
body, in order that Osiris might be worshipped in many places, and

that if Set searched for the real grave he might not be able to find it. However, the genital member of Osiris had been eaten by the fishes, so Isis made an image of it instead, and the image is used by the Egyptians at their festivals to this day. "Isis," writes the historian Diodorus Siculus, "recovered all the parts of the body except the genitals; and because she wished that her husband's grave should be unknown and honoured by all who dwell in the land of Egypt, she resorted to the following device. She moulded human images out of wax and spices, corresponding to the stature of Osiris, round each one of the parts of his body. Then she called in the priests according to their families and took an oath of them all that they would reveal to no man the trust she was about to repose in them. So to each of them privately she said that to them alone she entrusted the burial of the body, and reminding them of the benefits they had received she exhorted them to bury the body in their own land and to honour Osiris as a god. She also besought them to dedicate one of the animals of their country, whichever they chose, and to honour it in life as they had formerly honoured Osiris, and when it died to grant it obsequies like his. And because she would encourage the priests in their own interest to bestow the aforesaid honours, she gave them a third part of the land to be used by them in the service and worship of the gods. Accordingly it is said that the priests, mindful of the benefits of Osiris, desirous of gratifying the queen, and moved by the prospect of gain, carried out all the injunctions of Isis. Wherefore to this day each of the priests imagines that Osiris is buried in his country, and they honour the beasts that were consecrated in the beginning, and when the animals die the priests renew at their burial the mourning for Osiris. But the sacred bulls, the one called Apis and the other Mnevis, were dedicated to Osiris, and it was ordained that they should be worshipped as gods in common by all the Egyptians; since these animals above all others had helped the discoverers of corn in sowing the seed and procuring the universal benefits of agriculture."

Such is the myth or legend of Osiris, as told by Greek writers and eked out by more or less fragmentary notices or allusions in native Egyptian literature. A long inscription in the temple at Denderah has preserved a list of the god's graves, and other texts mention the parts of his body which were treasured as holy relics in each of the sanctuaries. Thus his heart was at Athribis, his backbone at Busiris, his neck at Letopolis, and his head at Memphis. As often happens in such cases, some of his divine limbs were miraculously multiplied.

His head, for example, was at Abydos as well as at Memphis, and his legs, which were remarkably numerous, would have sufficed for several ordinary mortals.

According to native Egyptian accounts, which supplement that of Plutarch, when Isis had found the corpse of her husband Osiris, she and her sister Nephthys sat down beside it and uttered a lament which in after ages became the type of all Egyptian lamentations for the dead. "Come to thy house," they wailed, "Come to thy house. O god On! come to thy house, thou who hast no foes. O fair youth, come to thy house, that thou mayest see me. I am thy sister, whom thou lovest; thou shalt not part from me. O fair boy, come to thy house. . . . I see thee not, yet doth my heart yearn after thee and mine eyes desire thee. Come to her who loves thee, who loves thee, Unnefer, thou blessed one! Come to thy sister, come to thy wife, to thy wife, thou whose heart stands still. Come to thy housewife. I am thy sister by the same mother, thou shalt not be far from me. Gods and men have turned their faces towards thee and weep for thee together. . . . I call after thee and weep, so that my cry is heard to heaven, but thou hearest not my voice; yet am I thy sister, whom thou didst love on earth; thou didst love none but me, my brother! my brother!" This lament for the fair youth cut off in his prime reminds us of the laments for Adonis. The title of Unnefer or "the Good Being" bestowed on him marks the beneficence which tradition universally ascribed to Osiris; it was at once his commonest title and one of his names as king.

The lamentations of the two sad sisters were not in vain. In pity for her sorrow the sun-god Ra sent down from heaven the jackal-headed god Anubis, who, with the aid of Isis and Nephthys, of Thoth and Horus, pieced together the broken body of the murdered god, swathed it in linen bandages, and observed all the other rites which the Egyptians were wont to perform over the bodies of the departed. Then Isis fanned the cold clay with her wings: Osiris revived, and thenceforth reigned as king over the dead in the other world. There he bore the titles of Lord of the Underworld, Lord of Eternity, Ruler of the Dead. There, too, in the great Hall of the Two Truths, assisted by forty-two assessors, one from each of the principal districts of Egypt, he presided as judge at the trial of the souls of the departed, who made their solemn confession before him, and, their heart having been weighed in the balance of justice, received the reward of virtue in a life eternal or the appropriate punishment of their sins.

In the resurrection of Osiris the Egyptians saw the pledge of a life everlasting for themselves beyond the grave. They believed that every man would live eternal in the other world if only his surviving friends did for his body what the gods had done for the body of Osiris. Hence the ceremonies observed by the Egyptians over the human dead were an exact copy of those which Anubis, Horus, and the rest had performed over the dead god. "At every burial there was enacted a representation of the divine mystery which had been performed of old over Osiris, when his son, his sisters, his friends were gathered round his mangled remains and succeeded by their spells and manipulations in converting his broken body into the first mummy, which they afterwards reanimated and furnished with the means of entering on a new individual life beyond the grave. The mummy of the deceased was Osiris; the professional female mourners were his two sisters Isis and Nephthys; Anubis, Horus, all the gods of the Osirian legend gathered about the corpse."

Thus every dead Egyptian was identified with Osiris and bore his name. From the Middle Kingdom onwards it was the regular practice to address the deceased as "Osiris So-and-So," as if he were the god himself, and to add the standing epithet "true of speech," because true speech was characteristic of Osiris. The thousands of inscribed and pictured tombs that have been opened in the valley of the Nile prove that the mystery of the resurrection was performed for the benefit of every dead Egyptian; as Osiris died and rose again from the dead, so all men hoped to arise like him from dead to life eternal. In an Egyptian text it is said of the departed that "as surely as Osiris lives, so shall he live also; as surely as Osiris did not die, so shall he not die; as surely as Osiris is not annihilated, so shall he too not be annihilated." The dead man, conceived to be lying, like Osiris, with mangled body, was comforted by being told that the heavenly goddess Nut, the mother of Osiris, was coming to gather up his poor scattered limbs and mould them with her own hands into a form immortal and divine. "She gives thee thy head, she brings thee thy bones, she sets thy limbs together and puts thy heart in thy body." Thus the resurrection of the dead was conceived, like that of Osiris, not merely as spiritual but also as bodily. "They possess their heart, they possess their senses, they possess their mouth, they possess their feet, they possess their arms, they possess all their limbs."

[Sir James Frazer, *The New Golden Bough*, ed. Theodor H. Gaster (New York, 1959), pp. 384–390.]

GREECE AND ROME: Adonis and Aphrodite

Adonis was a Greco-Roman version of a Semitic god of Mesopotamia who at
various times was identified with Osiris and Tammuz as well as with Jesus.
Adonis' Semitic name, Adonai, means "the Lord." In some versions of his story
he was born of a virgin (Myrrha), and some versions say that at his death he was
castrated. After his death the red anemone sprang in symbolic resurrection from
the earth. Early Christian writers—Origen, Jerome, and others—report joyous
celebrations of resurrection on the third day after his birth. The version here is
the most famous and literary one; it is taken from *The Metamorphoses* of Ovid. It
stresses the Aphrodite (Venus) relationship, which itself seems to point back to
an earlier emphasis on the return of the sacrificed savior and god-king to the
Great Mother, his castration or wound in the loins being a literal reaping of the
seed-bearing crop.

> The child conceived in sin had grown inside
> The wood and now was searching for some way
> To leave its mother and thrust forth. The trunk
> Swelled in the middle with its burdened womb.
> The load was straining, but the pains of birth
> Could find no words, nor voice in travail call
> Lucina. Yet the tree, in labour, stooped
> With groan on groan and wet with falling tears.
> Then, pitying, Lucina stood beside
> The branches in their pain and laid her hands
> Upon them and pronounced the words of birth.
> The tree split open and the sundered bark
> Yielded its living load; a baby boy
> Squalled, and the Naiads laid him on soft grass
> And bathed him in his mother's flowing tears.
> Envy herself would praise his looks; for like
> The little naked Loves that pictures show
> He lay there, give or take the slender bow.

VENUS AND ADONIS

> Time glides in secret and his wings deceive;
> Nothing is swifter than the years. That son,
> Child of his sister and his grandfather,
> So lately bark-enswathed, so lately born,
> Then a most lovely infant, then a youth.
> And now a man more lovely than the boy,

Was Venus' darling (Venus'!) and avenged
His mother's passion. Once, when Venus' son
Was kissing her, his quiver dangling down,
A jutting arrow, unbeknown, had grazed
Her breast. She pushed the boy away.
In fact the wound was deeper than it seemed,
Though unperceived at first. Enraptured by
The beauty of a man, she cared no more
For her Cythera's shores nor sought again
Her sea-girt Paphos nor her Cnidos, famed
For fish, nor her ore-laden Amathus.
She shunned heaven too: to heaven she preferred
Adonis. Him she clung to, he was her
Constant companion. She who always used
To idle in the shade and take such pains
To enhance her beauty, roamed across the hills,
Through woods and brambly boulders, with her dress
Knee-high like Dian's, urging on the hounds,
Chasing the quarry when the quarry's safe—
Does and low-leaping hares and antlered deer—
But keeping well away from brigand wolves
And battling boars and bears well-armed with claws
And lions soaked in slaughter of the herds.
She warned Adonis too, if warnings could
Have been of any use, to fear those beasts.
"Be brave when backs are turned, but when they're bold,
Boldness is dangerous. Never be rash,
My darling, to my risk; never provoke
Quarry that nature's armed, lest your renown
Should cost me dear. Not youth, not beauty, nor
Charms that move Venus' heart can ever move
Lions or bristly boars or eyes or minds
Of savage beasts. In his curved tusks a boar
Wields lightning; tawny lions launch their charge
In giant anger. Creatures of that kind
I hate."
Her warning given, Venus made her way,
Drawn by her silver swans across the sky;
But his bold heart rebuffed her warning words.
It chanced his hounds, hot on a well-marked scent,
Put up a boar, lying hidden in the woods,

And as it broke away Adonis speared it—
A slanting hit—and quick with its curved snout
The savage beast dislodged the bloody point,
And charged Adonis as he ran in fear
For safety, and sank its tusks deep in his groin
And stretched him dying on the yellow sand.
Venus was riding in her dainty chariot,
Winged by her swans, across the middle air
Making for Cyprus, when she heard afar
Adonis' dying groans, and thither turned
Her snowy birds and, when from heaven on high
She saw him lifeless, writhing in his blood,
She rent her garments, tore her lovely hair,
And bitterly beat her breast, and springing down
Reproached the Fates: "Even so, not everything
Shall own your sway. Memorials of my sorrow,
Adonis, shall endure; each passing year
Your death repeated in the hearts of men
Shall re-enact my grief and my lament.
But now your blood shall change into a flower:
Persephone of old was given grace
To change a woman's form to fragrant mint;
And shall I then be grudged the right to change
My prince?" And with these words she sprinkled nectar,
Sweet-scented, on his blood, which at the touch
Swelled up, as on a pond when showers fall
Clear bubbles form; and ere an hour had passed
A blood-red flower arose, like the rich bloom
Of pomegranates which in a stubborn rind
Conceal their seeds; yet is its beauty brief,
So lightly cling its petals, fall so soon,
When the winds blow that give the flower its name.

[Ovid, *Metamorphoses*, trans A. D. Melville
(Oxford University Press, 1986), pp. 241–242, 247–248.]

ASIA MINOR (PHRYGIA): Attis

Attis, too, is often identified with Jesus, because his death and renewal ritual includes a "Day of Blood" and a "Day of Joy," both in the early spring. Attis is hanged on a tree, and, as in so many dying god myths, the loss of genitals is an important theme, as is the death-union with the Great Goddess, represented in Phrygian myth by Cybele. An interesting aspect of this myth is the fact that Cybele is also—in her form as the virgin Nana—the mother of Attis. The son-lover theme underlies many of the dying god stories. The objective observer might well find it in the Jesus story. The Virgin Mary is made pregnant by God (the Holy Spirit), is the "mother of God" (Jesus, the Son), and is the "queen of heaven" (God the father is king of heaven).

A literary remnant of the son-lover motif occurs in the story of Oedipus and Jocasta, and, of course, the motif is a central element in the modern psychological "myth" propounded by Freud.

> One myth of Attis's birth is a virgin birth story in which the Great Goddess, in her form as the virgin Nana, placed a pomegranate on her lap only to have a seed enter her and result in the birth of Attis.
>
> Many stories of Attis's death exist. Some say he was killed by a boar, like Adonis. Others say he was attacked sexually by a brute called Agdistis, who had been conceived by Cybele as she slept on the Agdos Rock and semen from the sky god Pappas fell on her. According to that story, Attis had grown into a beautiful boy who was much loved by Cybele, and rather than commit an act of infidelity to the goddess with the monstrous Agdistis, Attis castrated himself and died. Attis returned to life in an Easter-like resurrection. In Rome the celebration of Attis's resurrection took place on March 25 in a saturnalia of sorts known as the Hilaria, or "Holiday of Joy."
>
> [David A. Leeming, *Oxford Companion to World Mythology* (Oxford University Press, 2005), p. 38.]

GREECE: Dionysos

The complicated myth of Dionysos is retold here by Sir James Frazer. In this story we find many of the elements already outlined in connection with the myth of the dying god in general.

> Like the other gods of vegetation whom we have considered, Dionysus was believed to have died a violent death, but to have been brought to life again; and his sufferings, death, and resurrection were enacted in his sacred rites. His tragic story is thus told by the poet Nonnus. Zeus in the form of a serpent visited Persephone, and she

bore him Zagreus, that is, Dionysus, a horned infant. Scarcely was he born, when the babe mounted the throne of his father Zeus and mimicked the great god by brandishing the lightning in his tiny hand. But he did not occupy the throne long; for the treacherous Titans, their faces whitened with chalk, attacked him with knives while he was looking at himself in a mirror. For a time he evaded their assaults by turning himself into various shapes, assuming the likeness successively of Zeus and Cronus [Kronos], of a young man, of a lion, a horse, and a serpent. Finally, in the form of a bull, he was cut to pieces by the murderous knives of his enemies. His Cretan myth, as related by Firmicus Maternus, ran thus. He was said to have been the bastard son of Jupiter, a Cretan king. Going abroad, Jupiter transferred the throne and sceptre to the youthful Dionysus, but, knowing that his wife Juno cherished a jealous dislike of the child, he entrusted Dionysus to the care of guards upon whose fidelity he believed he could rely. Juno, however, bribed the guards, and amusing the child with rattles and a cunningly-wrought looking-glass lured him into an ambush, where her satellites, the Titans, rushed upon him, cut him limb from limb, boiled his body with various herbs, and ate it. But his sister Minerva, who had shared in the deed, kept his heart and gave it to Jupiter on his return, revealing to him the whole history of the crime. In his rage, Jupiter put the Titans to death by torture, and, to soothe his grief for the loss of his son, made an image in which he enclosed the child's heart, and then built a temple in his honour. In this version a Euhemeristic turn has been given to the myth by representing Jupiter and Juno (Zeus and Hera) as a king and queen of Crete. The guards referred to are the mythical Curetes who danced a wardance round the infant Dionysus, as they are said to have done round the infant Zeus. Very noteworthy is the legend, recorded both by Nonnus and Firmicus, that in his infancy Dionysus occupied for a short time the throne of his father Zeus. So Proclus tells us that "Dionysus was the last king of the gods appointed by Zeus. For his father set him on the kingly throne, and placed in his hand the sceptre, and made him king of all the gods of the world." Such traditions point to a custom of temporarily investing the king's son with the royal dignity as a preliminary to sacrificing him instead of his father. Pomegranates were supposed to have sprung from the blood of Dionysus, as anemones from the blood of Adonis and violets from the blood of Attis: hence women refrain from eating seeds of pomegranates at the festival of the

Thesmophoria. According to some, the severed limbs of Dionysus were pieced together, at the command of Zeus, by Apollo, who buried them on Parnassus. The grave of Dionysus was shewn in the Delphic temple beside a golden statue of Apollo. However, according to another account, the grave of Dionysus was at Thebes, where he is said to have been torn in pieces. Thus far the resurrection of the slain god is not mentioned, but in other versions of the myth it is variously related. According to one version, which represented Dionysus as a son of Zeus and Demeter, his mother pieced together his mangled limbs and made him young again. In others it is simply said that shortly after his burial he rose from the dead and ascended up to heaven; or that Zeus raised him up as he lay mortally wounded; or that Zeus swallowed the heart of Dionysus and then begat him afresh by Semele, who in the common legend figures as mother of Dionysus. Or, again, the heart was pounded up and given in a potion to Semele, who thereby conceived him.

[Sir James Frazer, *The New Golden Bough*, ed. Theodor H. Gaster (New York, 1959), pp. 418–420.]

ICELAND (NORSE): Odin

In Norse mythology, as recorded originally in the ancient *Elder Edda* and as retold by Snorri Sturluson in the *Prose Edda* (c. 1220 C.E.), we find two stories that at least suggest the dying god motif. One concerns the great god Odin's hanging on a tree, and the other concerns the death of the god Baldr. Baldr, like Attis, Adonis, and Dionysos, is known as the "beautiful god." After his death he travels to the underworld, the womb of Mother Hel. He would return to Earth at the time of the great apocalypse, Ragnarök. The following selection recounts the story of Odin, found in *Havamal*, a poem of the *Elder Edda*. Odin's "death" upon the tree is really more of a shamanic ritual descent to discover magic runes than an actual death. But the tree, the sword piercing, and the sense of gaining knowledge through suffering recall the Christian story, for example, and suggest the dying god motif.

I know that I hung
on the windswept tree
for nine full nights,
wounded with a spear
and given to Odin,
myself to myself;
on that tree

of which none know
from what roots it rises.
They did not comfort me with bread,
and not with the drinking horn;
I peered downward,
I grasped the "runes,"
screeching I grasped them;
I fell back from there.
I learned nine mighty songs
from the famous son
of Bolthor, father of Bestla,
and I got a drink
of the precious mead,
I was sprinkled with Odrerir.
Then I began to be fruitful
and to be fertile,
to grow and to prosper;
one word sought
another word from me;
one deed sought
another deed from me.

[*Havamal*, in E. O. G. Turville-Petre, *Myth and Religion of the North:*
The Religion of Ancient Scandinavia (New York, 1964), p. 42.]

NATIVE NORTH AMERICAN (PENOBSCOT): Corn Mother

Corn Mother is a ubiquitous figure among Native Americans in both North
and South America. As the provider of essential nourishment, she is both a
Great Mother and a dying god.

One day, before there were people on the earth, a youth appeared,
born of the sea and the wind and the sun. Coming ashore, he
joined the All-Maker and, together, when the sun was at the zenith
and especially warm, they set about creating all sorts of things. At
that point, a drop of dew fell on a leaf and, warmed by the sun,
became a young girl. This beautiful maiden proclaimed, "I am
love, a giver of strength. I will provide for people and animals and
they will all love me."

The All-Maker was delighted, as was the youth, who married this
extraordinary girl. They made love and she conceived, becoming the

First Mother as their children, the people, were born. The All-Maker was happy again and handed down instructions about how the people should live and, with his tasks complete, retired to a place far in the north. The people became expert hunters, and they multiplied, eventually reaching such numbers that the game began to run out. Starvation stalked them, and their First Mother grew sad. She grew even sadder when her children came to her and asked her to feed them. She had nothing to give them, and she wept.

Seeing her cry, her husband was alarmed and asked what he could do to make her happy. First Mother said there was only one thing he could do that would stop her from weeping: "You must kill me." Her husband was thunderstruck and refused. Instead, he sought out the All-Maker in the north and asked his advice.

The wise old All-Maker told him that he had to do as she asked, and the husband returned home, now weeping himself. And First Mother told him that when the sun was at its highest in the sky, he should kill her and have two of her sons drag her body over the empty parts of the earth, pulling her back and forth by her silky hair until all her flesh had been scraped from her body. Afterward, they should take her bones and bury them in a clearing. Then they were to leave, waiting until seven moons had come and gone before returning.

At that time, they would find her flesh, lovingly given, and it would feed the people and make them strong for all time.

So these sad instructions were carried out, and after seven moons had come and gone, her children and their children returned. They found the earth covered by green plants with silken tassles, and the fruit—their mother's flesh—was sweet and tender. As instructed, they saved some of it to be planted in the earth at a later time. In this way, the First Mother's flesh and her spirit are renewed every seven moons and sustain the flesh and spirit of her children.

In the clearing where they had buried her bones, the people found another plant, a fragrant one that was their mother's breath. Her spirit told them that these leaves were sacred, that they should burn them to clear their minds and lift their hearts, and make their prayers effective.

And so the people remember their mother when they smoke and when they eat corn, and in this way she lives, her love renewing itself over and over from generation to generation.

[David A. Leeming and Jake Page, *Goddess*
(Oxford University Press, 1994), pp. 75–77.]

THE TRICKSTER

One of the most popular archetypal motifs in myth and literature is that of the trickster. Whether he be Hermes in Greece, Krishna in India, Loki in Northern Europe, Coyote or Raven among the Native Americans, or related popular figures such as Aesop's and La Fontaine's fable animals, Davy Crockett on the American frontier, Brer Rabbit in the American South, Inspector Clouseau in the film *The Pink Panther*, or any number of animated cartoon characters, the trickster is at once wise and foolish, the perpetrator of tricks and the butt of his own jokes. Always male, he is promiscuous and amoral; he is outrageous in his actions; he emphasizes the "lower" bodily functions; he often takes animal form. Yet the trickster is profoundly inventive, creative by nature, and in some ways a helper to humanity. Jung sees in him a hint of the later savior figure (*Four Archetypes*, p. 151).

The trickster, then, speaks to our animal nature, to our physical as opposed to our spiritual side, and reflects what Jung calls "an earlier, rudimentary stage of consciousness" (*Four Archetypes*, p. 141). He has the charming if sometimes dangerous appetites of the child, as yet untamed by the larger social conscience. And, of course, he is almost always funny.

MESOPOTAMIA (SUMER): Enki and the Me

Enki (Babylonian Ea) was one of the major Sumerian gods. He was lord (*en*) of the earth (*ki*). He lived in the underground sweet waters (*apsu*) and was associated with the irrigation so important to his particular city, Eridu, in the marshlands of what is now Iraq. Like most tricksters, Enki was an important force in the creation process and had magical powers and insatiable appetites. He also resembled culture heroes in that he taught the people, whom he created in the myth below, the art of survival through agriculture and the social order represented by the sacred *me*, which he controlled until he lost them to Inanna.

> To celebrate their newfound freedom and the creation of humans, the Anunnaki, the first generation of deities, had a banquet at which Enki and the goddess Ninmah drank too much. Ninmah challenged Enki to a creative contest. She would make new humans with any defects she saw fit. Enki agreed but with the idea that he would attempt to choose roles for the misfits that would negate their defects. A man with an eye problem he made a singer. A man who constantly leaked semen he cured with a magic water incantation. There were

six such creations and "cures." Then the combatants changed positions: Enki would create humans with defects for Ninmah to counteract. One of these was a being called an umul that was so helpless that it could neither talk, walk nor feed itself. Taunted by Enki to solve the being's problems, Ninmah asked it questions that it could not answer, offered it food that it could not use its hands to hold, and finally gave up in disgust. Enki had won the contest. It seems likely that the umal was the first human infant.

[David A. Leeming, *Oxford Companion to World Mythology* (Oxford University Press, 2005), p. 121.]

GREECE: Hermes Steals the Cattle

Hermes, who is best known as the messenger of the gods, was also a trickster. In this story, based on the *Homeric Hymns*, Hermes has the trickster qualities of deceitfulness, trickery, childishness, amorality, humor, extreme inventiveness, and great charm. He also has the proper sexual credentials. Robert Graves suggests that Hermes evolved from an earlier fertility cult that represented its god by means of stone phalli (*The Greek Myths*, vol. 1, p. 66). The herm, a marking stone with a human head and an erect phallus, was in common use in classical Greece.

The infant god secretly left his cradle on the morning he was born, came upon a tortoise, killed it, and with its shell invented a musical instrument, the lyre, upon which he proceeded to improvise a song. Feeling a longing for meat, baby Hermes ran to Pieria, where certain cattle belonging to the immortal gods had their pasture, and stole fifty cattle belonging to his older brother Apollon. Hermes drove the cattle backward to a fold in a distant cave, so that their footprints would not betray their hiding place, while he himself walked forward, having invented wicker sandals that made his own tracks hard to interpret. After rubbing two pieces of wood together, thereby inventing fire rocks, Hermes slaughtered two cows and roasted their meat. Their skins he stretched on a rock, perhaps as a trophy of his theft. Though tempted by the savor of the meat to feast upon it even though he was a god, he did not do so, but stored the meat in the cave as a sign of his theft. Then he burned up the heads and feet of the slaughtered cattle, threw his sandals into a river, put out the fire, and smoothed over the soil. By dawn of the next day, he was back at the cave on Mount Kyllenê that was his home and lay down with apparent innocence in his cradle. In the meantime, Apollon noticed that some of his cattle were missing and by inquiry and omens learned who the thief was. He confronted Hermes, threatening to hurl him into Tartaros, but Hermes denied stealing the cattle, pleading, that he was a day-old baby who cared only for sleep and mother's milk. Apollon laughed at the infant's lies, declaring that Hermes would have thievery and thieves as his divine province. They took the dispute to their father. Although Zeus also found Hermes's denials amusing, he ordered him to lead the way to the cattle, which he did. Once there, the two young gods made peace. Hermes gave Apollon the lyre he had invented, adding this instrument to Apollon's repertory as god of music, and Apollon gave Hermes a whip as a token of his becoming the deity of cattle-tending. Thereupon Hermes invented a different musical instrument for himself, shepherd's pipes, and Apollon presented him in addition with a golden caduceus, or herald's staff, in acknowledgment of his new honor as messenger of the gods.

[William Hansen, *Classical Mythology* (Oxford University Press, 2004), pp. 310–311.]

INDIA: Krishna and the Gopis

The Lord Krishna, one of the most important of the avatars of the god Vishnu, has many trickster characteristics, as these stories from the tenth-century *Bhagavata Purana* will demonstrate. He is a shapeshifter, he is erotic, and he possesses magical and creative powers. It should be noted, however, that Krishna's trickery has a moral purpose that transcends its apparent amorality. At the beginning of the myths retold here, he outsmarts his evil uncle, Kamsa.

Krishna was born with four hands holding the signs of Vishnu (conch, discus, club, and lotus). After instructing his father Vasudeva concerning past lives, Krishna revealed what needed to happen in this one. He then changed to a baby with more human characteristics. Vasudeva took Krishna and traded him with the baby who had been born to Nandagopa and Yashodâ in the village of Ambâdi. Vasudeva had to cross the Yamunâ River, but it changed its course to aid in his mission. Once Vasudeva returned with the substitute baby, he reported the birth to Kamsa. The evil uncle raced to the prison cell and attempted to kill the incarnation of Mâyâdevî as a baby girl, but she rose into the sky and spoke a chilling message: that the one who would kill Kamsa had already been born. Kamsa began a massacre of boy babies, so Nandagopa took Yashoda and Krishna as well as Rohinî and Balarâma and moved to Gokula.

Krishna spent his childhood in Ambâdi (Gokula) amongst the Gopâlas ("cow keepers") and the Gopîs ("female cowherds"), whose main profession was looking after cows, and selling milk and curd.

The childhood of Krishna was full of merrymaking and danger. He was attacked by many types of demons in the service of Kamsa: Pûtanâ, the nurse with poisoned breasts, whom Krishna sucked dry and left her dead; Sakata disguised as a cart, which Krishna kicked to pieces; Trinâvarta who was invisible in a whirl-wind, whom Krishna weighted down and choked to death; and an almost endless assortment of demons, beasts, and snakes. Some of these he killed dramatically, others he subdued and then converted, like Kâliya, the giant water serpent on whose head he danced. He performed miracles such as lifting Mount Govardhana on his finger to protect the Yâdavas, the local villagers, from Indra's torrential rain, sent by Indra in retaliation because Krishna had encouraged the villagers to stop worshipping Indra. Thus Krishna earned one of his many names, Govinda, "one who lifted the mountain." When his foster mother sought to catch him as the butter thief—or, some versions said, for putting dirt into his mouth, others, for eating sweets—he simply opened his mouth and showed her the entire universe.

Râdha became his best female friend, though each of the Gopîs thought that she was his favorite. Krishna was always accompanied by his brother Balarâma, who had been brought to Gokula by the sage Garga. Their play (lîlâ) with the Gopîs during this period became the subject of an extensive literature on devotion and love. On the surface it was highly erotic, including pranks like stealing the clothes of the Gopîs and making them come before him and beg, and calling all the women into the forest for lovemaking, even multiplying himself at least on one occasion so that each of them could have their own Krishna. The Gopîs were even called the 16,008 wives of Krishna. But good mythology, like good theology, has many levels of meaning—and at the deepest level that kind of love-making has been seen as pointing to a devotional relationship that risks everything for a personal experience of Krishna's presence and grace: loving, total, dangerous, and so much more.

[George M. Williams, *Handbook of Hindu Mythology* (Oxford University Press, 2003), pp. 187–188.]

ICELAND (NORSE): Loki

Like many tricksters, the great god Loki can take any form and is selfish, dangerous, and amoral. Yet, above all, he is a creator.

They say that you can hear Loki beating his children in the crackling of a fire on the hearth. They say that Loki was none other than Satan stalking the earth, and that he murdered Baldr, the beloved son of Odin, but none of that may ring true. . . .

To be sure, he was greedy, selfish, dangerous. He knew the foibles of all the gods and goddesses; indeed, he was himself the foible of many a goddess, having fast-talked his way into their beds. He was a handsome devil, a thief (there's no denying that), and he could be good company.

On one occasion, it was Loki's wiles that rescued Thor (not to mention his wife, Freya) from a terrible humiliation. Thor, it seems, woke up one morning to find his precious hammer missing. He mentioned this to Loki, who told him that it must have been taken by a giant, and he offered to go forth himself to find it.

In due course, he returned to Asgard, the home of the Aesir, with the news that a giant named Thrym had stolen the hammer, buried it deep in the earth, and would return it only if Freya would be given to him as his wife. This threw the entire assemblage of the Aesir, including Thor, into consternation and, not knowing what to do, they suggested to Freya that it might after all be best if she would . . . well, Freya flew into an indignant fury so great that her neck swelled up and burst her golden necklace.

And that gave Loki an idea. He snatched up the necklace and told Thor to dress up in Freya's bridal clothes. Then he put her necklace around his neck, and the two of them went to pay a visit on Thrym. Thrym was filled with desire when he saw his "bride" and set out a great feast which Thor (in disguise) wolfed down in a most unladylike fashion. Thrym was amazed, but Loki explained that his "bride" had fasted for eight days in anticipation of pleasuring the giant.

Then Thrym lifted her veil to kiss her and was startled at her ruddy skin and the fire in her eyes. Loki quickly explained that she had been unable to sleep those same eight days, so feverish had she been for Thrym's lusty attentions.

So Thrym sent for the hammer which, as was custom, he placed on his bride's lap by way of consecrating their union. His bride erupted with a great laugh, picked up the hammer, and struck Thrym dead, along with his entire company. And so Thor got his hammer back.

Oh, Loki was fast on his feet. One time he lost a wager by which his head belonged to the dwarf, Brokk, and the slow-witted Brokk announced his intention to claim his prize by separating it from Loki's body.

"My dear Brokk," Loki said, "it is quite true that you have every right to my head. It is yours, and you may take it. *But*," he went on, "nothing, you will recall, was said in our wager about my neck."

The dwarf blinked.

"In taking my head," Loki explained, "you may not take even the slightest shred of my neck."

The dwarf again blinked, his unfertile mind outpaced, and while he puzzled over this, Loki slipped away.

On another occasion, Loki was out wandering with Odin and another god and, famished, they stopped to roast an ox. An eagle settled into a nearby tree and cast a spell which kept the meat from cooking. He said he would lift the spell if the three Aesir would let him eat with them. They acceded, and the eagle settled in, taking all the best cuts of meat. Always quick to anger, Loki thrashed the eagle with a rod.

At this, the eagle flew off, with the rod magically stuck to his body and with Loki magically stuck to the rod. Loki bounced across the ground, bruised and cut, and never one to suffer physical hurt for long, he begged for mercy.

The eagle, who was in fact a giant named Thjazi, said that Loki could have his freedom on the condition that he deliver in his stead the luscious goddess Idun … and her apples. These were miraculous apples which kept all the Aesir from growing old. Without a thought for his fellows, Loki swore he would comply.

Back at Asgard, he approached the voluptuous Idun who carried with her, as always, her basket of apples, and he said, "My dear Idun, most sagacious of the goddesses, why don't you come with me for a stroll in the forest. I have something to show you. Something nobody else has ever seen."

"Not on your life," Idun said, for while she was not all that saga-cious, she knew Loki's reputation. "And anyway, there are many here who have indeed seen that thing."

"No, no," Loki protested, laughing ingratiatingly. "I came across some apples in the forest, apples even more beautiful than those with which you adorn yourself and so generously share with the Aesir." Idun was soon persuaded, her curiosity piqued, and the two set out into the forest.

Once they were among the trees, Thjazi leapt upon the goddess— as had been arranged—and dragged her off to his home while Loki slipped back into Asgard, free again.

Not long afterward, the Aesir noticed Idun's absence and won-dered where she might be. And then, Idun's apples being absent as well, they began to notice on each other the unmistakable ravages of age. They flew into a rage, blaming Loki for this, and threatened him with dismemberment and death until he agreed to bring the goddess and her apples back.

Changing himself into a hawk, he flew into the kingdom of the giants and alit near Thjazi's home. Finding Idun mourning her lost freedom and her fate at the hands of the gross and callous giant, Loki changed her into a nut and carried her back to Asgard.

In such ways did Loki torment the Aesir until the time came for them to vanish from the affairs of mankind. But these rumors . . . that it was Loki who arranged their disappearance . . . who could believe such a thing?

[David A. Leeming and Jake Page, *God* (Oxford University Press, 1995), pp. 30–33.]

UNDERSTAND GRIEF

NATIVE NORTH AMERICA (MAIDA): Coyote

Coyote is a ubiquitous trickster figure among Native North Americans. He is at once erotic, shapeshifting, and creative. In his role as a culture hero he teaches the people how to respond to certain conditions, but he is also amoral and dangerous.

In the beginning, when there was only night and water, a raft brought two persons—Turtle and Earth-Initiate. Working together, they created first some dry land, then the sun and the moon, and the stars, as well as a large tree with many kinds of acorns. Before long,

Coyote and his pet, Rattlesnake, emerged of their own accord, and Coyote watched with great interest as Earth-Initiate fashioned all the animals from clay. He watched with even greater interest when Earth-Initiate created the First Man and the First Woman.

Coyote thought it looked pretty easy, so he tried to make some people himself, but they didn't work out because he laughed while he was making them. Earth-Initiate said, "I told you not to laugh," and Coyote told the world's first lie, saying that he hadn't laughed.

Earth-Initiate wanted life to be easy and full for the people he had caused to exist, so every night he saw to it that their baskets were filled with food for the next day. No one had to work; no one got sick. One day, he told the people to go to a nearby lake, and he explained to the First Man that by the time he got there, he would be old.

Sure enough, when the people got to the lake, the First Man was white-haired and bent. He fell in the lake which shook, and the ground underneath roared, and soon he came to the top, a young man again. Earth-Initiate explained to all the people that, when they got old, all they needed to do was to plunge into the lake and they would be young again.

Then one day, Coyote visited the people and they told him how easy life was, how all they needed to do was eat and sleep.

"I can show you something better than that," Coyote said, and told them that he thought it would be better if people got sick and died. The people had no idea what he meant so he suggested that they begin by having a footrace. He told them how to line up to start the race.

At this moment his pet, Rattlesnake, went out along the race course and hid himself in a hole, with just his head sticking up. And then the race began.

Some of the people were faster than others and began to pull ahead from the pack, and one in particular ran the fastest. This was Coyote's son, and Coyote, watching from the sidelines, cheered him on with pride. But then his son came to a hole and Rattlesnake raised his head and bit him on the ankle. The boy, Coyote's son, fell over and within moments was dead.

The people all thought the boy was too ashamed to get up, but Coyote explained that he was dead. Coyote wept—the first tears—and gathered up his son and put him in the lake where the body floated for four days without reviving. So Coyote dug a grave and buried his son and told the people that this was what they would have to do from then on.

[David A. Leeming and Jake Page, *God* (Oxford University Press, 1995), pp. 52–53.]

AFRICA (FON): Legba — BROKEN TRUST   KARMA

The fon tribe of West Africa possesses a myth about a trickster called Legba, whose herm-like phallic symbol stands outside all tribal dwellings. Like most African tricksters, including the better-known Ananse, the Spider, Legba has all the traditional components of the archetype but is most notably an articulator of the divine.

In the beginning Legba lived on earth with God and only acted on his orders. Sometimes God told Legba to do something harmful and then people blamed Legba for it and came to hate him: They never gave him credit for his good deeds but thanked God instead. Legba got tired of this and went to ask God why he should always be blamed, since he was only doing the divine will. God replied that the ruler of a kingdom ought to be thanked for good things and his servants blamed for evil.

Now God had a garden in which fine yams were growing, and Legba told him that thieves were planning to plunder it. Therefore God called all men together and warned them that whoever stole his yams would be killed. During the night Legba crept into God's house and stole his sandals, put them on and went into the garden. He took away all the yams. It had rained not long before and the footprints were clearly seen. In the morning Legba reported the theft, saying that it would be easy to find the thief from the prints. All the people were called but nobody's feet fitted the prints since they were too big. Then Legba suggested that perhaps God had taken the yams in his sleep. God denied this and accused Legba of his usual mischief, but when he consented to put his foot down, it matched the prints exactly. The people cried out that God had stolen from himself, but God replied that his son had tricked him. So God left the world, and told Legba to come to the sky every night to give an account of what went on below.

A variant, giving another version of the stories of God retiring to heaven, says that when God and Legba lived near the earth, Legba was always being reprimanded for his mischief. He did not like this and persuaded an old woman to throw her dirty water into the sky after washing. God was annoyed at the water being constantly thrown into his face and he gradually moved away to his present distance. But Legba was left behind and that is why he has a shrine in every house and village, to report on human doings to God.

Legba is closely associated in Fon story and ritual with the oracle Fa. One myth says that Fa had sixteen eyes, the nuts of divination. He lived on a palm tree in the sky. From this height Fa could see all that went on in the world. Every morning Legba climbed the palm tree to open Fa's eyes. Fa did not wish to convey his wishes by speaking out loud, so he put one palm nut in Legba's hand if he wanted two eyes open, and two palm nuts to have one eye open. Then he looked round to see what was happening. And so today one palm nut thrown by the diviner is a sign for two marks to be made on the divining board, and two nuts make one mark.

Later God gave Fa the keys to the doors of the future, for the future is a house of sixteen doors. If men used the palm nuts correctly, they opened the eyes of Fa and showed the right door of the future. Legba worked with Fa, and when there was a great war on earth which threatened to destroy everything, God sent Legba to teach the method of the Fa divination so that men could consult the oracle and know the proper way of conduct.

[Geoffrey Parinder, *African Mythology*
(London, 1967), p. 91.]

BIBLIOGRAPHY

✦

For treatment of the concept of the archetype, the works of Carl Jung are indispensable. See especially his *Symbols of Transformation* (Princeton, NJ, 1967) and his *The Archetypes and the Collective Unconscious* (Princeton, NJ, 1971). For another definition of archetype—as a model or paradigm—see the works of Mircea Eliade, especially his *Patterns in Comparative Religion* (New York, 1958) and the first chapter of his *The Myth of the Eternal Return or, Cosmos and History* (New York, 1954). Numerous works of literary criticism make use of an archetypal approach to literature. The most prestigious of the archetypal or "myth critics" is Northrop Frye. See his *Anatomy of Criticism* (Princeton, NJ, 1957) for his general theory of a scientific approach to literature by way of myth. His *Fables of Identity* (New York, 1963) contains theoretical essays, including one titled "The Archetypes of Literature" and several applications of the theory to specific works. For treatments of the Supreme Being, see Chapter 2 of Eliade's *Patterns in Comparative Religion*; Raffaele Pettazzoni's "The Supreme Being: Phenomenological Structure and Historical Development," in *The History of Religions: Essays in Methodology*, edited by Eliade and Joseph M. Kitagawa (Chicago, 1959); and Lawrence E. Sullivan's comprehensive article, "Supreme Beings," in *The Encyclopedia of Religion* (vol. 14, pp. 166–181).

The classic work on the Great Goddess is Eric Neumann's *The Great Mother: An Analysis of the Archetype* (Princeton, NJ, 1963). Carl Jung has much to say about the Great Mother archetype in *The Archetypes and the Collective Unconscious*; his comments are also collected in *Four Archetypes* (Princeton, NJ, 1970). Useful articles on the Great Goddess by Merlin Stone, Momolina Marconi, and James Preston are to be found in *The Encyclopedia of Religion* (vol. 6, pp. 35–59). Preston's "Overview" and his "Theoretical Perspectives" in that volume are written from the point of view of anthropology and are particularly valuable. Robert Graves is always provocative on the question of the Goddess. The classic work is his *The White Goddess* (New York, 1966). His theories of the feminine principle in myth also pervade his two-volume *The Greek Myths* (Baltimore, MD, 1955). For more up-to-date and more feminist views of the Great Goddess, see Jean Markale's *The Great Goddess: Reverence of the Divine Feminine from the Paleolithic to the Present* (Inner Traditions, 1999) and Marija Gimbutas's *The Language of the Goddess* (Thames and Hudson, 2001). The Markale book traces goddess worship through various cultures. The Gimbutas work is a provocative and highly controversial argument for the ancient existence of matriarchal cultures later overrun by patriarchal force. See also David Leeming and Jake Page's *Goddess: Myths of the Female Divine* (New York: Oxford University Press, 1994).

On the dying god, Sir James Frazer's *The Golden Bough* (12 vols., London, 1907–1915)—especially volume 4, "The Dying and Reviving Gods," in which he has much to say about Attis, Osiris, Adonis, and the Mother Goddess—remains one of the great anthropological treatments of myth. See also Chapters 8 and 9 of Eliade's *Patterns in Comparative Religion*. For a somewhat skeptical view of the dying god archetype, see Jonathan Z. Smith's entry under "Dying and Rising Gods" in *The Encyclopedia of Religion* (vol. 4, pp. 521–527). A more recent view of the subject is David Livingstone's *The Dying God: The Hidden History of Western Civilization* (Thames and Hudson, 2001), in which the author finds the source of this important "Western" concept in Mesopotamia of the sixth century B.C.E. For the Inanna myth see Diane Wolkstein and Samuel Noah Kramer's Inanna: Queen of Heaven and Earth. New York: Harper & Row, 1983.

The classic archetypal consideration of the trickster is Paul Radin's *The Trickster: A Study in American Indian Mythology* (New York, 1956). Jung's comments on the subject appear in both *The Archetypes and the Collective Unconscious* and *Four Archetypes*. For further bibliographical information on the trickster and for a useful survey of the subject, see Lawrence E. Sullivan's overview and consideration by others of particular cultural manifestations of the archetype in *The Encyclopedia of Religion* (vol. 15, pp. 45–53). See also the trickster issue of *Parabola* (vol. 4, no. 1, Feb. 1979). Lewis Hyde's *Trickster Makes the World: Mischief, Myth, and Art* (Farrar, Strauss, and Giroux, 2010) is a good survey of the subject, which also treats contemporary trickster figures.

GODS, GODDESSES, AND LESSER SPIRITS

The stories included in this section are primarily of Greek origin and are relatively familiar to us because they are so frequently alluded to by our writers and other artists. Also included, however, is a sampling of less familiar myths of great importance to other cultures. Many of the stories in this section have religious significance, and many can be read in the light of the archetypal categories treated earlier. Some of them appear to be intended primarily for entertainment. All of them are part of the general vocabulary of the cultures from which they come, and all of them transcend these cultures as masks of the universal dream—part wish fulfillment, part nightmare—that is world mythology.

Greece and Rome
Prometheus

Prometheus is the archetype of the god who helps humankind. Other versions of this myth of the helper god are those of the Aztec god Quetzalcoatl and the Hittite Telipinu. In this case, the helper god incurs the wrath of the Supreme Being himself. This is Robert Graves's retelling of a story that has fascinated writers since the days of Homer and Hesiod. Included in this story are the popular tales of Atlas and Pandora.

Prometheus, the creator of mankind, whom some include among the seven Titans, was the son either of the Titan Eurymedon, or of Iapetus by the nymph Clymene; and his brothers were Epimetheus, Atlas, and Menoetius.

Gigantic Atlas, eldest of the brothers, knew all the depths of the sea; he ruled over a kingdom with a precipitous coastline, larger than Africa and Asia put together. This land of Atlantis lay beyond the Pillars of Heracles, and a chain of fruit-bearing islands separated it from a farther continent, unconnected with ours. Atlas's people canalized and cultivated an enormous central plain, fed by water from the hills which ringed it completely, except for a seaward gap. They also built palaces, baths, racecourses, great harbour works, and temples; and carried war not only westwards as far as the other continent, but eastward as far as Egypt and Italy. The Egyptians say that Atlas was the son of Poseidon, whose five pairs of male twins all swore allegiance to their brother by the blood of a Bull sacrificed at the pillar-top; and that at first they were extremely virtuous, bearing with fortitude the burden of their great wealth in gold and silver.

But one day greed and cruelty overcame them and, with Zeus's permission, the Athenians defeated them single-handed and destroyed their power. At the same time, the gods sent a deluge which, in one day and one night, overwhelmed all Atlantis, so that the harbour works and temples were buried beneath a waste of mud and the sea became unnavigable.

Atlas and Menoetius, who escaped, then joined Cronus [Kronos] and the Titans in their unsuccessful war against the Olympian gods. Zeus killed Menoetius with a thunderbolt and sent him down to Tartarus, but spared Atlas, whom he condemned to support Heaven on his shoulders for all eternity.

Atlas was the father of the Pleiades, the Hyades, and the Hesperides; and has held up the Heavens ever since, except on one occasion, when Heracles temporarily relieved him of the task. Some say that Perseus petrified Atlas into Mount Atlas by showing him the Gorgon's head; but they forget that Perseus was reputedly a distant ancestor of Heracles.

Prometheus, being wiser than Atlas, foresaw the issue of the rebellion against Cronus, and therefore preferred to fight on Zeus's side, persuading Epimetheus to do the same. He was, indeed, the wisest of his race, and Athene, at whose birth from Zeus's head he had assisted, taught him architecture, astronomy, mathematics, navigation, medicine, metallurgy, and other useful arts, which he passed on to mankind. But Zeus, who had decided to extirpate the whole race of man, and spared them only at Prometheus's urgent plea, grew angry at their increasing powers and talents.

One day, when a dispute took place at Sicyon, as to which portions of a sacrificial bull should be offered to the gods, and which should be reserved for men, Prometheus was invited to act as arbiter. He therefore flayed and jointed a bull, and sewed its hide to form two open-mouthed bags, filling these with what he had cut up. One bag contained all the flesh, but this he concealed beneath the stomach, which is the least tempting part of any animal; and the other contained the bones, hidden beneath a rich layer of fat. When he offered Zeus the choice of either, Zeus, easily deceived, chose the bag containing the bones and fat (which are still the divine portion); but punished Prometheus, who was laughing at him behind his back, by withholding fire from mankind. "Let them eat their flesh raw!" he cried.

Prometheus at once went to Athene, with a plea for a backstairs admittance to Olympus, and this she granted. On his arrival, he lighted a torch at the fiery chariot of the Sun and presently broke from it a fragment of glowing charcoal, which he thrust into the pithy hollow of a giant fennel-stalk. Then, extinguishing his torch, he stole away undiscovered, and gave fire to mankind.

Zeus swore revenge. He ordered Hephaestus to make a clay woman, and the four Winds to breathe life into her, and all the goddesses of Olympus to adorn her. This woman, Pandora, the most beautiful ever created, Zeus sent as a gift to Epimetheus, under Hermes's escort. But Epimetheus, having been warned by his brother to accept no gift from Zeus, respectfully excused himself. Now angrier even than before, Zeus had Prometheus chained naked to a pillar in the Caucasian mountains, where a greedy vulture tore at his liver all day, year in, year out; and there was no end to the pain, because every night (during which Prometheus was exposed to cruel frost and cold) his liver grew whole again.

But Zeus, loth to confess that he had been vindictive, excused his savagery by circulating a falsehood: Athene, he said, had invited Prometheus to Olympus for a secret love affair.

Epimetheus, alarmed by his brother's fate, hastened to marry Pandora, whom Zeus had made as foolish, mischievous, and idle as she was beautiful—the first of a long line of such women. Presently she opened a box, which Prometheus had warned Epimetheus to keep closed, and in which he had been at pains to imprison all the Spites that might plague mankind: such as Old Age, Labour, Sickness, Insanity, Vice, and Passion. Out these flew in a cloud, stung Epimetheus and Pandora in every part of their bodies, and then attacked the race of mortals. Delusive Hope, however, whom Prometheus had also shut in the box, discouraged them by her lies from a general suicide.

[Robert Graves, *The Greek Myths*
(Baltimore, MD, 1955), vol. 1, pp. 143–144.]

Pandora

Hesiod was perhaps the first to tell the story we have just read of the woman who, like Eve, was said to be the source of all human misery. Angry at Prometheus for having stolen fire from the gods to give to humanity, Zeus decides to punish the human species by creating one of the earliest examples of the archetypal femme fatale. It has been suggested by Jane Harrison (*Prolegomena to the Study of Greek Religion*, pp. 284–285) that this myth is a patriarchal perversion of a story that must originally have reflected the meaning of Pandora's name, the "All-Giver," a title that also belonged to the Earth Goddess Rhea, and suggests that Pandora was in reality an earth goddess as well. Here the myth is rewritten by Charlene Spretnak, and Pandora's earlier nature is restored.

Earth-Mother had given the mortals life. This puzzled them greatly. They would stare curiously at one another, then turn away to forage for food. Slowly they found that hunger has many forms.

One morning the humans followed an unusually plump bear cub to a hillside covered with bushes that hung heavy with red berries. They began to feast at once, hardly aware of the tremors beginning beneath their feet. As the quaking increased, a chasm gaped at the crest of the hill. From it arose Pandora with Her earthen pithos. The mortals were paralyzed with fear but the Goddess drew them into Her aura.

"I am Pandora, Giver of All Gifts." She lifted the lid from the large jar. From it She took a pomegranate, which became an apple, which became a lemon, which became a pear. "I bring you flowering trees that bear fruit, gnarled trees hung with olives and, this, the grapevine that will sustain you." She reached into the jar for a handful of seeds and sprinkled them over the hillside. "I bring you plants for hunger and illness, for weaving and dyeing. Hidden beneath My surface you will find minerals, ore, and clay of endless form." She took from the jar two flat stones. "Attend with care My plainest gift: I bring you flint."

Then Pandora turned the jar on its side, inundating the hillside with Her flowing grace. The mortals were bathed in the changing colors of Her aura. "I bring you wonder, curiosity, memory. I bring you wisdom. I bring you justice with mercy. I bring you caring and communal bonds. I bring you courage, strength, endurance. I bring you loving kindness for all beings. I bring you the seeds of peace."

[Charlene Spretnak, *Lost Goddesses of Early Greece*
(Boston, 1981), pp. 55–57.]

Tiresias, Echo, and Narcissus

The seer Tiresias predicted that Narcissus would live to an old age "provided that he never knows himself." Ovid retells the earlier Greek story of the seer and then the one of this fated youth, who became the first of many narcissists to carry the law of Apollo ("Know thyself") into the realm of absurdity. Jove here is Jupiter, the Roman vesion of Zeus. His wife, Juno, was Hera to the Greeks.

TIRESIAS

It chanced that Jove,
Well warmed with nectar, laid his weighty cares
Aside and, Juno too in idle mood,
The pair were gaily joking, and Jove said
"You women get more pleasure out of love
Than we men do, I'm sure." She disagreed.
So they resolved to get the views of wise
Tiresias. He knew both sides of love.
For once in a green copse when two huge snakes
Were mating, he attacked them with his stick,
And was transformed (a miracle!) from man
To woman; and spent seven autumns so;
Till in the eighth he saw the snakes once more
And said "If striking you has magic power
To change the striker to the other sex,
I'll strike you now again." He struck the snakes
And so regained the shape he had at birth.
Asked then to give his judgement on the joke,
He found for Jove; and Juno (so it's said)
Took umbrage beyond reason, out of all
Proportion, and condemned her judge to live
In the black night of blindness evermore.
But the Almighty Father (since no god
Has right to undo what any god has done)
For his lost sight gave him the gift to see
What things should come, the power of prophecy,
An honour to relieve that penalty.

NARCISSUS AND ECHO

So blind Tiresias gave to all who came
Faultless and sure reply and far and wide
Through all Boeotia's cities spread his fame.
To test his truth and trust the first who tried
Was wave-blue water-nymph Liriope,
Whom once Cephisus in his sinuous flow
Embracing held and ravished. In due time
The lovely sprite bore a fine infant boy,
From birth adorable, and named her son

Narcissus; and of him she asked the seer,
Would he long years and ripe old age enjoy,
Who answered "If he shall himself not know."
For long his words seemed vain; what they concealed
The lad's strange death and stranger love revealed.
    Narcissus now had reached his sixteenth year
And seemed both man and boy; and many a youth
And many a girl desired him, but hard pride
Ruled in that delicate frame, and never a youth
And never a girl could touch his haughty heart.
Once as he drove to nets the frightened deer
A strange-voiced nymph observed him, who must speak
If any other speak and cannot speak
Unless another speak, resounding Echo.
Echo was still a body, not a voice,
But talkative as now, and with the same
Power of speaking, only to repeat,
As best she could, the last of many words.
Juno had made her so; for many a time,
When the great goddess might have caught the nymphs
Lying with Jove upon the mountainside,
Echo discreetly kept her talking till
The nymphs had fled away; and when at last
The goddess saw the truth, "Your tongue," she said,
"With which you tricked me, now its power shall lose,
Your voice avail but for the briefest use."
The event confirmed the threat: when speaking ends,
All she can do is double each last word,
And echo back again the voice she's heard.
    Now when she saw Narcissus wandering
In the green byways, Echo's heart was fired;
And stealthily she followed, and the more
She followed him, the nearer flamed her love,
As when a torch is lit and from the tip
The leaping sulphur grasps the offered flame.
She longed to come to him with winning words,
To urge soft pleas, but nature now opposed;
She might not speak the first but—what she might—
Waited for words her voice could say again.
    It chanced Narcissus, searching for his friends,

Called "Anyone here?" and Echo answered "Here!"
Amazed he looked all round and, raising his voice,
Called "Come this way!" and Echo called "This way!"
He looked behind and, no one coming, shouted
"Why run away?" and heard his words again.
He stopped and, cheated by the answering voice,
Called "Join me here!" and she, never more glad
To give her answer, answered "Join me here!"
And graced her words and ran out from the wood
To throw her longing arms around his neck.
He bolted, shouting "Keep your arms from me!
Be off! I'll die before I yield to you."
And all she answered was "I yield to you."
Shamed and rejected in the woods she hides
And has her dwelling in the lonely caves;
Yet still her love endures and grows on grief,
And weeping vigils waste her frame away;
Her body shrivels, all its moisture dries;
Only her voice and bones are left; at last
Only her voice, her bones are turned to stone.
So in the woods she hides and hills around,
For all to hear, alive, but just a sound.

      Thus had Narcissus mocked her; others too,
Hill-nymphs and water-nymphs and many a man
He mocked; till one scorned youth, with raised hands, prayed,
"So may lie love—and never win his love!"
And Nemesis approved the righteous prayer.

      There was a pool, limpid and silvery,
Whither no shepherd came nor any herd,
Nor mountain goat; and never bird nor beast
Nor falling branch disturbed its shining peace;
Grass grew around it, by the water fed,
And trees to shield it from the warming sun.
Here—for the chase and heat had wearied him—
The boy lay down, charmed by the quiet pool,
And, while he slaked his thirst, another thirst
Grew; as he drank he saw before his eyes
A form, a face, and loved with leaping heart
A hope unreal and thought the shape was real.
Spellbound he saw himself, and motionless

Lay like a marble statue staring down.
He gazes at his eyes, twin constellation,
His hair worthy of Bacchus or Apollo,
His face so fine, his ivory neck, his cheeks
Smooth, and the snowy pallor and the blush;
All he admires that all admire in him,
Himself he longs for, longs unwittingly,
Praising is praised, desiring is desired,
And love he kindles while with love he burns.
How often in vain he kissed the cheating pool
And in the water sank his arms to clasp
The neck he saw, but could not clasp himself!
Not knowing what he sees, he adores the sight;
That false face fools and fuels his delight.
You simple boy, why strive in vain to catch
A fleeting image? What you see is nowhere;
And what you love—but turn away—you lose!
You see a phantom of a mirrored shape;
Nothing itself; with you it came and stays;
With you it too will go, if you can go!

　　No thought of food or rest draws him away;
Stretched on the grassy shade he gazes down
On the false phantom, staring endlessly,
His eyes his own undoing. Raising himself
He holds his arms towards the encircling trees
And cries "You woods, was ever love more cruel!
You know! For you are lovers' secret haunts.
Can you in your long living centuries
Recall a lad who pined so piteously?
My joy! I see it; but the joy I see
I cannot find" (so fondly love is foiled!)
"And—to my greater grief—between us lies
No mighty sea, no long and dusty road,
Nor mountain range nor bolted barbican.
A little water sunders us. He longs
For my embrace. Why, every time I reach
My lips towards the gleaming pool, he strains
His upturned face to mine. I surely could
Touch him, so slight the thing that thwarts our love.
Come forth, whoever you are! Why, peerless boy,

Elude me? Where retreat beyond my reach?
My looks, my age—indeed it cannot be
That you should shun—the nymphs have loved me too!
Some hope, some nameless hope, your friendly face
Pledges; and when I stretch my arms to you
You stretch your arms to me, and when I smile
You smile, and when I weep, I've often seen
Your tears, and to my nod your nod replies,
And your sweet lips appear to move in speech,
Though to my ears your answer cannot reach.
Oh, I am he! Oh, now I know for sure
The image is my own; it's for myself
I burn with love; I fan the flames I feel.
What now? Woo or be wooed ? Why woo at all?
My love's myself—my riches beggar me.
Would I might leave my body! I could wish
(Strange lover's wish!) my love were not so near!
Now sorrow saps my strength; of my life's span
Not long is left; I die before my prime.
Nor is death sad for death will end my sorrow;
Would he I love might live a long tomorrow!
But now we two—one soul—one death will die."
        Distraught he turned towards the face again;
His tears rippled the pool, and darkly then
The troubled water veiled the fading form,
And, as it vanished, "stay," he shouted, "stay!
Oh, cruelty to leave your lover so!
Let me but gaze on what I may not touch
And feed the aching fever in my heart."
Then in his grief he tore his robe and beat,
His pale cold fists upon his naked breast,
And on his breast a blushing redness spread
Like apples, white in part and partly red,
Or summer grapes whose varying skins assume
Upon the ripening vine a blushing bloom.
And this he saw reflected in the pool,
Now still again, and could endure no more.
But as wax melts before a gentle fire,
Or morning frosts beneath the rising sun,
So, by love wasted, slowly he dissolves

By hidden fire consumed. No colour now,
Blending the white with red, nor strength remains
Nor will, nor aught that lately seemed so fair,
Nor longer lasts the body Echo loved.
But she, though angry still and unforgetting,
Grieved for the hapless boy, and when he moaned
"Alas," with answering sob she moaned "alas,"
And when he beat his hands upon his breast,
She gave again the same sad sounds of woe.
His latest words, gazing and gazing still,
He sighed "alas! the boy I loved in vain!"
And these the place repeats, and then "farewell,"
And Echo said "farewell." On the green grass
He drooped his weary head, and those bright eyes
That loved their master's beauty closed in death.
Then still, received into the Underworld,
He gazed upon himself in Styx's pool.
His Naiad sisters wailed and sheared their locks
In mourning for their brother; the Dryads too
Wailed and sad Echo wailed in answering woe.
And then the brandished torches, bier and pyre
Were ready—but no body anywhere;
And in its stead they found a flower—behold,
White petals clustered round a cup of gold!

[Ovid, *Metamorphoses*, trans. A. D. Melville
(Oxford University Press, 2008), pp. 61–66.]

Hyacinth and Ganymede

Ovid's tale of another dying youth is a rare myth in that it places the god Apollo in a homosexual context. Sung by Orpheus, the myth of Hyacinth is immediately preceded by the story of Zeus' illicit love for the boy Ganymede. Conceivably, both the Narcissus and Hyacinth stories have their origins in earlier fertility rites or in the dying god myth, or both. As in the case of such figures as Adonis and Attis, spring flowers result directly from their deaths.

GANYMEDE

The King of Heaven once was fired with love
Of Ganymede, and something was devised

That Jove would rather be than what he was.
Yet no bird would he deign to be but one
That had the power to bear his thunderbolts.
At once his spurious pinions beat the breeze
And off he swept the Trojan lad; who now,
Mixing the nectar, waits in heaven above
(Though Juno frowns) and hands the cup to Jove.
     Hyacinth, too, Apollo would have placed
In heaven had the drear Fates given time
To place him there. Yet in the form vouchsafed
He is immortal. Year by year, when spring
Drives winter flying and the Ram succeeds
The watery Fish, he rises from the earth
And in the greensward brings his bloom to birth.

HYACINTH

Hyacinth was my father's favourite,
And Delphi, chosen centre of the world,
Lost its presiding god, who passed his days
Beside Eurotas in the martial land
Of unwalled Sparta, and no more esteemed
Zither or bow. Forgetting his true self,
He was content to bear the nets, to hold
The hounds in leash and join the daylong chase
Through the rough mountain ridges, nourishing
His heart's desire with long companionship.
     One day, near noon, when the high sun midway
Between the night past and the night to come
At equal distance stood from dawn and dusk,
They both stripped off their clothes and oiled their limbs,
So sleek and splendid, and began the game,
Throwing the discus; and Apollo first
Poised, swung and hurled it skywards through the air,
Up, soaring up, to cleave the waiting clouds.
The heavy disk at longest last fell back
To the familiar earth, a proof of skill,
And strength with skill. Then straightway Hyacinth,
Unthinking, in the excitement of the sport,
Ran out to seize it, but it bounded back

From the hard surface full into his face.
The god turned pale, pale as the boy himself,
And catching up the huddled body, tried
To revive him, tried to staunch the tragic wound
And stay the fading soul with healing herbs.
His skill was vain; the wound was past all cure.
And as, when in a garden violets
Or lilies tawny-tongued or poppies proud
Are bruised and bent, at once they hang their heads
And, drooping, cannot stand erect and bow
Their gaze upon the ground; so dying lies
That face so fair and, all strength ebbed away,
His head, too heavy, on his shoulder sinks.
      "My Hyacinth," Apollo cried, "laid low
And cheated of youth's prime! I see your wound,
My condemnation, you my grief and guilt!
I, I have caused your death; on my own hand,
My own, your doom is written. Yet what wrong
Is mine unless to join the game with you
Were wrong or I were wrong to love you well?
Oh, would for you—or with you—I might give
My life! But since the laws of fate forbid,
You shall be with me always; you shall stay
For ever in remembrance on my lips,
And you my lyre and you my song shall hymn.
A new flower you shall be with letters marked
To imitate my sobs, and time shall come
When to that flower the bravest hero born
Shall add his name on the same petals writ."
      So with prophetic words Apollo spoke,
And lo! the flowing blood that stained the grass
Was blood no longer; and a flower rose
Gorgeous as Tyrian dye, in form a lily,
Save that a lily wears a silver hue,
This richest purple. And, not yet content,
Apollo (who had wrought the work of grace)
Inscribed upon the flower his lament,
AI AI, AI AI, and still the petals show
The letters written there in words of woe.
And Sparta's pride in Hyacinth, her son,

Endures undimmed; with pomp and proud display
Each year his feast returns in the ancient way.

[Ovid, *Metamorphoses*, trans. A. D. Melville
(Oxford University Press, 2008), pp. 229–231.]

Eros and Psyche

The story of Eros (Cupid) and Psyche is a late one, told by Apuleius in *The Golden Ass*. It has been a favorite of poets, perhaps because of its allegorical implications, Eros standing for passion and the body, *psyche* being the Greek word for feminine soul or spirit. It is said that Eros (Cupid) fell in love with the mortal Psyche and she with him. The lovers met under cover of darkness each night until, urged on by her jealous sisters, Psyche shone a lamp on the sleeping Eros one night, causing him to awaken and depart while scolding her for her mistrust. After a period of aimless wandering in search of her lover, Psyche begged Aphrodite for assistance, and the lovers were eventually reunited.

Daphne and Apollo

As *Daphne* means "laurel" in Greek, this is an origin story, but it is also a celebration of the powers of Mother Earth, to whom Daphne prays for help in the myth as told by Apollodorus and retold by Ovid. A similar situation occurred in connection with the Pleiades, daughters of the world-bearing Titan Atlas and virgin companions of Artemis. They are saved from an unwanted lover, Orion, by being turned into doves and then into a constellation of stars that still carries their name.

APOLLO AND DAPHNE

Daphne, Peneus' child, was the first love
Of great Apollo, a love not lit by chance
Unwitting, but by Cupid's spiteful wrath.
The god of Delos, proud in victory,
Saw Cupid draw his bow's taut arc, and said:
"Mischievous boy, what are a brave man's arms
To you? That gear becomes my shoulders best.
My aim is sure; I wound my enemies,
I wound wild beasts; my countless arrows slew
But now the bloated Python, whose vast coils

Across so many acres spread their blight.
You and your loves! You have your torch to light them!
Let that content you; never claim my fame!"
And Venus' son replied: "Your bow, Apollo,
May vanquish all, but mine shall vanquish you.
As every creature yields to power divine,
So likewise shall your glory yield to mine."
Then winging through the air his eager way
He stood upon Parnassus' shady peak,
And from his quiver's laden armoury
He drew two arrows of opposing power,
One shaft that rouses love and one that routs it.
The first gleams bright with piercing point of gold;
The other, dull and blunt, is tipped with lead.
This one he lodged in Daphne's heart; the first
He shot to pierce Apollo to the marrow.
At once he loves; she flies the name of love,
Delighting in the forest's secret depths
And trophies of the chase, a nymph to vie
With heaven's virgin huntress, fair Diana;
A careless ribbon held her straying hair.

     Many would woo her; she, rejecting all,
Manless, aloof, ranged through the untrodden woods
Nor cared what love, what marriage rites might mean.
Often her father said, "My dearest daughter,
It is my due to have a son-in-law."
Often her father said, "It is my due,
Child of my heart, to be given grandchildren."
She hated like a crime the bond of wedlock,
And, bashful blushes tingeing her fair cheeks,
With coaxing arms embraced him and replied:
"My dear, dear father grant I may enjoy
Virginity for ever; this Diana
Was granted by her father." He, indeed,
Yielded, but Daphne—why, her loveliness
Thwarts her desire, her grace denies her prayer.

     Apollo saw her, loved her, wanted her—
Her for his bride, and, wanting, hoped—deceived
By his own oracles; and, as the stubble
Flames in the harvest fields or as a hedge

Catches alight when some late wayfarer
Chances his torch too close or, in the dawn,
Discards its smouldering embers, so love's fire
Consumed the god, his whole heart was aflame.
And high the hopes that stoked his fruitless passion.
He sees the loose disorder of her hair
And thinks what if it were neat and elegant!
He sees her eyes shining like stars, her lips—
But looking's not enough!—her fingers, hands,
Her wrists, her half-bare arms—how exquisite!
And sure her hidden charms are best! But she
Flies swifter than the lightfoot wind nor stops
To hear him calling: "Stay, sweet nymph! Oh, stay!
I am no foe to fear. Lambs flee from wolves
And hinds from lions, and the fluttering doves
From eagles; every creature flees its foes.
But love spurs my pursuit. Oh, you will fall
And briars graze your legs—for shame!—and I,
Alas, the cause of your distress! The ground
You race across is rough. You run too fast!
Check your swift flight, and I'll not chase so fast.
Yet ask who loves you. No rough forester
Am I, no unkempt shepherd guarding here
His flocks and herds. You do not know—you fly,
You madcap girl, because you do not know.
I am the lord of Delphi; Tenedos
And Patara and Claros are my realms.
I am the son of Jupiter. By me
Things future, past and present are revealed;
I shape the harmony of song and strings.
Sure are my arrows, but one surer still
Has struck me to the heart, my carefree heart.
The art of medicine I gave the world
And all men call me "healer"; I possess
The power of every herb. Alas! that love
No herb can cure, that skills which help afford
To all mankind fail now to help their lord!"
        More he had tried to say, but she in fear
Fled on and left him and his words unfinished.
Enchanting still she looked—her slender limbs

Bare in the breeze, her fluttering dress blown back,
Her hair behind her streaming as she ran;
And flight enhanced her grace. But the young god,
Could bear no more to waste his blandishments,
And (love was driving him) pressed his pursuit.
And as a beagle sees across the stubble
A hare and runs to kill and she for life—
He almost has her; now, yes now, he's sure
She's his; his straining muzzle scrapes her heels;
And she half thinks she's caught and, as he bites,
Snatches away; his teeth touch—but she's gone.
So ran the god and girl, he sped by hope
And she by fear. But he, borne on the wings
Of love, ran faster, gave her no respite,
Hot on her flying heels and breathing close
Upon her shoulders and her tumbling hair.
Her strength was gone; the travail of her flight
Vanquished her, and her face was deathly pale.
And then she saw the river, swift Peneus,
And called, "Help, father, help! If mystic power
Dwells in your waters, change me and destroy
My baleful beauty that has pleased too well."
Scarce had she made her prayer when through her limbs
A dragging languor spread, her tender bosom
Was wrapped in thin smooth bark, her slender arms
Were changed to branches and her hair to leaves;
Her feet but now so swift were anchored fast
In numb stiff roots, her face and head became
The crown of a green tree; all that remained
Of Daphne was her shining loveliness.
　　　And still Apollo loved her; on the trunk
He placed his hand and felt beneath the bark
Her heart still beating, held in his embrace
Her branches, pressed his kisses on the wood;
Yet from his kisses still the wood recoiled.
"My bride," he said, "since you can never be,
At least, sweet laurel, you shall be my tree.
My lyre, my locks, my quiver you shall wreathe;
You shall attend the conquering lords of Rome

When joy shouts triumph and the Capitol
Welcomes the long procession; you shall stand
Beside Augustus' gates, sure sentinel
On either side, guarding the oak between.
My brow is ever young, my locks unshorn;
So keep your leaves' proud glory ever green."
Thus spoke the god; the laurel in assent
Inclined her new-made branches and bent down,
Or seemed to bend, her head, her leafy crown.

[Ovid, *Metamorphoses*, trans. A. D. Melville
(Oxford University Press, 2008), pp. 14–18.]

The Eumenides

The Eumenidies (or Erinnyes or Furies) are disgusting flying crones who
harass people for breaking social codes or taboos. Homer knew of them, and
the playwright Aeschylus treats them in the third play of his Orestes trilogy
(the *Eumenides*). Orestes is hounded by the Furies for having committed matricide
in order to avenge his mother Clytemnestra's murder of his father, King
Agamemnon. The ordeal of Orestes ends at his famous trial at Athens, during
which Apollo argues for Orestes against the Furies and Athena acts as judge
and in which the ancient power of the earth-oriented Furies gives way to the
rational power of the two great sky gods. The trial itself can be seen as a metaphor for this important change in Greek religion.

Zeus and Europa

Ovid tells this bizarre tale of one of Zeus' many philandering escapades. Zeus
takes the form of a bull to carry away Europa, the daughter of Agenor.

JUPITER AND EUROPA

Jove called his son aside and, keeping dark
His secret passion, "Mercury," he said,
"Trusty executant of my commands,
Make haste, glide swiftly on your usual course
Down to the land that sees your mother's star
High in the southern sky, named by its people
The land of Sidon; in the distance there,
Grazing the mountain pastures, you will find
The royal herd; drive them to the sea-shore."

And presently (as Jove had bidden) the herd,
Driven from the hillside, headed for the shore,
Where with her girls of Tyre for company
The great king's daughter often used to play.
        Ah, majesty and Jove go ill together,
Nor long share one abode! Relinquishing
Sceptre and throne, heaven's father, God of gods,
Who wields the three-forked lightning, at whose nod
The world is shaken, now transforms himself
Into a bull and, lowing, joins the herd,
Ambling—so handsome—through the tender grass.
His hide was white, white as untrodden snow
Before the south wind brings the melting rain.
The muscles of his neck swelled proud; below
The dewlap hung; his horns, though small, you'd swear
A master hand had made, so jewel-like
Their pure and pearly sheen; upon his brow
No threat, no menace in his eye; his mien
Peaceful. Europa marvelled at his beauty
And friendliness that threatened naught of harm.
Yet, gentle as he seemed, she feared at first
To touch him, but anon came up to him
And offered flowers to his soft white lips.
        Glad was the lover's heart and, till the joy
Hoped for should come, he kissed her hand, and then—
Hardly, oh, hardly, could postpone the rest!
And now he frolicked, prancing on the greensward;
Then on the yellow sand laid his white flank;
And gradually she lost her fear, and he
Offered his breast for her virgin caresses,
His horns for her to wind with chains of flowers,
Until the princess dared to mount his back,
Her pet bull's back, unwitting whom she rode.
Then—slowly, slowly down the broad dry beach—
First in the shallow waves the great god set
His spurious hooves, then sauntered further out
Till in the open sea he bore his prize.
Fear filled her heart, as, gazing back, she saw
The fast receding sands. Her right hand grasped

A horn, the other leant upon his back;
Her fluttering tunic floated in the breeze.
Now, safe in Crete, Jove shed the bull's disguise
And stood revealed before Europa's eyes.
Meanwhile her father, baffled, bade his son
Cadmus, set out to find the stolen girl
And threatened exile should he fail—in one
Same act such warmth of love, such wickedness!

[Ovid, *Metamorphoses*, trans. A. D. Melville
(Oxford University Press, 2008), pp. 50–51.]

Non-Greek
Iran (Persia): Mithras

The god Mithras (or Mithra) was a major influence on Christianity until the fourth century c.e. In this version of his story by Barbara Walker, the parallels between the two cults are emphasized.

Mithra [was the] Persian savior, whose cult was the leading rival of Christianity in Rome, and more successful than Christianity for the first four centuries of the "Christian" era. In 307 A.D. the emperor officially designated Mithra "Protector of the Empire."

Christians copied many details of the Mithraic mystery-religion, explaining the resemblance later with their favorite argument, that the devil had anticipated the true faith by imitating it before Christ's birth. Some resemblances between Christianity and Mithraism were so close that even St. Augustine declared the priests of Mithra worshipped the same deity as he did.

Mithra was born on the 25th of December, called "Birthday of the Unconquered Sun," which was finally taken over by Christians in the 4th century A.D. as the birthday of Christ. Some said Mithra sprang from an incestuous union between the sun god and his own mother, just as Jesus, who was God, was born of the Mother of God. Some claimed Mithra's mother was a mortal virgin. Others said Mithra had no mother, but was miraculously born of a female Rock, the petra genetrix, fertilized by the Heavenly Father's phallic lightning.

Mithra's birth was witnessed by shepherds and by Magi who brought gifts to his sacred birth-cave of the Rock. Mithra performed the usual assortment of miracles: raising the dead, healing the sick, making the blind see and the lame walk, casting out devils. As a Peter, son of the petra, he carried the keys of the kingdom of heaven. His triumph and ascension to heaven were celebrated at the spring equinox (Easter), when the sun rises toward its apogee.

Before returning to heaven, Mithra celebrated a Last Supper with his twelve disciples, who represented the twelve signs of the zodiac. In memory of this, his worshippers partook of a sacramental meal of bread marked with a cross. This was one of seven Mithraic sacraments, the models for the Christians' seven sacraments. It was called mizd, Latin missa, English mass. Mithra's image was buried in a rock tomb, the same sacred cave that represented his Mother's womb. He was withdrawn from it and said to live again.

Like early Christianity, Mithraism was an ascetic, anti-female religion. Its priesthood consisted of celibate men only. Women were forbidden to enter Mithraic temples. The women of Mithraic families had nothing to do with the men's cult, but attended services of the Great Mother in their own temples of Isis, Diana, or Juno.

To eliminate the female principle from their creation myth, Mithraists replaced the Mother of All Living in the primal garden of paradise (Pairidaeza) with the Bull named Sole-Created. Instead of Eve, this Bull was the partner of the first man. All creatures were born from the bull's blood. Yet the bull's birth-giving was oddly female-imitative. The animal was castrated and sacrificed, and its blood was delivered to the moon for magical fructification, the moon being the source of women's magic lunar "blood of life" that produced real children on earth.

Persians have been called the Puritans of the heathen world. They developed Mithraism out of an earlier Aryan religion that was not so puritanical or so exclusively male-oriented. Mithra seems to have been the Indo-Iranian sun god Mitra, or Mitravaruna, one of the twelve zodiacal sons of the Infinity-goddess Aditi. Another of Aditi's sons was Aryaman, eponymous ancestor of "Aryans," whom the Persians transformed into Ahriman, the Great Serpent of Darkness, Mithra's enemy.

Early on, there seems to have been a feminine Mithra. Herodotus said the Persians used to have a sky-goddess Mitra, the same as Mylitta, Assyria's Great Mother. Lydians combined Mithra with his archaic spouse Anahita as an androgynous Mithra-Anahita, identified with Sabazius-Anaitis, the Serpent and Dove of Anatolian mystery cults.

Anahita was the Mother of Waters, traditional spouse of the solar god whom she bore, loved, and swallowed up. She was identified with the Anatolian Great Goddess Ma. Mithra was naturally coupled with her, as her opposite, a spirit of fire, light, and the sun. Her "element," water, overwhelmed the world in the primordial flood, when one man built an ark and saved himself, together with his cattle, according to Mithraic myth. The story seems to have been based on the Hindu Flood of Manu, transmitted through Persian and Babylonian scriptures to appear in a late, rather corrupt version in the Old Testament.

What began in water would end in fire, according to Mithraic eschatology. The great battle between the forces of light and darkness in the Last Days would destroy the earth with its upheavals and burnings. Virtuous ones who followed the teachings of the Mithraic priesthood would join the spirits of light and be saved. Sinful ones who followed other teachings would be cast into hell with Ahriman and the fallen angels. The Christian notion of salvation was almost wholly a product of this Persian eschatology, adopted by Semitic eremites and sun-cultists like the Essenes, and by Roman military men who thought the rigid discipline and vivid battle-imagery of Mithraism appropriate for warriors. Under emperors like Julian and Commodus, Mithra became the supreme patron of Roman armies.

After extensive contact with Mithraism, Christians also began to describe themselves as soldiers for Christ; to call their savior Light of the World, Helios the Rising Sun, and Sun of Righteousness; to celebrate their feasts on Sun-day rather than the Jewish sabbath; to claim their savior's death was marked by an eclipse of the sun; and to adopt the seven Mithraic sacraments. Like Mithraists, Christians practiced baptism to ascend after death through the planetary spheres to the highest heaven, while the wicked (unbaptized) would be dragged down to darkness.

Mithra's cave-temple on the Vatican Hill was seized by Christians in 376 A.D. Christian bishops of Rome pre-empted even the Mithraic high priest's title of Pater Patrum, which became Papa, or Pope. Mithraism entered into many doctrines of Manichean Christianity and continued to influence its old rival for over a thousand years. The Mithraic festival of Epiphany, marking the arrival of sun-priests or Magi at the Savior's birthplace, was adopted by the Christian church only as late as 813 A.D.

[Barbara Walker, *The Woman's Encyclopedia of Myths and Secrets* (New York, 1983), pp. 663–665.]

Japan: Izanami and Izanagi

The motif of the struggle between the male and female creator gods is common. It occurs in Japanese mythology between the creator gods Izanagi and Izanami.

IZANAMI

She arrived, divine, among eight pairs of deities at the beginning of time, and it was she who would bring forth all that was to exist in the world.

And be dishonored.

In the freshness of youth, she stood high in the heavens and conceived the notion of having her brother Izanagi as her mate. They agreed to circumambulate all of heaven, she from the left and her brother from the right. When they met, Izanami explained her idea to her brother, singing of her great desire for him, and so they mated.

From this mating came a water serpent, an ugly beast, and everyone declared that its birth was most tragic. It was, everyone said, because Izanami had committed an unforgiveable breach of manners by speaking to Izanagi of her desire. It was the male who should speak first in all such matters.

And so the pair, with the brother speaking first, circled heaven again and mated, bringing forth the isles of Japan. Izanami bore the sun and the moon, the features of the land, the oceans and rivers and streams . . . and all things that grow, and she filled them with kami spirit.

Finally, Izanami labored and brought forth the kami of fire, but in doing so, her womb was frightfully burned—indeed, mortally so. In pain and grieving to leave all that she had created, Izanami made her way to the Land of the Dead, where she built a castle to spend her lonely eternity of days.

Overtaken by an urge to see the mother of all his children, Izanagi one day undertook a journey to the Land of the Dead. He went even though it was known that Izanami wanted never to be seen in death. When he arrived and looked on his mate, he was disgusted and ran off. Enraged, Izanami sent the female spirits of death after Izanagi. But he escaped, rolled a gigantic rock between the Lands of the Dead and of the Living, and called out to Izanami, "I divorce you, I divorce you!"

And so the one who had given birth to all creation, and mortally wounded herself by giving birth even to fire, spent the rest of time alone in her castle in the Land of the Dead.

[David A. Leeming and Jake Page, *Goddess* (Oxford University Press, 1994), pp. 96–97.]

Hawaii: Pele and Hiiaka'

The Hawaiian tale of the goddesses Pele and Hiiaka' is at once a typical quest narrative and a story of resurrection.

At one time Pele fell in love with a mortal; and this is the story of the fiery wooing. Pele, her brothers, and sisters one day, to amuse themselves with a taste of mortal enjoyments, left their lurid caves in the crater of Kilauea, and went down to the coast of Puna to bathe, surf-ride, sport in the sands, and gather squid, limpets, edible seaweed, and like delicacies. As they had assumed human forms for the time, so for the time they experienced human appetites.

While the others were amusing themselves in various ways, Pele, in the guise of an old woman, sought repose and sleep in the shade of a hala-tree. Her favourite sister was Hiiaka', her full name being Hiiaka-i-ka-pali-o-Pele. She was younger than Pele, and they frequently occupied the same grotto under the burning lake of Kilauea.

Hiiaka' accompanied her sister, and, sitting beside her, kept her cool with a kahili (feather plume). Her eyelids growing heavy, Pele settled herself to sleep, instructing Hiiaka' to allow her under no circumstances to be disturbed, no matter how long she might sleep, be it for hours or be it for days; she then fell into a sound sleep.

Hardly was she lapped in the silence of forgetfulness when the sound of a beaten drum fell on her ear; a distant beating, but regular as if to the impulse of music. Before leaving the crater she had heard the same sound, but had paid little attention to it. Now in her dreams, however, her curiosity was awakened, and assuming her spiritual form she set off in the direction from which the sound seemed to come. Leaving her slumbering body in the care of Hiiaka', Pele followed the sound all over Hawaii; and always it seemed just before her, but never there, so that she could not overtake it. At Upolu it came to her from over the sea, and she followed it to the island of Maui. It was still beyond, and she followed to Molokai; still beyond, and she followed to Oahu; still beyond, and she followed to Kauai. She stood on the peak of Haupu, when she saw at last that the sound came from the beach at Kaena.

Hovering unseen over the place, she observed that the sound she had so long followed was that of the pahu-hula, or hula drum, beaten by Lohiau, the young and handsome Prince of Kauai, who was noted not only for the splendour of his hula entertainments, where danced the most beautiful women of the island, but also for his own personal graces as dancer and musician. The favourite deity of Lohiau was Laka-kane, the god of the hula and similar sport, and it was this god who, in a spirit of mischief, had conveyed the sound to Pele, awaking in her the curiosity that urged her on and on.

The beach was thronged with dancers, musicians, and spectators, all enjoying themselves under the shade of the hala- and coconut-trees, with the Prince as leader and the centre of attraction. Assuming the form of a beautiful woman, Pele suddenly appeared among them. Displaying every imaginable charm of form and feature, her presence was at once noted; and, a way being opened for her to the Prince, he received her graciously and invited her to a seat near him, where she could best witness the entertainment.

Glancing at the beautiful stranger from time to time in the midst of his performances, Lohiau at length became so fascinated that he failed to follow the music, when he yielded the instrument to another, and seated himself beside the enchantress. In answer to his inquiry she informed the Prince that she was a stranger in Kauai, and had come from the direction of the rising sun.

"You are most welcome," said Lohiau, adding, after a pause, "but I cannot rejoice that you have come."

"And why, since I do not come as your enemy?" asked Pele, increasing, with her glances, the turmoil within him.

"Because until now," answered the Prince, "my thought has been that there are beautiful women in Kauai."

"I see you know how to shape your speech to suit the fancies of women," said Pele provocatively.

"Not better than I know how to love them," answered Lohiau. "Would you be convinced?"

"Lohiau is in his own kingdom, and has but to command," was her reply; and her play of modesty completed the enthralment of the Prince.

Thus Pele became the wife of Lohiau. He knew nothing of her but what delighted him, nor did he care to inquire about that which he could not discover without inquiry. He saw that she was beautiful above all women, and for a few days they lived so happily together that life seemed a dream to him, as it was a dream to her. But the time had to come when she must return to Hawaii; and, pledging him to remain true to her, she left him with protestations of affection and the promise of a speedy return; and on the wings of the wind she was wafted back to the shores of Puna, where her sister was still patiently watching and waiting in the shade of the hala.

Lohiau was inconsolable. As each day passed, he thought she would be with him the next, until more than a month went by, when he refused food, and died in grief at her absence. The strange death of the Prince caused much comment, for he was physically strong, and suffered from no malady. Some declared that he had been prayed to death by enemies; some that he had been poisoned; but an old kaula (prophet), who had seen Pele at Kaena and noted her actions, advised against further inquiry concerning the cause of death, offering as a reason the opinion that the strangely beautiful and unknown woman he had taken as wife was an immortal, who had become attached to her earthly husband and called his spirit to her.

The Prince was much loved by his people; and his body, wrapped in many folds of tapa, was kept in state for some time in the royal house. It was guarded by the high chiefs of the kingdom, and every night funeral hymns were chanted round it, and mele recited of the deeds of the dead prince and his ancestors.

Let us return now to Pele. Her body had been carefully watched by her brothers and sisters, who had not dared to disturb it; and her return was greeted with joy, for the fires of Kilauea had almost died out with neglect. Pele rose to her feet in the form of the old woman she had assumed when falling asleep in the care of Hiiaka'; and without referring to her adventures in Kauai, or to the cause of her long slumber, she returned with the others to Kilauea, and with a breath renewed the dying fires of the crater. Hiiaka' asked and received from Pele permission to remain for a few days at the beach with her loved friend Hopoe, a young woman of Puna, who had lost both her parents in an eruption of Kilauea.

It is probable that Pele, on leaving Kauai, notwithstanding her fervent words to the contrary, never expected, or particularly desired, to see Lohiau again; but he had so endeared himself to her during their brief union that she found it difficult to forget him; and, after struggling against the feeling for some time, she resolved to send for him. But to whom could she entrust the important mission? She applied to her sisters at the crater one after another; but the way was beset with evil spirits, and one after another refused to go.

In this dilemma Pele sent her brother Lono-i-ka-onolii to bring Hiiaka' from the beach, well knowing that she would not refuse to undertake the journey, however hazardous. Hiiaka' accepted the mission, with the understanding that during her absence her friend Hopoe should remain in the guardianship of Pele.

Arrangements were made for her immediate departure. Pele conferred upon her some of her own powers, and for a companion servant gave her Pauo-palae, a woman of proved sagacity and prudence.

With a farewell from the relatives of Hiiaka' and many an admonition from Pele they took their departure; and, travelling as mortals, they were subject to the fatigues and perils of mortals. They met a woman, whose name was Omeo, and who was leading a hog to the volcano as a sacrifice to Pele. She desired to accompany them; and, they agreeing, she hastened to the crater with her offering, returned, and followed Hiiaka' and her companion. Proceeding through the forests toward the coast of Hilo, they were impeded by a hideous demon, who threw himself across their path in a narrow defile and attempted to destroy them; but Pele was aware of their danger, and ordered her brothers to protect them with a rain of fire and thunder, which drove the monster to his den and enabled them to escape.

The forests abounded in mischievous gnomes and fairies, nymphs and monsters guarded the streams; the air was peopled with spirits, for a thin veil only separated the living from the dead, the natural from the supernatural.

Again they had not gone far when they encountered a man of fierce appearance who was either insane or possessed of demons; but he lacked the power or the disposition to injure them, and they passed on unharmed. Coming to a small stream, they found the waters dammed by a huge mo'o, or lizard (moko), lying in the bed. He was more than a hundred paces in length, with eyes the size of great calabashes. He glared viciously, and opened his mouth as if to devour the travellers; but Hiiaka' tossed a stone into his mouth which on touching his throat became red-hot, and with a roar of pain that made the trees tremble he disappeared down the stream.

After many adventures with monsters and evil spirits they reached the coast at Honoipo, where they found a number of men and women engaged in the sport of surf-riding. As they were about to start on another trial, Hiiaka' in a spirit of mischief turned their surf-boards into stone, and they fled from the beach in terror, fearing that some sea-god was preparing to devour them.

Observing a fisherman drawing in a line, Hiiaka' caused a human head to be fastened to the submerged hook. The man raised it to the surface, stared at it in horror for a moment, then dropped the line and paddled swiftly away, to the great amusement of Hiiaka' and her companions.

Embarking in a canoe, the travellers reached Maui, crossed it with further adventures, then sailed with a fisherman for Oahu. They landed at Maka-puu, journeyed overland to Kou—now Honolulu—and from Haena made sail for Kauai. Arriving at Kaena, Hiiaka' saw the spirit hand of Lohiau beckoning to her from the mouth of a cave up in the cliffs. Turning to her companion, she said, "We have failed; the lover of Pele is dead! I see his spirit beckoning from the pali [cliff] where it is held and hidden by the lizard-women Kilioa and Kalamainu."

Instructing her companions to proceed to the puoa where the body of Lohiau was lying in state, Hiiaka' started at once up the pali, to give battle to the demons and rescue the spirit of the dead prince. Ascending the cliff and entering the cave, she waved her pau, and with angry hisses the demons disappeared. She searched for the spirit of Lohiau, and at last found it in a niche of the rocks where it had been imprisoned by a moonbeam. Taking it tenderly in her hand, she folded it in her pau and in an invisible form floated down with it to the puoa.

Waiting until after nightfall, Hiiaka' entered the chamber of death unseen, and restored the spirit to the body of Lohiau. Recovering life and consciousness, the bewildered Prince looked about him. The guards were filled with fear when he raised his head, and would have fled in alarm had they not been prevented by Hiiaka', who that instant appeared before them in mortal form. Holding up her hand to command obedience, she said, "Fear nothing; say nothing of this to anyone living, and do nothing except as you may be ordered. The Prince has returned to life, and may recover if properly cared for. His body is weak and wasted. Let him at once be secretly removed to the seashore. The night is dark, and this may be done without observation."

Not doubting that these instructions were from the gods, the guards obeyed, and Lohiau was soon comfortably resting in a hut by the seashore, with Hiiaka' and her companion attending to his wants.

The return of the Prince to health and strength was rapid, and in a few days he reappeared among his friends, to their amazement and great joy. In answer to their inquiries he told them that he owed to the gods his restoration to life. This did not altogether satisfy them, but no other explanation was offered.

[Johannes Andersen, *Myths and Legends of the Polynesians* (Rutland and Tokyo, 1969), pp. 268–274.]

India: Indra and the Parade of Ants

One thing mythologies attempt to do is to provide humans with a sense of their relative importance in the universe, a sense of proportion. We need such a perspective, such an understanding of our significance or lack of it on the cosmic scale. In this famous tale of the parade of ants from the *Brahmavaivarta Purana*, retold by Heinrich Zimmer, we find the god Indra himself in need of this understanding.

Indra slew the dragon, a giant titan that had been couching on the mountains in the limbless shape of a cloud serpent, holding the waters of heaven captive in its belly. The god flung his thunderbolt into the midst of the ungainly coils; the monster shattered like a stack of withered rushes. The waters burst free and streamed in ribbons across the land, to circulate once more through the body of the world.

This flood is the flood of life and belongs to all. It is the sap of field and forest, the blood coursing in the veins. The monster had appropriated the common benefit, massing his ambitious, selfish hulk between heaven and earth, but now was slain. The juices again were pouring. The titans were retreating to the underworlds; the gods were returning to the summit of the central mountain of the earth, there to reign from on high.

During the period of the supremacy of the dragon, the majestic mansions of the lofty city of the gods had cracked and crumbled. The first act of Indra was to rebuild them. All the divinities of the heavens were acclaiming him their savior. Greatly elated in his triumph and in the knowledge of his strength, he summoned Vishvakarman, the god of arts and crafts, and commanded him to erect such a palace as should befit the unequaled splendor of the king of the gods.

The miraculous genius, Vishvakarman, succeeded in constructing in a single year a shining residence, marvelous with palaces and gardens, lakes and towers. But as the work progressed, the demands of Indra became even more exacting and his unfolding visions vaster. He required additional terraces and pavilions, more ponds, groves, and pleasure grounds. Whenever Indra arrived to appraise the work, he developed vision beyond vision of marvels remaining to be contrived. Presently the divine craftsman, brought to despair, decided to seek succor from above. He would turn to the demiurgic creator, Brahmā, the pristine embodiment of the Universal Spirit, who abides far above the troubled Olympian sphere of ambition, strife, and glory.

When Vishvakarman secretly resorted to the higher throne and presented his case, Brahmā comforted the petitioner. "You will soon be relieved of your burden," he said. "Go home in peace." Then, while Vishvakarman was hurrying down again to the city of Indra, Brahmā himself ascended to a still higher sphere. He came before Vishnu, the Supreme Being, of whom he himself, the Creator, was but an agent. In beatific silence Vishnu gave ear, and by a mere nod of the head let it be known that the request of Vishvakarman would be fulfilled.

Early next morning a brahmin boy, carrying the staff of a pilgrim, made his appearance at the gate of Indra, bidding the porter announce his visit to the king. The gate-man hurried to the master, and the master hastened to the entrance to welcome in person the auspicious guest. The boy was slender, some ten years old, radiant with the luster of wisdom. Indra discovered him amidst a cluster of enraptured, staring children. The boy greeted the host with a gentle glance of his dark and brilliant eyes. The king bowed to the holy child and the boy cheerfully gave his blessing. The two retired to the hall of Indra, where the god ceremoniously proffered welcome to his guest with oblations of honey, milk, and fruits, then said: "O Venerable Boy, tell me of the purpose of your coming."

The beautiful child replied with a voice that was as deep and soft as the slow thundering of auspicious rain clouds. "O King of Gods, I have heard of the mighty palace you are building, and have come to refer to you the questions in my mind. How many years will it require to complete this rich and extensive residence? What further feats of engineering will Vishvakarman be expected to accomplish? O Highest of the Gods,"—the boy's luminous features moved with a gentle, scarcely perceptible smile—"no Indra before you has ever succeeded in completing such a palace as yours is to be."

Full of the wine of triumph, the king of the gods was entertained by this mere boy's pretension to a knowledge of Indras earlier than himself. With a fatherly smile he put the question: "Tell me, Child! Are they then so very many, the Indras and Vishvakarmans whom you have seen—or at least, whom you have heard of?"

The wonderful guest calmly nodded. "Yes, indeed, many have I seen." The voice was as warm and sweet as milk fresh from the cow, but the words sent a slow chill through Indra's veins. "My dear child," the boy continued, "I knew your father, Kashyapa, the Old Tortoise Man, lord and progenitor of all the creatures of the earth. And I knew your grandfather, Marīchi, Beam of Celestial Light, who was the son of Brahā. Marīchi was begotten of the god Brahmā's pure spirit; his only wealth and glory were his sanctity and devotion. Also, I know Brahmā, brought forth by Vishnu from the lotus calix growing from Vishnu's navel. And Vishnu himself—the Supreme Being, supporting Brahmā in his creative endeavor—him too I know.

"O King of Gods, I have known the dreadful dissolution of the universe. I have seen all perish, again and again, at the end of every cycle. At that terrible time, every single atom dissolves into the primal, pure waters of eternity, whence originally all arose. Everything then goes back into the fathomless, wild infinity of the ocean, which is covered with utter darkness and is empty of every sign of animate being. Ah, who will count the universes that have passed away, or the creations that have risen afresh, again and again, from the formless abyss of the vast waters? Who will number the passing ages of the world, as they follow each other endlessly? And who will search through the wide infinities of space to count the universes side by side, each containing its Brahmā, its Vishnu, its Shiva? Who will count the Indras in them all—those Indras side by side, who reign at once in all the innumerable worlds; those others who passed away before them; or even the Indras who succeed each other in any given line, ascending to godly kingship, one by one, and, one by one, passing away? King of Gods, there are among your servants certain who maintain that it may be possible to number the grains of sand on earth and the drops of rain that fall from the sky, but no one will ever number all those Indras. This is what the Knowers know.

"The life and kingship of an Indra endure seventy-one eons, and when twenty-eight Indras have expired, one Day and Night of Brahmā has elapsed. But the existence of one Brahmā, measured in such Brahmā Days and Nights, is only one hundred and eight years. Brahmā follows Brahmā; one sinks, the next arises; the endless series cannot be told. There is no end to the number of those Brahmās—to say nothing of Indras.

"But the universes side by side at any given moment, each harboring a Brahmā and an Indra: who will estimate the number of these? Beyond the farthest vision, crowding outer space, the universes come and go, an innumerable host. Like delicate boats they float on the fathomless, pure waters that form the body of Vishnu. Out of every hair-pore of that body a universe bubbles and breaks. Will you presume to count them? Will you number the gods in all those worlds—the worlds present and the worlds past?"

A procession of ants had made its appearance in the hall during the discourse of the boy. In military array, in a column four yards wide, the tribe paraded across the floor. The boy noted them, paused, and stared, then suddenly laughed with an astonishing peal, but immediately subsided into a profoundly indrawn and thoughtful silence.

"Why do you laugh?" stammered Indra. "Who are you, mysterious being, under this deceiving guise of a boy?" The proud king's throat and lips had gone dry, and his voice continually broke. "Who are you, Ocean of Virtues, enshrouded in deluding mist?"

The magnificent boy resumed: "I laughed because of the ants. The reason is not to be told. Do not ask me to disclose it. The seed of woe and the fruit of wisdom are enclosed within this secret. It is the secret that smites with an ax the tree of worldly vanity, hews away its roots, and scatters its crown. This secret is a lamp to those groping in ignorance. This secret lies buried in the wisdom of the ages, and is rarely revealed even to saints. This secret is the living air of those ascetics who renounce and transcend mortal existence; but worldlings, deluded by desire and pride, it destroys."

The boy smiled and sank into silence. Indra regarded him, unable to move. "O Son of a Brahmin," the king pleaded presently, with a new and visible humility, "I do not know who you are. You would seem to be Wisdom Incarnate. Reveal to me this secret of the ages, this light that dispels the dark."

Thus requested to teach, the boy opened to the god the hidden wisdom. "I saw the ants, O Indra, filing in long parade. Each was once an Indra. Like you, each by virtue of pious deeds once ascended to the rank of a king of gods. But now, through many rebirths, each has become again an ant. This army is an army of former Indras.

"Piety and high deeds elevate the inhabitants of the world to the glorious realm of the celestial mansions, or to the higher domains of Brahmā and Shiva and to the highest sphere of Vishnu; but wicked acts sink them into the worlds beneath, into pits of pain and sorrow, involving reincarnation among birds and vermin, or out of the wombs of pigs and animals of the wild, or among trees, or among insects. It is by deeds that one merits happiness or anguish,and becomes a master or a serf. It is by deeds that one attains to the rank of a king or brahmin, or of some god, or of an Indra or a Brahmā. And through deeds again, one contracts disease, acquires beauty and deformity, or is reborn in the condition of a monster.

"This is the whole substance of the secret. This wisdom is the ferry to beatitude across the ocean of hell.

"Life in the cycle of the countless rebirths is like a vision in a dream. The gods on high, the mute trees and the stones, are alike apparitions in this phantasy. But Death administers the law of time. Ordained by time, Death is the master of all. Perishable as bubbles are the good and the evil of the beings of the dream. In unending cycles the good and evil alternate. Hence, the wise are attached to neither, neither the evil nor the good. The wise are not attached to anything at all."

The boy concluded the appalling lesson and quietly regarded his host. The king of gods, for all his celestial splendor, had been reduced in his own regard to insignificance. Meanwhile, another amazing apparition had entered the hall.

The newcomer had the appearance of a kind of hermit. His head was piled with matted hair; he wore a black deerskin around his loins; on his forehead was painted a white mark; his head was shaded by a paltry parasol of grass; and a quaint, circular cluster of hair grew on his chest: it was intact at the circumference, but from the center many of the hairs, it seemed, had disappeared. This saintly figure strode directly to Indra and the boy, squatted between them on the floor, and there remained, motionless as a rock. The kingly Indra, somewhat recovering his hostly role, bowed and paid obeisance, offering sour milk with honey and other refreshments; then he inquired, falteringly but reverently, after the welfare of the stern guest, and bade him welcome. Whereupon the boy addressed the holy man, asking the very questions Indra himself would have proposed.

"Whence do you come, O Holy Man? What is your name and what brings you to this place? Where is your present home, and what is the meaning of this grass parasol? What is the portent of that circular hair-tuft on your chest: why is it dense at the circumference but at the center almost bare? Be kind enough, O Holy Man, to answer, in brief, these questions. I am anxious to understand."

Patiently the old saint smiled, and slowly began his reply. "I am a brahmin. Hairy is my name. And I have come here to behold Indra. Since I know that I am short-lived, I have decided to possess no home, to build no house, and neither to marry nor to seek a livelihood. I exist by begging alms. To shield myself from sun and rain I carry over my head this parasol of grass.

"As to the circle of hair on my chest, it is a source of grief to the children of the world. Nevertheless, it teaches wisdom. With the fall of an Indra, one hair drops. That is why, in the center all the hairs have gone. When the other half of the period allotted to the present Brahmā will have expired, I myself shall die. O Brahmin Boy, it follows that I am somewhat short of days; what, therefore, is the use of a wife and a son, or of a house?

"Each flicker of the eyelids of the great Vishnu registers the passing of a Brahmā. Everything below that sphere of Brahmā is as insubstantial as a cloud taking shape and again dissolving. That is why I devote myself exclusively to meditating on the incomparable lotus-feet of highest Vishnu. Faith in Vishnu is more than the bliss of redemption; for every joy, even the heavenly, is as fragile as a dream, and only interferes with the one-pointedness of our faith in Him Supreme.

"Shiva, the peace-bestowing, the highest spiritual guide, taught me this wonderful wisdom. I do not crave to experience the various blissful forms of redemption: to share the highest god's supernal mansions and enjoy his eternal presence, or to be like him in body and apparel, or to become a part of his august substance, or even to be absorbed wholly in his ineffable essence."

Abruptly, the holy man ceased and immediately vanished. It had been the god Shiva himself; he had now returned to his supramundane abode. Simultaneously, the brahmin boy, who had been Vishnu, dis-appeared as well. The king was alone, baffled and amazed.

The king, Indra, pondered; and the events seemed to him to have been a dream. But he no longer felt any desire to magnify his heav-enly splendor or to go on with the construction of his palace. He summoned Visvakarman. Graciously greeting the craftsman with honeyed words, he heaped on him jewels and precious gifts, then with a sumptuous celebration sent him home.

The king, Indra, now desired redemption. He had acquired wisdom, and wished only to be free. He entrusted the pomp and burden of his office to his son, and prepared to retire to the hermit life of the wilderness. Whereupon his beautiful and passionate queen, Shachi, was overcome with grief.

Weeping, in sorrow and utter despair, Shachi resorted to Indra's ingenious house-priest and spiritual advisor, the Lord of Magic Wisdom, Brihaspati. Bowing at his feet, she implored him to divert her husband's mind from its stern resolve. The resourceful coun-selor of the gods, who by his spells and devices had helped the heav-enly powers wrest the government of the universe from the hands of their titan rivals, listened thoughtfully to the complaint of the volup-tuous, disconsolate goddess, and knowingly nodded assent. With a wizard's smile, he took her hand and conducted her to the presence of her spouse. In the role, then, of spiritual teacher, he discoursed sagely on the virtues of the spiritual life, but on the virtues also, of the secular. He gave to each its due. Very skillfully he developed his theme. The royal pupil was persuaded to relent in his extreme re-solve. The queen was restored to radiant joy.

This Lord of Magic Wisdom, Brihaspati, once had composed a treatise on government, in order to teach Indra how to rule the world. He now issued a second work, a treatise on the polity and stratagems of married love. Demonstrating the sweet art of wooing ever anew, and of enchaining the beloved with enduring bonds, this priceless book established on sound foundations the married life of the reunited pair.

Thus concludes the marvelous story of how the king of gods was humiliated in his boundless pride, cured of an excessive ambition, and through wisdom, both spiritual and secular, brought to a knowl-edge of his proper role in the wheeling play of unending life.

[Heinrich Zimmer, *Myths and Symbols in Indian Art and Civilization* (Princeton, NJ, 1946, 1972), pp. 3–11.]

BIBLIOGRAPHY

✦

Only a few of the many good collections of mythological tales can be mentioned here. For the Greek myths, Edith Hamilton's *Mythology* (New York, 1969) is useful if somewhat dated in approach. The same can be said of the other great standard collection, a nineteenth-century work by Thomas Bulfinch, *Bulfinch's Mythology* (New York, 1962), which includes a volume on medieval myths. Robert Graves's two-volume *The Greek Myths* (Baltimore, MD, 1955) is still a lively if controversial interpretation of the myths—with special emphasis on the struggle between the patriarchal and the feminine in myth. His work is also the best source for the origins and derivations of the myths, even if his accuracy is sometimes questionable. Mark Morford and Robert Lenardon present thorough interpretations of many of the classical myths in their *Classical Mythology* (New York: Oxford University Press, 2011), as does William Hansen in his *Classical Mythology* (New York: Oxford University Press, 2004). Lively retellings of small selections of myths from other parts of the world are to be found in *The Oldest Stories in the World* (Boston, 1952) by Theodor Gaster and in *Myths of the World* (New York, 1932, 1972) by Padraic Colum. David Leeming's *Oxford Companion to World Mythology* (New York: Oxford University Press, 2005) is a comprehensive dictionary/encyclopedia of world mythology. J. F. Bierlein's *Parallel Myths* (New York: Ballantine Books, 1994) emphasizes the "common threads" of world mythology. For a feminist reading of mythology, see Barbara Walker's *The Woman's Encyclopedia of Myths and Secrets* (New York, 1983).

✦ Rama and Sita

PART 3 ✦

HERO MYTHS

Mythology comes alive for us most clearly in the stories of heroes, for the "hero with a thousand faces," wherever he or she comes from, is our persona, our representative in the world dream that is myth. Joseph Campbell tells us that the universal hero pattern or "monomyth" (here he uses a word coined by James Joyce) involves a process by which the hero leaves the ordinary world of waking consciousness, enters the dark world of the supernatural, overcomes those who would destroy him there, and then returns to the ordinary, possessed of powers and new knowledge for his people.

When the hero, be he the Irish Cuchulainn or the Greek Herakles, journeys on his quest into the world of mysteries, he resembles the shamans of certain cultures who journey into the spirit world to retrieve lost or sick tribe members. Some heroes are, in fact, perhaps shamanic in origin or are metaphors for shamanic rituals and beliefs. We feel this especially in the hero stories that involve a literal descent into the underworld to retrieve a lost lover or relative such as in the Orpheus myth. Whoever the hero may be, he or she journeys for us, carries us metaphorically into our darker side, into the unconscious realm that we tentatively explore in our own dreams—into the world where our nightmares become real, where the monsters inside of us take on terrifyingly real forms, where our deepest wishes sometimes are fulfilled.

The myth that emerges from the many cultural versions of the hero, then, can be seen as a universal metaphor for the human search for self-knowledge, for what Teilhard de Chardin might have called the evolutionary path to full consciousness. And, of course, on the individual level it speaks to our attempts to achieve individuation. To follow the hero is to lose ourselves in order to find ourselves, to recognize our true selves in what Campbell calls "the wonderful song of the soul's high adventure" (*The Hero with a Thousand Faces*, p. 6).

The monomyth contains many elements. This is not to say that every hero acts out each element. Many heroes have miraculous conceptions and births, while some do not. Some descend to the underworld, and others do not. But a comparison of mythical heroes from all over the world reveals the common identity behind their highly differentiated cultural masks: they all experience the majority of the ritual acts—the rites of passage—outlined below.

More often than not the hero is miraculously conceived and born under unusual circumstances. Jesus and Quetzalcoatl and many others are born of virgins; the Buddha conceives himself in his mother's dream; Adonis is born of a tree. Heroes are born when they are needed, during a culture's dark period, often symbolized by the winter solstice. The pure or virgin birth provides a special status for the hero and announces the primordial hope for a new beginning. Mithras was born of a rock on December 25 and was attended by shepherds. The founders of the early Christian church chose the same date for the birth of Jesus in a stable and reported that shepherds attended him there.

The darkest time of the year, the darkest period in a culture's history, can be for us metaphors for a psychological reality and need. The hero's conception and birth represent the birth of the hero process within us—that is, of the process of individuation by which we agree to a shamanic journey into our own unknown in order eventually to discover our relationship with the overall significance of things, what in myth is called the Supreme Being or, in patriarchal cultures, the Father. So it is that one of the important leitmotifs of myth and literature is the hero's search for his father. This is the real father, the universal source, the agent of conception that transcends even the biological father.

By the same token, the virgin who gives birth to the hero is the Great Goddess herself—the Mother of us all, the provider of the physical existence in which we must carry the divine energy. The hero may be fathered by that intangible energy, but to be truly human, truly us, he must enter the element of flesh and blood by the only doorway available. As a metaphor for our psychological journey within, therefore, the hero story gains strength from the fact that the hero's birth often takes place in a hidden place—a cave, a rock, a stable, a grove, a water pot—which may be seen as a symbolic Mother Earth womb that prefigures the tomb. The body of the Mother and our reality on earth are, after all, death defined.

A further dimension is added by the threat to the young hero's life. If one side—the heroic side—of the individual or the society desires a new beginning, the other, more ordinary side prefers the status quo and struggles against the birth. The Herods, the demons, the jealous or angry fathers—all are only too willing to murder the hero, to leave him unattended in the wilderness, or to place him in a basket and leave him to his fate on a river's current. In psychological terms a part of us, representing everything we have been taught about safety and the nest, resists this dangerous journey within. Perhaps this is why heroes so often must separate themselves from or be separated from their human families in order to go about "my father's business."

The quest itself is the predominant aspect of the hero myth. It usually begins with a call to adventure: the voice of God calls Moses from the burning bush; the appearance of the Holy Grail calls Arthur's knights; the young Buddha is called by the "Four Signs" that appear to him as he rides about with his charioteer. Often the hero refuses the summons. We all resist radical change, and the hero, as our persona in the universal dream, is no exception. "Who am I" to perform such a task, asks Moses. In effect, Jonah asks the same question, as does Jesus in the Garden of Gethsemane.

The quest is marked by trials, by confrontations with and the defeat of our inner monsters. These monsters appear, as they would in dreams, in forms that reflect the social beliefs and concerns of the particular cultures that give them life. In the Indian epics the

Ramayana and the *Mahabharata* heroines are threatened by demons and demonic acts. Rama's wife Sita is threatened by the demon Ravana in the *Ramayana*. In the *Mahabharata* Draupadi must confront the monstrous and shameful actions of her husbands' enemies. In the patriarchal cultures out of which most of our extant myths emerge, we nearly always see the hero as being threatened by a femme fatale or temptress—Circe, the Sirens, Samson's Delilah. Cultures that stress the division of nature into good and evil place the hero against some epitome of evil, a satanic figure or a true monster, as is the case with Perseus' killing of Medusa.

However, the monsters of the inner world are balanced by sources of strength. Heroes are often guided—Aeneas by the Sibyl, countless fairy tale heroes and heroines by a spirit who takes the form of a fairy godmother, a wise old man, or a wise fool (the last perhaps a remnant of our trickster god).

At some point in the hero's journey quest he or she must confront the ultimate nemesis, death itself, and must undertake a journey to the Land of the Dead. The Indonesian heroine Hainuwele descends, and so do the African heroine Wanjiru and so many other heroes. Through this descent, the hero takes us to the very depths of the unconscious world where individual destiny and human destiny lie. In the death motif we confront the essence of what we are. In facing our death-defined nature, we rob death of "dominion" and emerge in rebirth from the womb of the earth into a new individuated existence, a new wisdom or wholeness. It remains only for the hero to return to the Supreme Being in an act of apotheosis or ascension signifying that wholeness. In many of the myths the hero, like the dying god, descends into death and in returning brings great boons to his or her culture. Often the gift is a new crop—corn or wheat—or some new spiritual knowledge. The hero's descent into the Mother is, as in the dying god motif, a form of planting associated with the Great Goddess, and even in the myths of patriarchal cultures we find in this aspect of the hero cycle an important female presence, signifying the psyche or spiritual energy—what Jung called the *anima*—without which the hero cannot achieve wholeness or full individuation.

Each of these heroic rites becomes for the literary artist an archetypal form that speaks to our common human experience and lends power and reality to the creative work. When we read that the hero of Henry Fielding's novel *Tom Jones* is a foundling, we associate him in our minds with all those heroes who are abandoned in the wilderness, and Tom's actions take on added significance in light of the lives of those heroes who, like him, go on to be questers in their cultures and metaphors for our own individual quests for wholeness, for the union with wisdom symbolized by Tom's eventual marriage with Sophia (Greek, "wisdom"), by Jesus' ascension into heaven, and by the mysterious apotheosis of Oedipus at the end of *Oedipus at Colonus*. The characters these heroes confront—the guides such as Dante's Beatrice or Lambert Strether's Maria Gostrey or the enchantresses such as Henry James's Madame Merle or John Keats's "belle dame sans merci" or the satanic figures such as William Shakespeare's Iago or Nathaniel Hawthorne's Chillingworth—take their power to communicate with our psyches from the archetypal guides, femmes fatales, and satanic characters of myth. When we read William Faulkner's *The Bear* or James Joyce's *A Portrait of the Artist as a Young Man*, the very images chosen by the two authors lead us to myths and rituals of childhood initiation; as a result, these stories, which on the surface seem to be about hunting in the American South and growing up a Catholic in Ireland, become clear and moving metaphors for our own initiations into adulthood and into the mysteries of our own "other" selves. In the same way, Fyodor Dostoevsky turns Raskolnikov's wanderings in St. Petersburg in *Crime and Punishment* into a modern antihero's pilgrimage through a modern hell. Raskolnikov's situation takes its irony from the presence in our mythic heritage of all those heroes who descend to the underworld to discover a father, a lover, or themselves. And when we realize that Shakespeare's Lear and Hamlet must die before their nations can rediscover normality under their much more ordinary successors, we realize that we are experiencing anew the sacred mythic ritual of the scapegoat, that, like dying gods and heroes, Lear and Hamlet speak to the psychological process by which we die to the old and are reborn to the new in the path toward individuation.

The hero stories collected here are from various parts of the world, with some emphasis on myths that have been most important to the imagery and subject matter of the arts in Western culture.

Some of the figures treated as heroes could have been treated as gods as well. Jesus, the Buddha, and Quetzalcoatl, for example, are seen sometimes as primarily human, sometimes as primarily divine. The stories here are meant to illustrate the existence of that "hero with a thousand faces" who lives within us all.

NATIVE NORTH AMERICA (TEWA): Water Jar Boy

Divinity finds many paths to the doorway to human life. The Aztec Quetzalcoatl was conceived when his mother, Chimalman, was breathed upon
by the Supreme Being in his form as the morning; the Phrygian Nana
conceived Attis by losing a pomegranate in her lap. Many heroes, while
not actually born of virgins, are miraculously conceived. The Blackfoot
Indian Kutoyis was born of a clot of blood; Isaac, the Virgin Mary, and
John the Baptist were all born to women who were barren or postmeno-
pausal. Although perhaps, strictly speaking, a simple folktale hero rather
than a hero of a religiously based myth, Water Jar Boy is a wonderfully
unusual representation of the classic myth of the virgin birth, and his
story also contains the familiar motif of the hero's search for the
Father.

The people were living at Sikyatki. There was a fine looking girl who
refused to get married. Her mother made water jars all the time. One
day as she was using her foot to mix some clay, she told her daughter
to go on with this while she went for water. The girl tried to mix the
clay on a flat stone by stepping on it. Somehow some of it entered
her. This made her pregnant, and after a time she gave birth. The
mother was angry about this, but when she looked she saw it was not
a baby that had been born, but a little jar. When the mother asked
where it came from, the girl just cried. Then the father came in. He
said he was very glad his daughter had a baby. When he found out
that it was a water jar, he became very fond of it.

He watched it and saw it move. It grew, and in twenty days it had
become big. It could go about with the other children and was able
to talk. The children also became fond of it. They found out from
his talk that he was Water Jar Boy. His mother cried, because he had
no legs or arms or eyes. But they were able to feed him through the
jar mouth.

When snow came, the boy begged his grandfather to take him along
with the men to hunt rabbits. "My poor grandson, you can't hunt rabbits; you have no arms or legs."

"Take me anyway," said the boy. "You are so old, you can't kill
anything." His grandfather took him down under the mesa where he
rolled along. Pretty soon he saw a rabbit track and followed it. Then

a rabbit ran out, and he began to chase it. He hit himself against a rock. The jar broke, and up jumped a boy.

He was very glad his skin had been broken and that he was a big boy. He had lots of beads around his neck, earstrings of turquoise, a dance kilt and moccasins, and a buckskin shirt. He was fine-looking and handsomely dressed. He killed four jackrabbits before sunset, because he was a good runner.

His grandfather was waiting for him at the foot of the mesa, but did not know him. He asked the fine looking boy, "Did you see my grandson anywhere?"

"No, I did not see him."

"That's too bad; he's late."

"I didn't see anyone anywhere," said the boy. Then he said, "I am your grandson." He said this because his grandfather looked so disappointed.

"No, you are not my grandson."

"Yes, I am."

"You are only teasing me. My grandson is a round jar and has no arms and legs."

Then the boy said, "I am telling you the truth. I am your grandson. This morning you carried me down here. I looked for rabbits and chased one, just rolling along. Pretty soon I hit myself on a rock. My skin was broken, and I came out of it. I am the very one who is your grandson. You must believe me." Then the old man believed him, and they went home together.

When the grandfather came to the house with a fine looking man, the girl was ashamed, thinking the man was a suitor. The old man said, "This is Water Jar Boy, my grandson." The grandmother then asked how the water jar became a boy, and the two men told her. Finally, the women were convinced.

The boy went about with the other boys of the village. One day he said to his mother, "Who is my father?"

"I don't know," she replied. He kept on asking, but it just made her cry. Finally he said, "I am going to find my father, tomorrow."

"You can't find him. I have never been with any man, so there is no place for you to look for a father," she said.

"But I know I have one," the boy said. "I know where he lives. I am going to see him."

The mother begged him not to go, but he insisted. The next day she fixed food for him, and he went off toward the southwest to a place called Horse Mesa Point. There was a spring at this place. As he approached, he saw a man walking a little way from the spring. He said to the boy, "Where are you going?"

"To the spring," the boy answered.

"Why are you going there?"

"I want to see my father."

"Who is your father?"

"He lives in this spring."

"Well, you will never find your father," said the man.

"Well, I want to go to the spring. My father is living in it," said the boy.

"Who is your father?" asked the man again.

"Well, I think you are my father."

"How do you know that?"

"I just know, that's all."

Then the man stared hard at the boy, trying to scare him. The boy just kept on saying, "You are my father." At last the man said, "Yes, I am your father. I came out of the spring to meet you." He put his arms around the boy's neck. He was very glad his boy had come, and he took him down to the spring.

There were many people living there. The women and the girls ran up to the boy and put their arms around him, because they were glad he had come. This way he found his father and his father's relatives. He stayed there one night. The next day he went to his own home and told his mother he had found his father.

Soon his mother got sick and died. The boy thought to himself, "It's no use for me to stay with these people," so he went to the spring. There he found his mother among the other women. He learned that his father was Red Water Snake. He told his boy that he could not live over at Sikyatki, so he had made the boy's mother sick so she would die and come to live with him. After that they all lived together.

[T. P. Coffin, ed., *Indian Tales of North America* (Philadelphia, 1961), pp. 99–101.]

GREECE: Theseus

In the case of Theseus, as with so many other heroes—for example, Jesus, Herakles, Helen of Troy—the father-god chooses a mortal woman to be the hero's vessel. Theseus' call to a life of adventure, which will fulfill his destiny as the son of a god and as a great hero, is represented by the existence of his foster father's sword and sandals under a magic rock. He goes on to participate in many of the ritual deeds of the world hero—for example, the search for his father, the confrontation with a monster (the Minotaur), and the descent into the underworld.

According to the mythographer Apollodoros, King Aigeus of Athens consulted the Delphic oracle about his childlessness and received a cryptic response instructing him not to release the mouth of his wineskin until he reached Athens again (that is, not to have sexual intercourse until he was home). Returning to Athens by way of Troizen, he lodged there with King Pittheus, telling him of the oracular response. Although Aigeus did not perceive its meaning, his host Pittheus did, made Aigeus drunk, and put him in bed with his daughter Aithra. During the same night Poseidon also lay with Aithra. Before departing, Aigeus instructed Aithra that if she should give birth to a boy, she should raise him without naming his father; and Aigeus left a sword and sandals beneath a certain rock, telling Aithra that when their son could roll away the rock and take up these items, she should send him with them to Aigeus.

Upon his return to Athens, the king celebrated the athletic games that were part of the Panathenaic festival. Androgeos, son of King Minos of Crete, won the events, whereupon Aigeus sent the youth against the Bull of Marathon, but Androgeos was destroyed by the animal. Minos then attacked Athens with a fleet, praying to Zeus that he might punish the Athenians. A famine and pestilence came upon Athens, so that the Athenians consulted an oracle about what they should do. The response was that they should give Minos whatever satisfaction he might choose. Minos ordered the Athenians annually to send seven unarmed youths and seven unarmed maidens as food for the Minotaur, a creature with the head of a bull and the body of a man. The monster was confined in the Labyrinth, a maze in which it was impossible for a person, once he had entered it, to find the exit.

Aithra bore a son, Theseus. When he grew up, he pushed aside the rock, retrieved the sword and sandals, and set out for Athens on foot. In the course of his journey he rid the road of several evildoers. First Theseus dispatched Periphetes the Clubman, who used to kill passersby with his iron club. The youth next killed Sinis the

Pine-Bender, who forced passersby to bend pine trees, which then flung them into the air, killing them. Theseus dispatched Sinis in the same way. Third, he killed the monstrous Krommyon Sow. Fourth, he slew Skeiron (Latinized form = Sciron), who used to compel passersby to wash his feet, and as they did so he kicked them into the sea to be food for a giant turtle. Theseus threw Skeiron into the sea. Fifth, he slew Kerkyon (Latinized form = Cercyon), who killed passersby after forcing them to wrestle with him. Theseus's sixth victim was Damastes, who lived beside the road and used to offer one of his two beds to passersby. He placed short men on his large bed, hammering their bodies to lengthen them, and tall men on his short bed, sawing off the parts of their body that extended beyond the bed. (Other ancient sources call this nightmarish host Prokrustes [Latinized form = Procrustes], whence our expression "Procrustean bed.")

When Theseus reached Athens, his father's wife, Medeia, was hostile to him, persuading Aigeus that the stranger was plotting against him. Aigeus sent him against the Marathonian Bull, which he succeeded in killing. Then Aigeus planned to poison Theseus, but seeing the youth's sword, he knocked the cup from his hands. Perceiving Medeia's plotting, he expelled her from Athens.

Voluntarily or by lot, Theseus was included among the annual tribute of youths and maidens to the Minotaur. Before the ship with its black sails departed, Aigeus instructed Theseus to change the sails to white if he should return alive. The ship reached Crete, where Minos's daughter Ariadnê fell in love with Theseus and offered to help him on the condition that he take her as his wife and take her away to Athens, which he agreed to do. Ariadnê learned from Daidalos, the constructor of the Labyrinth, how a person might find his way out, namely, by tying a of clew of thread to the door upon entering. So Ariadnê supplied Theseus with a ball of thread, one end of which he tied to the door. Then he found the Minotaur in the depths of the maze, killed him with his fists, and followed the thread back to the door. Theseus, Ariadnê, and the other young persons departed by night and reached the island of Naxos. There Dionysos, having fallen in love with Ariadnê, carried her off.

Pained at the loss of Ariadnê, Theseus forgot to change the sails to white. In Athens Aigeus stood on the Akropolis, looking for the ship, and when he saw the ship approach with black sails, he believed that Theseus had perished and so threw himself from the heights. Theseus succeeded his father as ruler of Athens.

[William Hansen, *Classical Mythology*
(Oxford University Press, 2004), pp. 299–301.]

GREECE: Herakles (Hercules) and the Twelve Labors

Herakles, the illegitimate son of Zeus, is one of the greatest and most complex of Greek heroes—at once unbelievably powerful and surprisingly unintelligent. His conception and birth, and especially the threat to his life, follow the pattern of the hero's childhood. Other great heroes who overcome early threats to their lives include the Persian Zoroaster (Zarathustra), Siegfried, and Jesus, who are threatened by demons, a dragon, and a wicked king, respectively. In the Greek tradition especially, the hero must often prove himself by accomplishing an impossible series of tasks. The twelve labors of Herakles (or Hercules), which include a descent into the underworld, have echoes in the only slightly less onerous labors of Perseus, who struggled against and killed the monstrous Gorgon (Medusa), and of Bellerophon, who, with the help of the winged horse Pegasus, killed the horrible Chimaera. Heroes of all traditions must confront monsters of the collective nightmare. Oedipus must destroy the Sphinx before he can enter Thebes. Saint George and many other medieval heroes must kill the dragon. The Buddha, Jesus, and other heroes whose adventures are as much spiritual as physical must confront the monsters within.

According to the mythographer Apollodoros, Amphitryon wooed Alkmenê (Alcmena), who agreed to marry him after he had avenged the death of her brother. He did so, but before he returned to Alkmenê in Thebes, Zeus assumed Amphitryon's likeness and lay with Alkmenê, lengthening the night threefold. After the god departed, the real Amphitryon reached home and found he was not received as warmly as he had expected. Subsequently, he learned from the seer Teiresias of Zeus's imposture. Alkmenê bore a son Herakles by Zeus and, a day later, a son Iphikles by Amphitryon. When the babes were eight months old, Hera sent two immense serpents to their bed, wishing to destroy Zeus's son. But Herakles, holding one serpent in each hand, strangled them.

Young Herakles had many tutors. His father taught him to drive a chariot, Autolykos to wrestle, Eurytos to shoot with the bow, Kastor to wield sword and javelin, and Linos, a brother of Orpheus, to play the lyre. When Linos once struck him, Herakles hit him back with the lyre, killing him, whereupon Amphitryon, fearing that he might do the same again, sent him out to tend the cattle. Herakles presently exceeded all others in size and strength, and it became obvious that he was a son of Zeus. His body was huge, his eyes flashed fire, and he never missed with either the bow or the javelin.

When he was eighteen years old, the Cithaeronian Lion, a lion using Mount Kithairon (Latinized form = Cithaeron) as its base, was killing cattle belonging to Amphitryon and Thespios, a nearby ruler. Wishing to catch the lion, Herakles went to Thespios, in whose house he stayed for fifty days while hunting the creature. Thespios had fifty daughters, and each night he bedded one of his daughters with Herakles, wishing them all to have children by him. Herakles, thinking he was with the same girl each night, lay with them all. Eventually he overcame the lion and dressed himself in its skin, using its gaping scalp as a helmet.

After Herakles distinguished himself in a conflict between Thebans and Minyans, King Kreon (Latinized form = Creon) of Thebes gave him his daughter Megara in marriage. Hermes moreover gave him a sword, Apollon a bow and arrows, Hephaistos a breastplate of gold, and Athena a peplos, or robe. He equipped himself with a club, which he had cut at Nemea. But Hera in her jealousy drove Herakles mad, and in this state he killed his own children as well as those of his brother Iphikles by flinging them into the fire. Condemning himself to exile, he went to Thespios, who purified him of the killings. Then he went to Delphi to ask the god where he should live. The Pythia, or priestess, instructed him to dwell in Tiryns, where he should serve Eurystheus for twelve years, performing ten tasks that Eurystheus would assign him, and when the tasks were completed, he would become immortal. She also addressed him for the first time as Herakles, for his given name was Alkides.

Herakles went to Eurystheus at Tiryns. His first task was to bring the skin of the Nemean Lion, which was invulnerable. Herakles caught up with the animal in Nemea, put his arm around its neck, choked it to death, and carried the beast back to his taskmaster. Astonished at Herakles's manliness, Eurystheus forbade him henceforth to enter the city, instructing him rather to display the results of his tasks before the city gates. Furthermore, Eurystheus concealed himself in a subterranean bronze jar and from then on conveyed his commands via a herald.

As his second task Herakles was commanded to kill the Lernaean Hydra, or water-serpent, which lived by a swamp at Lerna and used to sally out to kill cattle. It had an immense body and nine heads, one of which was immortal. Herakles grappled with the monster, smashing its heads with his club, but for every smashed head two new ones sprouted. So he told his companion Iolaos to cauterize each smashed head with fire in order to prevent new heads from growing, which he did. Then Herakles cut off the immortal head and buried it under a heavy rock. Before departing he dipped his arrows in the gall of the hydra's body. Eurystheus said, however, that this task should not count, since Herakles overcame the hydra with the aid of a helper.

His third labor was to capture the Cerynitian Hind and bring it back alive. The animal had golden horns and was sacred to Artemis. Not wishing to kill or wound it, Herakles chased it for a year, but finally he shot it with an arrow and captured it alive. As he was carrying it on his shoulders, he encountered Artemis, who rebuked him for trying to kill an animal that was sacred to her, but he soothed the goddess's anger by pointing out that Eurystheus was to blame. Then he carried the animal alive to Eurystheus.

Next he was ordered to fetch the Erymanthian Boar alive. Using Mount Erymanthos as its base, this beast caused much harm. On his way there Herakles was entertained by the centaur Pholos, whom he persuaded to open the jar of wine that belonged to the centaurs in common. Smelling the wine, the other centaurs presently arrived at Pholos's cave armed with rocks and sticks. Herakles repelled them, and when they retreated to Cheiron's cave at Malea, he shot an arrow at them that happened to strike Cheiron, who received thereby an incurable wound but, being immortal, could not die. Zeus transferred Cheiron's immortality to another, and Cheiron died. The other centaurs fled in all directions, but Pholos drew one of Herakles's arrows from the body of a slain centaur, wondering how so small a thing could kill such large beings, and the arrow slipped from his hand and landed on his foot, killing him also. After that Herakles resumed his hunt for the boar, exhausted it, trapped it, and conveyed it alive to Eurystheus.

His fifth task was to remove the cattle dung from the cattle yard of King Augeias of Elis in a single day. Herakles offered to clear out the dung in return for a tenth of the cattle, a proposal to which the incredulous king agreed. Herakles did not mention that he was obliged to clear away the dung anyway. Then he diverted the course of two rivers through the cattle yard, which got rid of the dung.

But when Augeias learned that Herakles had acted at the command of Eurystheus, he refused payment, and when Eurystheus learned that Herakles had performed the task for hire, he did not accept it as one of the ten.

Herakles's sixth labor was to chase away the Stymphalian Birds from Lake Stymphalis, where they had taken refuge. When he was at a loss how to do so, Athena provided him with brazen castanets, which she had gotten from Hephaistos. Clashing these together, Herakles frightened the birds away.

Eurystheus then ordered him to bring the Cretan Bull. He captured it, showed it to Eurystheus, and set it free.

His eighth task was to bring the cannibalistic mares that belonged to Diomedes the Thracian, ruler of the fierce Bistones. Herakles overpowered the men in charge of the mares, drove them away, and turned them over to Eurystheus, who let them go.

Herakles's ninth labor was to fetch the Belt of Ares, which belonged to Hippolytê, queen of the warlike Amazons. Coming to the land of the Amazons, Herakles was visited by Hippolytê, who learned of his quest and promised him the belt. In the meantime Hera, in the likeness of an Amazon, spread a false rumor among the Amazons that Herakles and his companions were carrying away their queen. When the Amazons attacked, Herakles believed that Hippolytê was acting treacherously, so that he killed her, took her belt, and sailed away. He went to Troy, where he found that Hesionê, daughter of King Laomedon, was being sacrificed to a sea-monster. Apollon and Poseidon had wished secretly to test Laomedon's hubris, so that disguised as humans they had hired themselves out to the king to fortify Pergamon, but when they had finished the job and the monarch refused to pay them their wages, Apollon sent a pestilence and Poseidon sent a monster from the sea. Oracles foretold that the people could escape these misfortunes if Laomedon should set out his daughter as food for the monster. Herakles now offered to rescue her in return for certain mares, and when Laomedon agreed to this condition, the hero killed the monster. But Laomedon once again reneged on his agreement, and as Herakles sailed away he said he would come back and make war on Troy. Returning to Eurystheus for the time being, he gave him the belt.

Next he was ordered to bring the Cattle of Geryon from Erythia, an island near the River Ocean. Geryon had the bodies of three men fused together. His cattle were herded by Eurytion, who was aided by his two-headed watchdog, Orthos. As Herakles was crossing from Europe to Libya (Africa), he set up two pillars as signs of his journey. When he was heated by Helios (Sun), he aimed his bow at the god, and Helios in admiration of his courage gave him a golden goblet, by means of which Herakles crossed the River Ocean. Reaching Erythia, Herakles smote both Orthos and his master, Eurytion, with his club, killing them, and when Geryon attacked him, Herakles killed him, too. Taking the cattle, he crossed back over the River Ocean on the golden goblet, returning the goblet to the sun-god and giving the cattle to Eurystheus.

Since Eurystheus did not acknowledge the task concerning Augeias's cattle or that concerning the hydra, he now ordered Herakles to perform an eleventh labor, to fetch golden apples from the Hesperides. These apples, a gift from Gaia (Earth) to Zeus upon his marriage to Hera, were guarded by an immortal hundred-headed dragon and by the Hesperides. Learning the location of the sea-god Nereus from certain nymphs, Herakles seized Nereus as he was sleeping. Nereus changed himself into all sorts of forms, but the hero did not let him go until he had learned where to find the apples. On his way through Libya he encountered Antaios (Latinized form = Antaeus), a son of Poseidon who ruled Libya at that time. Antaios killed strangers by making them wrestle with him. Since Antaios's strength increased every time he touched the earth, Herakles lifted him off the ground with a hug and crushed him to death. Reaching the Caucasus, Herakles shot the eagle that devoured the liver of Prometheus and unbound the Titan. On Prometheus's advice, Herakles relieved Atlas of the sky and sent him after the golden apples, but Atlas, returning with three apples from the Hesperides and not wishing to resume his support of the sky, said he himself would deliver them to Eurystheus. Advised by Prometheus once again, Herakles asked Atlas to take back the sky until he should place a pad on his head. After Atlas set the apples on the ground and took the sky, Herakles picked up the apples and departed. He gave them to Eurystheus, who gave them back as a gift to Herakles, but he passed them on to Athena, who returned them to their rightful place, for it was improper for them to be laid down anywhere.

Herakles's twelfth labor was to bring from Hades's realm Cerberus (Greek Kerberos), a three-headed dog with the tail of a dragon. Herakles descended down to the realm of the dead through Tainaron (Latinized form = Taenarum), a cave in Laconia. Plouton told him he could take Cerberus away, provided that he overcame the hound without the use of weapons. So Herakles put his arms around the animal's head and squeezed, despite his being bitten by the dragon at the dog's tail, until Cerberus gave in. He carried the dog up to the earth's surface, showed it to Eurystheus, and returned it to Hades's realm.

After he had completed his labors, he returned to Thebes and bestowed his wife, Megara, on Iolaos and sought the hand of Iolê, daughter of Eurytos, ruler of Oichalia. But his madness recurred, and he killed a son of Eurytos. As a result of the killing he contracted a disease, and an oracle revealed that in order to be cured he must be sold and serve someone for three years. So Hermes sold him to Omphalê, queen of Lydia, and Herakles served her as a slave for three years, after which he was rid of his sickness.

Gathering volunteers, Herakles went to Troy and took the city, killing King Laomedon. He had many other adventures and accomplishments, including helping the gods in their war against the Giants and founding the Olympic Games. In time he went to Calydon in order to woo Deianeira, for whom the river god Acheloos (Latinized form = Achelous) was also a suitor. Herakles and Acheloos wrestled for her hand. Although Acheloos transformed himself into a Bull, Herakles overcame him and wed Deianeira. Traveling together, Herakles and Deianeira came to the Euenos River, across which the centaur Nessos ferried travelers for a fee. Herakles crossed it on his own, but he entrusted his wife to the centaur, who attempted to rape her as he carried her across. When she screamed, Herakles fatally shot Nessos. But before he died, the centaur privately told Deianeira that if she wanted a love potion to give her husband, she could make one by mixing the semen that the centaur had ejaculated and the blood that was flowing from his wound. Deianeira did so.

Herkles now gathered together an army to attack Oichalia in order to punish Eurytos, and he and his companions killed Eurytos and his sons, captured the city, and took Iolê captive. Deianeira, learning about Iolê and fearing that Herakles might love her more than herself, resorted to the love potion made from Nessos's blood and semen, which she smeared on one of her husband's garments. When Herakles donned it, however, the hydra's poison began to mortify his flesh. The poisoned clothing clung to his skin so that when he ripped it off, he tore his flesh. When Deianeira saw what had happened, she hanged herself. After arranging for one of his sons to marry Iolê, Herakles climbed Mount Oirê, built a pyre, mounted it, and had someone set it afire. As it burned, a cloud came down and, with a peal of thunder, carried him up to the sky, where he obtained immortality and was reconciled with Hera, who gave him her daughter Hebê in marriage.

[William Hansen, *Classical Mythology*
(Oxford University Press, 2004), pp. 189–195.]

INDIA: The Buddha

Siddhartha Gautama, the Buddha, was said to have been miraculously conceived and born, like so many other heroes, without any impurity. His mother, Maya—the embodiment of tangible reality—dies soon after the hero's birth (again, like the mothers of other heroes—for example, the mothers of Quetzalcoatl and of Water Jar Boy). The boy, in the tradition of Quetzalcoatl, Water Jar Boy, Siegfried, and others, is possessed of adult qualities almost at birth. These two motifs indicate the Buddha's special status as the *puer aeternus* or divine child. The story of the Buddha under the Bodhi, or Bo, Tree is as central to the mythology and philosophy of Buddhism as the Crucifixion and Resurrection are to those of Christianity. The story itself bears a strong resemblance to the story of Jesus' temptation by the Devil in the wilderness (Luke 4).

It is related that at that time the midsummer festival had been proclaimed in the city of Kapilavatthu, and the multitude were enjoying the feast. And queen Maha-Maya, abstaining from strong drink, and brilliant with garlands and perfumes, took part in the festivities for the six days previous to the day of full moon. And when it came to be the day of full moon, she rose early, bathed in perfumed water, and dispensed four hundred thousand pieces of money in great largess. And decked in full gala attire, she ate of the choicest food; after which she took the eight vows, and entered her elegantly furnished chamber of state. And lying down on the royal couch, she fell asleep and dreamed the following dream:

The four guardian angels came and lifted her up, together with her couch, and took her away to the Himalaya Mountains. There, in the Manosila table-land, which is sixty leagues in extent, they laid her under a prodigious sal-tree, seven leagues in height, and took up their positions respectfully at one side. Then came the wives of these guardian angels, and conducted her to Anotatta Lake, and bathed her, to remove every human stain. And after clothing her with divine garments, they anointed her with perfumes and decked her with divine flowers. Not far off was Silver Hill, and in it a golden mansion. There they spread a divine couch with its head toward the east, and laid her down upon it. Now the future Buddha had become a superb white elephant, and was wandering about at no great distance, on Gold Hill. Descending thence, he ascended Silver Hill, and approaching from the north, he plucked a white lotus with his silvery trunk, and trumpeting loudly, went into the golden mansion. And three times he walked round his mother's couch, with his right side towards it, and striking her on her right side, he seemed to enter her womb. Thus the conception took place in the midsummer festival.

On the next day the queen awoke, and told the dream to the king. And the king caused sixty-four eminent Brahmanas to be summoned, and spread costly seats for them on ground festively prepared with green leaves, dalbergia flowers, and so forth. The Brahmanas being seated, he filled gold and silver dishes with the best of milk-porridge compounded with ghee, honey, and treacle; and covering these dishes with others, made likewise of gold and silver, he gave the Brahmanas to eat. And not only with food, but with other gifts, such as new garments, tawny cows, and so forth, he satisfied them completely. And when their every desire had been satisfied, he told them the dream and asked them what would come of it.

"Be not anxious, great king!" said the Brahmanas; "a child has planted itself in the womb of your queen, and it is a male child and not a female. You will have a son. And he, if he continue to live the household life, will become a universal monarch; but if he leave the household life and retire from the world, he will become a Buddha, and roll back the clouds of sin and folly of this world." . . .

Now the instant the future Buddha was conceived in the womb of his mother, all the ten thousand worlds suddenly quaked, quivered, and shook. And the thirty-two prognostics appeared, as follows: an immeasurable light spread through ten thousand worlds; the blind recovered their sight, as if from desire to see this his glory; the deaf received their hearing; the dumb talked; the hunchbacked became straight of body; the lame recovered the power to walk; all those in bonds were freed from their bonds and chains; the fires went out in all the hells; the hunger and thirst of the departed ancestors were stilled; wild animals lost their timidity; diseases ceased among men; all mortals became mild-spoken; horses neighed and elephants trumpeted in a manner sweet to the ear; all musical instruments gave forth their notes without being played upon; bracelets and other ornaments jingled; in all quarters of the heavens the weather became fair; a mild, cool breeze began to blow, very refreshing to men; rain fell out of season; water burst forth from the earth and flowed in streams; the birds ceased flying through the air; the rivers checked their flowing; in the mighty ocean the water became sweet; the ground became everywhere covered with lotuses of the five different colours; all flowers bloomed, both those on land and those that grow in the water; trunk-lotuses bloomed on the trunks of trees, branch-lotuses on the branches, and vine-lotuses on the vines; on the ground, stalk-lotuses, as they are called, burst through the overlying rocks and came up by sevens; in the sky were produced others, called hanging-lotuses; a shower of flowers fell all about; celestial music was heard to play in the sky; and the whole ten thousand worlds became one mass of garlands of the utmost possible magnificence, with waving chowries, and saturated with the incenselike fragrance of flowers, and resembled a bouquet of flowers sent whirling through the air, or a closely woven wreath, or a superbly decorated altar of flowers.

From the time the future Buddha was thus conceived, four angels with swords in their hands kept guard, to ward off all harm from both the future Buddha and the future Buddha's mother. No lustful thought sprang up in the mind of the future Buddha's mother; having reached the pinnacle of good fortune and of glory, she felt comfortable and well, and experienced no exhaustion of body. And within her womb she could distinguish the future Buddha, like a white thread passed through a transparent jewel. And whereas a womb that has been occupied by a future Buddha is like the shrine of a temple, and can never be occupied or used again, therefore it was that the mother of the future Buddha died when he was seven days old, and was reborn in the Tusita heaven.

Now other women sometimes fall short of and sometimes run over the term of ten lunar months, and bring forth either sitting or lying down; but not so the mother of a future Buddha. She carries the future Buddha in her womb for just ten months, and then brings forth while standing up. This is a characteristic of the mother of a future Buddha. So also queen Maha-Maya carried the future Buddha

in her womb, as it were oil in a vessel, for ten months; and being then
far gone with child, she grew desirous of going home to her relatives, and said to king Suddhodana,

"Sire, I should like to visit my kinsfolk in their city Devadaha."

"So be it," said the king; and from Kapilavatthu to the city of
Devadaha he had the road made even, and garnished it with plan-
tain-trees set in pots, and with banners, and streamers; and, seating
the queen in a golden palanquin borne by a thousand of his courtiers, he sent her away in great pomp.

Now between the two cities, and belonging to the inhabitants of
both, there was a pleasure-grove of sal-trees, called Lumbini Grove.
And at this particular time this grove was one mass of flowers from
the ground to the topmost branches, while amongst the branches and
flowers hummed swarms of bees of the five different colours, and
blocks of various kinds of birds flew about warbling sweetly. Throughout the whole of Lumbini Grove the scene resembled the Chittalata
Grove in Indra's paradise, or the magnificently decorated banqueting
pavilion of some potent king.

When the queen beheld it, she became desirous of disporting
herself therein, and the courtiers therefore took her into it. And
going to the foot of the monarch sal-tree of the grove, she wished to
take hold of one of its branches. And the sal-tree branch, like the tip
of a well-stemmed reed, bent itself down within reach of the queen's
hand. Then she reached out her hand, and seized hold of the branch,
and immediately her pains came upon her. Thereupon the people
hung a curtain about her, and retired. So her delivery took place
while she was standing up, and keeping fast hold of the sal-tree
branch.

At that very moment came four pure-minded Maha-Bramha
angels bearing a golden net; and, receiving the future Buddha on
this golden net, they placed him before his mother and said,

"Rejoice, O queen! A mighty son has been born to you."

Now other mortals on issuing from the maternal womb are
smeared with disagreeable, impure matter; but not so the future
Buddha. He issued from his mother's womb like a preacher descending from his preaching-seat, or a man coming down a stair, stretching out both hands and both feet, unsmeared by any impurity from
his mother's womb, and flashing pure and spotless, like a jewel
thrown upon a vesture of Benares cloth. Notwithstanding this, for
the sake of honouring the future Buddha and his mother, there

came two streams of water from the sky, and refreshed the future Buddha and his mother.

Then the Brahma angels, after receiving him on their golden net, delivered him to the four guardian angels, who received him from their hands on a rug which was made of the skins of black antelopes, and was soft to the touch, being such as is used on state occasions; and the guardian angels delivered him to men who received him on a coil of fine cloth; and the men let him out of their hands on the ground, where he stood and faced the east. There, before him, lay many thousands of worlds, like a great open court; and in them, gods and men, making offerings to him of perfumes, garlands, and so on, were saying,

"Great Being! There is none your equal, much less your superior."

When he had in this manner surveyed the four cardinal points, and the four intermediate ones, and the zenith, and the nadir, in short, all the ten directions in order, and had nowhere discovered his equal, he exclaimed, "This is the best direction," and strode forward seven paces, followed by Maha-Brahma holding over him the white umbrella, Suyama bearing the fan, and other divinities having the other symbols of royalty in their hands. Then, at the seventh stride, he halted, and with a noble voice he shouted the shout of victory, beginning,

"The chief am I in all the world."

Now at the very time that our future Buddha was born in Lumbini Grove there also came into existence the mother of Rahula, and Channa the courtier, Kaludayi the courtier, Kanthaka the king of horses, the great Bo-tree, and the four urns full of treasure. Of these last, one was a quarter of a league in extent, another a half-league, the third three-quarters of a league, and the fourth a league. These seven are called the connate ones.

Then the inhabitants of both cities took the future Buddha, and carried him to Kapilavatthu.

[Henry Clarke Warren, introduction to the *Jataka* in *Buddhism in Translations* (Cambridge, MA, 1896), pp. 183–187.]

✦

Now during the time that Gautama had been dwelling in the forest near by Uruvela, the daughter of the village headman, by name Sujata, had been accustomed to make a daily offering of food to eight hundred Brahmans, making the prayer—"May the Bodhisatta

at length, receive an offering of food from me, attain enlightenment, and become a Buddha!" And now that the time had come
when he desired to receive nourishing food, a Deva appeared in the
night to Sujata and announced that the Bodhisatta had put aside his
austerities and desired to partake of good and nourishing food,
"and now shall your prayer be accomplished." Then Sujata with all
speed arose early and went to her father's herd. Now for a long time
she had been accustomed to take the milk of a thousand cows and
to feed therewith five hundred, and again with their milk to feed
two hundred and fifty, and so on until eight only were fed with the
milk of the rest, and this she called "working the milk in and in." It
was the full-moon day of the month of May when she received the
message of the gods, and rose early, and milked the eight cows, and
took the milk and boiled it in new pans, and prepared milk-rice. At
the same time she sent her maid Punna to the foot of the great tree
where she had been wont to lay her daily offerings. Now the
Bodhisatta knowing that he would that day attain Supreme Enlightenment, was sitting at the foot of the tree, awaiting the house for
going forth to beg his food; and such was his glory that all the region
of the East was lit up. The girl thought that it was the spirit of the
tree who would deign to receive the offering with his own hands.
When she returned to Sujata and reported this, Sujata embraced her
and bestowed on her the jewels of a daughter, and exclaimed,
"Henceforth thou shalt be to me in the place of an elder daughter!"
And sending for a golden vessel she put the well-cooked food
therein, and covered it with a pure white cloth, and bore it with
dignity to the foot of the great Nigrodha-tree; and there she too saw
the Bodhisatta, and believed him to be the spirit of the tree. Sujata
approached him, and placed the vessel in his hand, and she met his
gaze and said: "My lord, accept what I have offered thee," and she
added, "May there arise to thee as much of joy as has come to me!"
and so she departed.

The Bodhisatta took the golden bowl, and went down to the
bank of the river and bathed, and then dressing himself in the garb
of an Arahat, he again took his seat, with his face towards the East.
He divided the rice into forty-nine portions, and this food sufficed
for his nourishment during the forty-nine days following the Enlightenment. When he had finished eating the milk rice, he took the
golden vessel and cast it into the stream, saying, "If I am able to
attain Enlightenment to-day, let this pot go up stream, but if not,

may it go down stream." And he threw it into the water, and it went swiftly up the river until it reached the whirlpool of the Black Snake King, and there it sank.

The Bodhisatta spent the heat of the day in a grove of Saltrees beside the stream. But in the evening he made his way to the foot of the tree of wisdom, and there, making the resolution: "Though my skin, my nerves and my bones should waste away and my life-blood dry, I will not leave this seat until I have attained Supreme Enlightenment," he took his seat with his face towards the East.

At this moment Mara the Fiend became aware that the Bodhisatta had taken his seat with a view to attaining Perfect Enlightenment; and thereupon, summoning the hosts of the demons, and mounting his elephant of war, he advanced towards the Tree of Wisdom. And there stood Maha Brahma holding above the Bodhisatta a white canopy of state, and Sakka, blowing the great trumpet, and with them were all the companies of gods and angels. But so terrible was the array of Mara that there was not one of all this host of the Devas that dared to remain to face him. The Great Being was left alone.

First of all, however, Mara assumed the form of a messenger, with disordered garments, and panting in haste, bearing a letter from the Sakya princes. And in the letter it was written that Devadatta had usurped the kingdom of Kapilavatthu and entered the Bodhisatta's palace, taken his goods and his wife, and cast Suddhodana into prison and they prayed him to return to restore peace and order. But the Bodhisatta reflected lust it was that had caused Devadatta thus to misuse the women, malice had made him imprison Suddhodana, while the Sakyas neutralized by cowardice failed to defend their King: and so reflecting on the folly and weakness of the natural heart, his own resolve to attain a higher and better state was strengthened and confirmed.

Failing in this device, Mara now advanced to the assault with all his hosts, striving to overcome the Bodhisatta first by a terrible whirlwind, then by a storm of rain, causing a mighty flood: but the hem of the Bodhisatta's robe was not stirred, nor did a single drop of water reach him. Then Mara cast down upon him showers of rocks, and a storm of deadly and poisoned weapons, burning ashes and coals, and a storm of scorching sand and flaming mud; but all these missiles only fell at the Bodhisatta's feet as a rain of heavenly flowers, or hung in the air like a canopy above his head. Nor could he be moved by an onset of thick and fourfold darkness. Then finding all these means to fail, he addressed the Bodhisatta and said: "Arise, Siddhattha, from that seat, for it is not thine, but mine!" The Bodhisatta replied, "Mara! thou hast not accomplished the Ten Perfections, nor even the minor virtues. Thou hast not sought for knowledge, nor for the salvation of the world. The seat is mine." Then Mara was enraged, and cast at the Bodhisatta his Sceptre-javelin, which cleaves asunder a pillar of solid rock like a tender shoot of cane: and all the demon hosts hurled masses of rock. But the javelin hung in the air like a canopy, and the masses of rock fell down as garlands of flowers.

Then the Great Being said to Mara: "Mara, who is the witness that thou hast given alms?" Mara stretched forth his hand, and a shout arose from the demon hosts, of a thousand voices crying: "I am his witness!" Then the Fiend addressed the Bodhisatta, and enquired: "Siddhattha! who is the witness that thou has given alms?" and the Great Being answered: "Mara, thou hast many and living witnesses that thou hast given alms, and no such witnesses have I. But apart from the alms I have given in other births, I call upon this solid earth to witness to my supernatural generosity when I was born as Vessantara." And drawing his right hand from his robe, he stretched it forth to touch the earth, and said: "Do you or do you not witness to my supernatural generosity when I was born as Vessantara?" And the great Earth replied with a voice of thunder: "I am witness of that." And thereat the great elephant of Mara bowed down in adoration, and the demon hosts fled far away in dread.

Then Mara was abashed. But he did not withdraw, for he hoped to accomplish by another means what he could not effect by force: he summoned his three daughters, Tanha, Rati, and Raga, and they danced before the Bodhisatta like the swaying branches of a young leafy tree, using all the arts of seduction known to beautiful women. Again they offered him the lordship of the earth, and the companionship of beautiful girls: they appealed to him with songs of the season of spring, and exhibited their supernatural beauty and grace. But the Bodhisatta's heart was not in the least moved, and he answered:

Pleasure is brief as a flash of lightning
Or like an Autumn shower, only for a moment . . .
Why should I then covet the pleasures you speak of?

I see your bodies are full of all impurity:
Birth and death, sickness and age are yours.
I seek the highest prize, hard to attain by men—
The true and constant wisdom of the wise.

And when they could not shake the Bodhisatta's calm, they were filled with shame, and abashed: and they made a prayer to the Bodhisatta, wishing him the fruition of his labour:

That which your heart desires, may you attain,
And finding for yourself deliverance, deliver all!

And now the hosts of heaven, seeing the army of Mara defeated, and the wiles of the daughters of Mara vain, assembled to honour the Conqueror, they came to the foot of the Tree of Wisdom and cried for joy:

The Blessed Buddha—he hath prevailed!
And the Tempter is overthrown!

The victory was achieved while the sun was yet above the horizon. The Bodhisatta sank into ever deeper and deeper thought. In the first watch of the night he reached the Knowledge of Former States of being, in the middle watch he obtained the heavenly eye of Omniscient Vision, and in the third watch he grasped the perfect understanding of the Chain of Causation which is the Origin of Evil, and thus at break of day he attained to Perfect Enlightenment. Therewith there broke from his lips the song of triumph:

Through many divers births I passed
Seeking in vain the builder of the house.[1]
But O framer of houses, thou art found—
Never again shalt thou fashion a house for me!
Broken are all thy beams,
The king-post shattered!
My mind has passed into the stillness of Nibbana
The ending of desire has been attained at last!

---

[1] The house is, of course, the house—or rather the prison—of individual existence: the builder of the house is desire (tankā)—the will to enjoy and possess [Coomaraswamy's note].

Innumerable wonders were manifest at this supreme hour. The earth quaked six times, and the whole universe was illuminated by the supernatural splendour of the sixfold rays that proceeded from the body of the seated Buddha. Resentment faded from the hearts of all men, all lack was supplied, the sick were healed, the chains of hell were loosed, and every creature of whatsoever sort found peace and rest.

Gautama, who was now Buddha, the Enlightened, remained seated and motionless for seven days, realizing the bliss of Nibbana; and thereafter rising, he remained standing for seven days more, steadfastly regarding the spot where had been won the fruit of countless deeds of heroic virtue performed in past births: then for seven days more he paced to and fro along a cloistered path from West to East, extending from the throne beneath the Wisdom Tree to the place of the Steadfast Gazing; and again for seven days he remained seated in a god-wrought pavilion near to the same place, and there reviewed in detail, book by book, all that is taught in the Abhidhamma Pitaka, as well as the whole doctrine of causality; then for seven days more he sat beneath the Nigrodha tree of Sujata's offering, meditating on the doctrine and the sweetness of Nibbana— and according to some books it was at this time the temptation by the daughters of Mara took place; and then for seven days more while a terrible storm was raging, the snake king Mucalinda sheltered him with his sevenfold hood; and for seven days more he sat beneath a Rajayatana tree, still enjoying the sweetness of liberation.

And so passed away seven weeks, during which the Buddha experienced no bodily wants, but fed on the joy of contemplation, the joy of the Eightfold Path, and the joy of its fruit, Nibbana.

Only upon the last day of the seven weeks he desired to bathe and eat, and receiving water and a tooth-stick from the god Sakka, the Buddha bathed his face and seated himself at the foot of a tree. Now at that time two Brahman merchants were travelling with a caravan from Orissa to the middle country, and a Deva, who had been a blood relation of the merchants in a former life, stopped the carts, and moved their hearts to make an offering of rice and honey cakes to the Lord. They went up to him accordingly, saying: "O Blessed One, have mercy upon us, and accept this food." Now the Buddha no longer possessed a bowl, and as the Buddhas never receive an offering in their hands, he reflected how he should take it. Immediately the Four Great Kings, the Regents of the Quarters appeared before him, each of them with a bowl; and in order that none of them should be disappointed, the Buddha received the four bowls, and placing them one above the other made them to be one, showing only the four lines round the mouth, and in this bowl the Blessed One received the food, and ate it, and gave thanks. The two merchants took refuge in the Buddha, the Norm, and the Order, and became professed disciples. Then the Buddha rose up and returned again to the tree of Sujata's offering and there took his seat. And there, reflecting upon the depth of truth which he had found, a doubt arose in his mind whether it would be possible to make it known to others: and this doubt is experienced by every Buddha when he becomes aware of the Truth. But Maha Brahma exclaiming: "Alas! the world will be altogether lost!" came thither in haste, with all the Deva hosts, and besought the Master to proclaim the Truth; and he granted their prayer.[2]

[Ananda Coomaraswamy, *Buddha and the Gospel of Buddhism* (London, 1928), pp. 30–38.]

IRELAND: Cuchulainn

Cuchulainn resembles Krishna, Herakles, and Theseus. As a child he already possesses the powers of the world hero.

Before his fifth year, when already possessed of man's strength, he heard of the "boy corps" of his uncle Conchobar and went to test them, taking his club, ball, spear, and javelin, playing with these as he went. At Emain he joined the boys at play without permission; but this was an insult, and they set upon him, throwing at him clubs, spears, and balls, all of which he fended off, besides knocking down fifty of the boys, while his "contortion" seized him—the first reference to this curious phenomenon. Conchobar now interfered, but Cuchulainn would not desist until all the boys came under his protection and guarantee.

---

[2] "Great truths do not take hold of the hearts of the masses. . . . And now, as all the world is in error, I, though I know the true path—how shall I, how shall I guide? If I know that I cannot succeed and yet try to force success, this would be but another source of error. Better, then, to desist and strive no more. But if I strive not, who will?"—Chuang Tzu. It is highly characteristic of the psychology of genius that when this doubt assails the Buddha he nevertheless immediately responds to a definite request for guidance; the moment the pupil puts the right questions, the teacher's doubts are resolved [Coomaraswamy's note].

At Conchobar's court he performed extraordinary feats and expelled a band of invaders when the Ulstermen were in their yearly weakness. He was first known as Setanta, and was called Cuchulainn in the following way. Culann the smith had prepared a banquet for Conchobar, who, on his way to it, saw the youth holding the field at ball against three hundred and fifty others; and though he bade him follow, Setanta refused to come until the play was over. While the banquet was progressing, Culann let loose his great watch-dog, which had the strength of a hundred, and when Setanta reached the fort, the beast attacked him, whereupon he thrust his ball into its mouth, and seizing its hind legs, battered it against a rock. Culann complained that the safe-guard of his flocks and herds was destroyed, but the boy said that he would act as watch-dog until a whelp of its breed was ready; and Cathbad the Druid now gave him a name—Cu Chulainn, or "Culann's Dog." This adventure took place before he was seven years old. Baudis suggests that as Cuchulainn was not the hero's birth-name, a dog may have been his manito, his name being given him in some ceremonial way at puberty, a circumstance afterward explained by the mythical story of Culann's Hound.

One day Cuchulainn overheard Cathbad saying that whatever stripling assumed arms on that day would have a short life, but would be the greatest of warriors. He now demanded arms from Conchobar, but broke every set of weapons given him until he received Conchobar's own sword and shield; and he also destroyed seventeen chariots, so that nothing but Conchobar's own chariot sufficed him. Cuchulainn made the charioteer drive fast and far until they reached the *dun* of the sons of Nechtan, each of whom he fought and slew, cutting off their heads; while on his return he killed two huge stags and then captured twenty-four wild swans, fastening all these to the chariot. From afar Levarcham the prophetess saw the strange cavalcade approaching Emain and bade all be on their guard, else the warrior would slay them; but Conchobar alone knew who he was and recognized the danger from a youth whose appetite for slaughter had been whetted. A stratagem was adopted, based upon Cuchulainn's well-known modesty. A hundred and fifty women with uncovered breasts were sent to meet him, and while he averted his face, he was seized and plunged into vessels of cold water. The first burst asunder; the water of the second boiled with

the heat from his body; that of the third became warm; and thus his
rage was calmed.

[Louis Gray, ed., *The Mythology of All Races*, vol. 3,
Celtic (Boston, MA, 1916–1932), pp. 141–143.]

GREECE: Antigone

Sophocles' trilogy of plays about Oedipus and his family begins with *Oedipus
the King*, which is concerned with a quest that is the most important event in the
hero-king's life. It is a quest for identity (albeit ironic, since at first he is not even
aware that he is the object of his quest), for self, and therefore for the father. It
is an acceptance of a call from the oracle to remove the moral pollution that is
destroying Thebes, and it is a quest that will confirm the king's eventual fear
that he has killed his father and married his mother. In the second play, *Antigone*,
Antigone, the brave daughter of King Oedipus, answers the call that comes to
her through her reverence for religious codes and her sense of the irrationality
of the male-dominated society in which she must live. In the excerpt from
Sophocles' *Antigone* that follows, the heroine argues her point with her uncle,
King Creon, the representative of the patriarchal arbitrariness that refuses the
call. As a result of her defiance, Antigone will die, but Creon (like the stubborn
Pentheus, who refuses the call of Dionysos in Euripides' *Bacchae*) will pay a high
price for his moral blindness.

Antigone is brought before her uncle to be charged with having broken the
edict that denied burial to her treasonous brother, one of the unfortunate sons of
the even more unfortunate Oedipus.

CREON: Explain the circumstance of the arrest.
GUARD: She was burying the man. You have it all.
CREON: Is this the truth? And do you grasp its meaning?
GUARD: I saw her burying the very corpse you had forbidden. Is this adequate?
CREON: How was she caught and taken in the act?
GUARD: It was like this: when we got back again
struck with those dreadful threatenings of yours,
we swept away the dust that hid the corpse.
We stripped it back to slimy nakedness.
And then we sat to windward on the hill
so as to dodge the smell.
We poked each other up with growling threats

if anyone was careless of his work.
For some time this went on, till it was noon.
The sun was high and hot. Then from the earth
up rose a dusty whirlwind to the sky,
filling the plain, smearing the forest-leaves,
clogging the upper air. We shut our eyes,
sat and endured the plague the gods had sent.
So the storm left us after a long time.
We saw the girl. She cried the sharp and shrill
cry of a bitter bird which sees the nest
bare where the young birds lay.
So this same girl, seeing the body stripped,
cried with great groanings, cried a dreadful curse
upon the people who had done the deed.
Soon in her hands she brought the thirsty dust,
and holding high a pitcher of wrought bronze
she poured the three libations for the dead.
We saw this and surged down. We trapped her fast;
and she was calm. We taxed her with the deeds
both past and present. Nothing was denied.
And I was glad, and yet I took it hard.
One's own escape from trouble makes one glad;
but bringing friends to trouble is hard grief.
Still, I care less for all these second thoughts
than for the fact that I myself am safe.
CREON: You there, whose head is drooping to the ground,
do you admit this, or deny you did it?
ANTIGONE: I say I did it and I don't deny it.
CREON: (*to the guard*) Take yourself off wherever you wish to go
free of a heavy charge.
CREON: (*to Antigone*) You—tell me not at length but in a word.
You knew the order not to do this thing?
ANTIGONE: I knew, of course I knew. The word was plain.
CREON: And still you dared to overstep these laws?
ANTIGONE: For me it was not Zeus who made that order.
Nor did that Justice who lives with the gods below
mark out such laws to hold among mankind.
Nor did I think your orders were so strong
that you, a mortal man, could over-run

the gods' unwritten and unfailing laws.
Not now, nor yesterday's, they always live,
and no one knows their origin in time.
So not through fear of any man's proud spirit
would I be likely to neglect these laws,
draw on myself the gods' sure punishment.
I knew that I must die; how could I not?
even without your warning. If I die
before my time, I say it is a gain.
Who lives in sorrows many as are mine
how shall he not be glad to gain his death?
And so, for me to meet this fate, no grief.
But if I left that corpse, my mother's son,
dead and unburied I'd have cause to grieve
as now I grieve not.
And if you think my acts are foolishness
the foolishness may be in a fool's eye.
CHORUS: The girl is bitter. She's her father's child.
She cannot yield to trouble; nor could he.
CREON: These rigid spirits are the first to fall.
The strongest iron, hardened in the fire,
most often ends in scraps and shatterings.
Small curbs bring raging horses back to terms.
Slave to his neighbor, who can think of pride?
This girl was expert in her insolence
when she broke bounds beyond established law.
Once she had done it, insolence the second,
to boast her doing, and to laugh in it.
I am no man and she the man instead
if she can have this conquest without pain.
She is my sister's child, but were she child
of closer kin than any at my hearth,
she and her sister should not so escape
their death and doom. I charge Ismene too.
She shared the planning of this burial.
Call her outside. I saw her in the house,
maddened, no longer mistress of herself.
The sly intent betrays itself sometimes
before the secret plotters work their wrong.
I hate it too when someone caught in crime

then wants to make it seem a lovely thing.

ANTIGONE: Do you want more than my arrest and death?

CREON: No more than that. For that is all I need.

ANTIGONE: Why are you waiting? Nothing that you say

fits with my thought. I pray it never will.

Nor will you ever like to hear my words.

And yet what greater glory could I find

than giving my own brother funeral?

All these would say that they approved my act

did fear not mute them.

(A king is fortunate in many ways,

and most, that he can act and speak at will.)

CREON: None of these others see the case this way.

ANTIGONE: They see, and do not say. You have them cowed.

CREON: And you are not ashamed to think alone?

ANTIGONE: No, I am not ashamed. When was it shame

to serve the children of my mother's womb?

CREON: It was not your brother who died against him, then?

ANTIGONE: Full brother, on both sides, my parents' child.

CREON: Your act of grace, in this regard, is crime.

ANTIGONE: The corpse below would never say it was.

CREON: When you honor him and the criminal just alike?

ANTIGONE: It was a brother, not a slave, who died.

CREON: Died to destroy this land the other guarded.

ANTIGONE: Death yearns for equal law for all the dead.

CREON: Not that the good and bad draw equal shares.

ANTIGONE: Who knows that this is holiness below?

CREON: Never the enemy, even in death, a friend.

ANTIGONE: I cannot share in hatred, but in love.

CREON: Then go down there, if you must love, and love the dead.

No woman rules me while I live.

[Sophocles, *Antigone*, in *Sophocles I*, trans. Elizabeth Wyckoff
(New York, 1967), pp. 176–181.]

EUROPE: King Arthur — LEAD

King Arthur is called to adventure by the existence of a magic sword in a rock, the removal of which is possible only for the true king. Eventually, Arthur's quest will be for unity and renewal, represented by the Holy Grail. Arthur's birth is marked by mysterious circumstances, and he and his knights must face such familiar obstacles as the femme fatale in the persons of Morgan le Fay, Viviane, the Lady of the Lake, and Queen Guinevere herself, whose attraction to Sir Lancelot was the cause of much pain in Arthur's realm.

Arthur, though only fifteen years old at his father's death, was elected king at a general meeting of the nobles. It was not done without opposition, for there were many ambitious competitors; but Bishop Brice, a person of great sanctity, on Christmas eve addressed the assembly and represented that it would well become them, at that solemn season, to put up their prayers for some token which should manifest the intentions of Providence respecting their future sovereign. This was done, and with such success, that the service was scarcely ended when a miraculous stone was discovered, before the church door, and in the stone was firmly fixed a sword, with the following words engraven on its hilt:

I am hight Escalibore,
Unto a king fair tresore.

Bishop Brice, after exhorting the assembly to offer up their thanksgivings for this signal miracle, proposed a law that, whoever should be able to draw out the sword from the stone, should be acknowledged as sovereign of the Britons; and his proposal was decreed by general acclamation. The tributary kings of Uther and the most famous knights successively put their strength to the proof, but the miraculous sword resisted all their efforts. It stood till Candlemas; it stood till Easter, and till Pentecost, when the best knights in the kingdom usually assembled for the annual tournament. Arthur, who was at that time serving in the capacity of squire to his foster-brother, Sir Kay, attended his master to the lists. Sir Kay fought with great valor and success, but had the misfortune to break his sword, and sent Arthur to his mother for a new one. Arthur hastened home, but did not find the lady; but having observed near the church a sword, sticking in a stone, he galloped to the place, drew out the sword with great ease, and delivered it to his master. Sir Kay would willingly have assumed to himself the distinction conferred by the possession of the sword; but when, to confirm the doubters, the sword was replaced in the stone, he was utterly unable to withdraw it, and it would yield a second time to no hand but Arthur's.

Thus decisively pointed out by Heaven as their king, Arthur was by general consent proclaimed as such, and an early day appointed for his solemn coronation.

[Thomas Bulfinch, *Bulfinch's Mythology: The Age of Chivalry* (New York, 1962), pp. 72–73.]

EUROPE: Parcival and the Holy Grail

Parcival (or Percival), one of the greatest knights of King Arthur's Round Table, goes on a quest for the Holy Grail. His initial failure is a particularly poignant example of the quest hero's refusal of the call.

The Sangreal [or Holy Grail] was the cup from which [Jesus] drank at his last supper. He was supposed to have given it to Joseph of Arimathea, who carried it to Europe, together with the spear with which the soldier pierced the Saviour's side. From generation to generation, one of the descendants of Joseph of Arimathea had been devoted to the guardianship of these precious relics; but on the sole condition of leading a life of purity in thought, word, and deed. For a long time the Sangreal was visible to all pilgrims, and its presence conferred blessings upon the land in which it was preserved. But, at length, one of those holy men to whom its guardianship had descended so far forgot the obligation of his sacred office as to look with unhallowed eye upon a young female pilgrim whose robe was accidentally loosened as she knelt before him. The sacred lance instantly punished his frailty, spontaneously falling upon him and inflicting a deep wound. The marvellous wound could by no means be healed, and the guardian of the Sangreal was ever after called "Le Roi Pecheur"—the Sinner King [the Fisher King]. The Sangreal withdrew its visible presence from the crowds who came to worship, and an iron age succeeded to the happiness which its presence had diffused among the tribes of Britain. . . .

Merlin, . . . that great prophet and enchanter, sent a message to King Arthur by Sir Gawain, directing him to undertake the recovery of the Sangreal, informing him at the same time that the knight who should accomplish that sacred quest was already born, and of a suitable age to enter upon it. Sir Gawain delivered his message, and the king was anxiously revolving in his mind how best to achieve the enterprise when, at the vigil of Pentecost, all the fellowship of the

Round Table being met together at Camelot, as they sat at meat, suddenly there was heard a clap of thunder, and then a bright light burst forth, and every knight, as he looked on his fellow, saw him, in seeming, fairer than ever before. All the hall was filled with sweet odors, and every knight had such meat and drink as he best loved. Then there entered into the hall the Holy Grail, covered with white samite, so that none could see it, and it passed through the hall suddenly, and disappeared. During this time no one spoke a word, but when they had recovered breath to speak, King Arthur said, "Certainly we ought greatly to thank the Lord for what he hath showed us this day." Then Sir Gawain rose up and made a vow that for twelve months and a day he would seek the Sangreal, and not return till he had seen it, if so he might speed. When they of the Round Table heard Sir Gawain say so, they arose, the most part of them, and vowed the same. When King Arthur heard this, he was greatly displeased, for he knew well that they might not gainsay their vows. "Alas!" said he to Sir Gawain, "you have nigh slain me with the vow and promise that ye have made, for ye have bereft me of the fairest fellowship that ever were seen together in any realm of the world; for when they shall depart hence, I am sure that all shall never meet more in this world."

One day [Percival] came to a great lake which he had never seen before. He saw a man seated in a boat, fishing. The man was richly dressed, but pale and sad. Percival asked if he could get food and shelter anywhere about for himself and his tired horse, and was told that if he went straight on, and did not lose his way, he would come to a castle, where he would be kindly received. He started in the direction indicated by the fisherman, and reached the castle at nightfall, after a long and toilsome search. There he met with so much kindness and consideration, garments even being provided for him "by Queen Repanse's orders," that he was filled with amazement. When freshly attired, he was taken into the hall, which was brilliantly lighted. Four hundred knights were seated on softly-cushioned seats at small tables, each of which was laid for four. They all sat grave and silent, as though in expectation. When Percival entered, they rose and bowed, and a ray of joy passed over each woeful countenance.

The master of the house, who much resembled the fisherman Percival had seen on the lake, sat in an armchair near the fire, wrapped in sables, and was apparently suffering from some wasting disease.

The deep silence that reigned in the hall was at length broken by the host, who invited Percival, in a low, weak voice, to sit down beside him, telling him that he had been long expected and, at the same time, giving him a sword of exquisite workmanship. The young knight was filled with astonishment. A servant now entered carrying the head of a lance stained with blood, with which he walked round the room in silence. Percival would much have liked to ask the meaning of this strange ceremony and also how his arrival had come to be expected, but he feared lest he should be deemed unwarrantably curious. While thus thinking, the door opened again and a number of beautiful blue-eyed maidens came in, two and two, with a velvet cushion embroidered with pearls, an ebony stand, and various other articles. Last of all came Queen Repanse bearing a costly vessel, whose radiance was more than the human eye could steadfastly gaze upon.

"The holy Grail," Percival heard whispered by one voice after another. He longed to question someone; but felt too much awed by the strangeness and solemnity of all he saw.

The maidens withdrew, and the squires and pages of the knights came forward. Then from the shining vessel streamed an endless supply of the costliest dishes and wines, which they set before their masters. The lord of the castle, however, only ate of one dish, and but a small quantity of that. Percival glanced round the great hall. What could this strange stillness and sadness mean?

When the meal was at an end, the lord of the castle dragged himself to his feet, leaning on two servants. He looked eagerly at his guest, and then retired with a deep sigh. Servants now came to conduct Percival to his sleeping apartment. Before leaving the hall they opened the door of a room in which a venerable old man slept on a low couch. His still handsome face was framed in a coronal of white curls. His sleep was uneasy, and his lips quivered as though he were trying to speak. The servants closed the door again, and led Percival to his chamber.

When he entered the room he looked about him, and at once became aware of a picture embroidered on the silken tapestry, that arrested his attention. It was the picture of a battle, in which the most prominent figure, a knight strangely like the lord of the castle in appearance, was sinking to the ground, wounded by a spear of the same kind as the broken weapon that had been carried round the hall. Much as he desired to know the meaning of this, he determined to ask no questions till the following morning, though the servants told him that his coming had been long expected, and deliverance was looked for at his hands; and they went away, sighing deeply.

His sleep was disturbed by bad dreams, and he awoke next morning unrefreshed. He found his own clothes and armour beside his bed; but no one came to help him. He got up and dressed. All the doors in the castle were locked except those that led out to the ramparts, where his horse stood saddled and bridled at the drawbridge. No sooner had he crossed the bridge than it was drawn up behind him, and a voice called from the battlements:

"Accursed of God, thou that wast chosen to do a great work, and hast not done it. Go, and return no more. Walk they evil way till it leads thee down to hell."

[Thomas Bulfinch, *Bulfinch's Mythology: The Age of Chivalry*
(New York, 1962), pp. 157–159;
and W. Wagner, *Romances and Epics of Our Northern Ancestors*
(London, 1907), pp. 302–305.]

ISRAEL: Jonah

One of the better-known biblical stories of the refusal of the call is that of Jonah. Perhaps Jonah and others, such as the Greek Pentheus, who, as Euripides tells us in his play the *Bacchae*, refused the call of Dionysos and paid the full price for denying the god in his life, are not properly called heroes. By definition, the hero is the one who finally accepts the call and confronts his destiny, his true being.

Chapter 1

Now the word of the Lord came unto Jonah the son of Ă-mit'-tai, saying,

2 Arise, go to Nin'-ĕ-vēh, that great city, and cry against it; for their wickedness is come up before me.
3 But Jonah rose up to flee unto Tar-shish from the presence of the Lord, and went down to Joppa; and he found a ship going to Tarshish: so he paid the fare thereof, and went down into it, to go with them unto Tarshish from the presence of the Lord.
4 But the Lord sent out a great wind into the sea, and there was a mighty tempest in the sea, so that the ship was like to be broken.

5 Then the mariners were afraid, and cried every man unto his god, and cast forth the wares that were in the ship into the sea, to lighten it of them. But Jonah was gone down into the sides of the ship; and he lay, and was fast asleep.

6 So the shipmaster came to him, and said unto him, What meanest thou, O sleeper? arise, call upon thy God, if so be that God will think upon us, that we perish not.

7 and they said every one to his fellow, Come, and let us cast lots, that we may know for whose cause this evil is upon us. So they cast lots, and the lot fell upon Jonah.

8 Then said they unto him, Tell us, we pray thee, for whose cause this evil is upon us; What is thine occupation? and whence comest thou? what is thy country? and of what people art thou?

9 And he said unto them, I am an Hebrew; and I fear the Lord, the God of heaven, which hath made the sea and the dry land.

10 Then were the men exceedingly afraid, and said unto him, Why hast thou done this? For the men knew that he fled from the presence of the Lord, because he had told them.

11 Then said they unto him, What shall we do unto thee, that the sea may be calm unto us? for the sea wrought, and was tempestuous.

12 And he said unto them, Take me up, and cast me forth into the sea; so shall the sea be calm unto you: for I know that for my sake this great tempest is upon you.

13 Nevertheless the men rowed hard to bring it to the land; but they could not: for the sea wrought, and was tempestuous against them.

14 Wherefore they cried unto the Lord, and said, We beseech thee, O Lord, we beseech thee, let us not perish for this man's life, and lay not upon us innocent blood: for thou, O Lord, hast done as it pleased thee.

15 So they took up Jonah, and cast him forth into the sea: and the sea ceased from her raging.

16 Then the men feared the Lord exceedingly, and offered a sacrifice unto the Lord, and made vows.

17 Now the Lord had prepared a great fish to swallow up Jonah. And Jonah was in the belly of the fish three days and three nights.

Chapter 2

Then Jonah prayed unto the Lord his God out of the fish's belly,

2 And said, I cried by reason of mine affliction unto the Lord, and he heard me; out of the belly of hell cried I, and thou heardest my voice.

3   For thou hadst cast me into the deep, in the midst of the seas; and the floods compassed me about: all thy billows and thy waves passed over me.

4   Then I said, I am cast out of thy sight; yet I will look again toward thy holy temple.

5   The waters compassed me about, even to the soul: the depth closed me round about, the weeds were wrapped about my head.

6   I went down to the bottoms of the mountains; the earth with her bars was about me for ever; yet hast thou brought up my life from corruption, O Lord my God.

7   When my soul fainted within me I remembered the Lord: and my prayer came in unto thee, into thine holy temple.

8   They that observe lying vanities forsake their own mercy.

9   But I will sacrifice unto thee with the voice of thanksgiving; I will pay that that I have vowed. Salvation is of the Lord.

10   And the Lord spake upon the fish, and it vomited out Jonah upon the dry land.

Chapter 3

And the word of the Lord came unto Jonah the second time, saying,

2   Arise, go unto Nĭn'-e-vēh, that great city, and preach unto it the preaching that I bid thee.

3   So Jonah arose, and went unto Nĭn'-ĕ-vēh, according to the word of the Lord. Now Nineveh was an exceeding great city of three days' journey.

4   And Jonah began to enter into the city a day's journey, and he cried, and said, Yet forty days, and Nĭn'-ĕ-vēh shall be overthrown.

5   So the people of Nĭn'-ĕ-vēh believed God, and proclaimed a fast, and put on sackcloth, from the greatest of them even to the least of them.

[Jonah 1–3:5.]

GREECE: Jason and the Golden Fleece

In the quest that is central to the hero's life, he or she searches for a particular person, object, or concept. The Buddha searches for enlightenment under the Bodhi Tree; Aeneas looks for Rome, the new Troy; Odysseus strives to return home; Rama searches for his wife, Sita, in the Indian epic the *Ramayana.*

One of the most famous quest stories is that of Jason and the Golden Fleece. Like so many heroes of the patriarchal tradition, Jason becomes involved with a woman who might in earlier times have been a guiding goddess but is now a femme fatale. This pattern is present as well in the story of Helen of Troy, who in the *Odyssey* is a wise woman with prophetic powers (reminiscent of the priestly role

permitted for some women in preclassical societies), but who in the more patriarchal *Iliad* is a wanton woman whose sexual attraction is the cause of the Trojan
War. Similar origins may exist in the story of Clytemnestra, who, with her lover,
killed her husband, Agamemnon, when he returned from the Trojan War and was
killed in turn by her son Orestes at the urging of her daughter Elektra. The story
as told by Aeschylus in the *Oresteia* trilogy is a patriarchal condemnation of what
in earlier times might have been a ritual sacrificing of the old king for the sake of
renewal in the person of a new mate for the matriarch.

The story of Jason and Medea is told by Apollonius of Rhodes in the third-
century B.C.E. epic the *Argonauts,* by Pindar in the fourth *Pythian Ode* of the fifth
century B.C.E., and by Euripides in the fifth-century B.C.E. tragedy *Medea.*

> The son of Aeson, King of Iolcus in Thessaly, the child Jason was
> threatened with death by his uncle Pelias, who usurped Aeson's
> throne. Jason escaped his uncle and grew under the care of the cen-
> taur Chiron. When Jason was fully grown, he returned to Iolcus and
> demanded the throne as its rightful heir. Pelias, a son of Poseidon,
> agreed to give up the throne in return for the Golden Fleece. So
> began the adventures described in the *Argonautica.* After Jason re-
> turned to Iolcus with the Golden Fleece and his new wife, Medea,
> who had helped him obtain the prize, Pelias reneged on his promise,
> and Medea used her magic to kill him, convincing his daughters that
> by cutting him up and boiling him they would restore his youth. As
> he was now an accessory to a terrible crime, Jason was still not made
> king. In fact, he and Medea were exiled by the new king, Pelias's son
> Acastus.
>
> Jason and Medea were accepted in Corinth, where they lived until
> the events described by Euripides in his play the *Medea.* As Euripides
> tells us, Jason became enamored of Glauce (Creusa), the daughter of
> Creon, King of Corinth and, spurred on by political reasoning,
> abandoned Medea for Glauce. Furious and consumed by a desire for
> revenge, Medea sent Glauce a beautiful but magical garment that,
> when the girl put it on, caused her to burst into flames. Her father,
> too, died in the conflagration. Then Medea killed her own children
> by Jason and fled to Athens in a chariot drawn by dragons. There she
> is said by some to have married Theseus's father, King Aegeus.
> There are many stories of Jason's end. Perhaps the most popular is
> the one of his being crushed by a falling part of the ship *Argo.*
>
> [David A. Leeming, *Oxford Companion to World Mythology*
> (Oxford University Press, 2005), p. 215.]

ROME: Aeneas

The femme fatale figure is by no means always evil. As in the case of Dido, with whom the Trojan-Roman hero Aeneas falls in love in Carthage during his quest for the new Troy, she can be the representation of true love or honest passion. Nevertheless, this love can prevent the hero from doing his patriarchal "duty." The story of Dido and Aeneas was first told by Virgil in Book IV of the *Aeneid*. Later in the poem, Aeneas makes the tradional heroic descent into the Underworld.

When Aeneas and his cohorts arrived at Carthage on the North African coast, the city's queen, Dido, was building a state that would eventually become the primary rival of Rome. The queen greeted the visitors. In due course Dido and Aeneas fell in love, and had the gods not reminded him of the importance of his quest to found a new Troy (Rome), the hero might well have remained happily in Carthage. Pulling himself together, Aeneas took leave of a now grieving and angry Dido. Before, in her despair, Dido commits suicide, she curses her departed lover. When he meets her in the underworld, she refuses to accept his apology and ignores him.

O Sun, you who traverse all earth's works with your flames, and you, O Juno, mediator in these troubles and witness, and Hecate, called on with weird cries by night at the crossways in the cities, and dire avenging goddesses (*Dirae*), and gods of dying Elissa [i.e., Dido], accept my words and hear my prayer! If it is necessary for his cursed head to reach harbor and come to land, and if Jupiter's fate so demands and this ending is fixed, then let him beg for help, harried by war with a brave and well-armed people, an exile with no home, torn from the embrace of Iulus, and let him see the untimely death of his companions. And when he has yielded himself to the terms of an unfair peace, then may he not enjoy his kingdom nor the light he longed for. Let him fall before his time and lie unburied on the shore. This is my prayer, this is my final word as I shed my blood. Then may you, O my Tyrians, harass his family and all his future descendants with hatred and send this offering to my ashes. Let there be no love, no treaty between our peoples. May you arise, some avenger, from my bones, and may you pursue the Trojan settlers with fire and sword, now, in the future, whenever time gives you strength. This is my curse—shore with opposing

shore, sea with sea, arms with arms, let them and their descendants fight!

[Morford et al., *Classical Mythology*
(Oxford University Press, 2011), p. 685.]

ARABIA: Muhammad and the Night Journey

One of the world's great quest stories is that of the Islamic prophet Muhammad
and his journey to Jerusalem and Heaven on the flying horse al Buraq.

The myth of the Night Journey (*Isra*), the Journey to Jerusalem and
Ascension (*Mi'raj*), is referred to in the *Qur'an* (17:1), where Allah is
praised for bringing his Prophet from the Sacred Mosque (Mecca) to
the Farthest Mosque (usually interpreted as the Al-Aqsa in Jerusalem,
but for some it might refer to Allah's Heaven). This is a central myth
in Islam. In tradition the story has developed from what was perhaps
the reporting of a dream to a fully developed myth with several
versions. It usually begins with Muhammad's rising from sleep
and going during the night to the Ka'bah to worship. There he fell
asleep, only to be awakened by Jibril (Gabriel) and two other angels
who washed his heart with the waters of the ancient well Zamzam,
thus instituting a ritual followed by Muslims and suggesting the idea
of a heart cleansed of sin and idolatry. The winged mule, al-Buraq,
arrived and was told by Jibril to carry Muhammad on a journey.
According to some, this animal possessed a human soul and had
in ancient times carried Ibrahim (Abraham) to the Zamzam well to
find Hajar (Hagar) and Ismail (Ishmael). As Jan Knappert suggests,
the fact that Muhammad was permitted to ride on Buraq signifies
that he was, in fact, continuing the mission of Ibrahim. Eventually
Muhammad came to Jerusalem, where he prayed at the Temple-
Mosque of the Rock as the de facto imam in front of Ibrahim, Musa,
and Isa (Abraham, Moses, and Jesus), who thus recognized his
supremacy among them and, in effect, trumped the events of the
Transfiguration of Jesus in the New Testament. Presented with a
glass of wine and a glass of milk, the Prophet chose the milk and was
praised by Jibril for having chosen the "true religion." With Jibril
Muhammad made the steep and difficult climb up the ladder (*mi'raj*)
through the seven heavens, each with its own prophet, learning
aspects of the future Islam on the way and finally reaching the place

of divinity, where, according to some, Muhammad saw Allah, and according to others, he saw not Allah himself but signs of Allah.

[David A. Leeming, *Oxford Companion to World Mythology* (Oxford University Press, 2005), p. 288.]

UNWILLING

AFRICA (KIKUYU): Wanjiru   BETRYAL / GREED

The greatest of tests that faces the quest hero is death itself. Heroes who die and are later reborn resemble the dying god, and this aspect of their stories is closely related to that theme. The dying hero is the sacrificial victim whose death is part of a ritual act by which his or her society will be renewed or "saved." The story of the African maiden Wanjiru also contains the descent motif and the story of the rescue of the victim from the dark world that must remind us of the shamanistic rescues performed by Dionysos, Inanna, Jesus, Herakles, and others.

The sun was very hot and there was no rain, so the crops died and hunger was great. This happened one year; and it happened again a second, and even a third year, that the rain failed. The people all gathered together on the great open space on the hilltop, where they were wont to dance, and they said to each other, "Why does the rain delay in coming?" And they went to the Medicine-Man and they said to him, "Tell us why there is no rain, for our crops have died, and we shall die of hunger."

And he took his gourd and poured out its contents. This he did many times; and at last he said, "There is a maiden here who must be bought if rain is to fall, and the maiden is named Wanjiru. The day after tomorrow let all of you return to this place, and every one of you from the eldest to the youngest bring with him a goat for the purchase of the maiden."

On the day after the morrow, old men and young men all gathered together, and each brought in his hand a goat. Now they all stood in a circle, and the relations of Wanjiru stood together, and she herself stood in the middle. As they stood there, the feet of Wanjiru began to sink into the ground, and she sank in to her knees and cried aloud, "I am lost!"

Her father and mother also cried and exclaimed, "We are lost!"

Those who looked on pressed close and placed goats in the keeping of Wanjiru's father and mother. Wanjiru sank lower to her waist, and again she cried aloud, "I am lost, but much rain will come!"

She sank to her breast; but the rain did not come. Then she said again, "Much rain will come."

Now she sank in to her neck, and then the rain came in great drops. Her people would have rushed forward to save her, but those who stood around pressed upon them more goats, and they desisted.

Then Wanjiru said, "My people have undone me," and she sank down to her eyes. As one after another of her family stepped forward to save her, someone in the crowd would give to him or her a goat, and he would fall back. And Wanjiru cried aloud for the last time, "I am undone, and my own people have done this thing." Then she vanished from sight; the earth closed over her, and the rain poured down, not in showers, as it sometimes does, but in a great deluge, and all the people hastened to their own homes.

Now there was a young warrior who loved Wanjiru and he lamented continually, saying, "Wanjiru is lost, and her own people have done this thing." And he said, "Where has Wanjiru gone? I will go to the same place." So he took his shield and spear. And he wandered over the country day and night until, at least, as the dusk fell, he came to the spot where Wanjiru had vanished. Then he stood where she had stood and, as he stood, his feet began to sink as hers had sunk; and he sank lower and lower until the ground closed over him, and he went by a long road under the earth as Wanjiru had gone and, at length, he saw the maiden. But, indeed, he pitied her sorely, for her state was miserable, and her raiment had perished. He said to her, "You were sacrificed to bring the rain; now the rain has come, and I shall take you back." So he took Wanjiru on his back as if she had been a child and brought her to the road he had traversed, and they rose together to the open air, and their feet stood once more on the ground.

Then the warrior said, "You shall not return to the house of your people, for they have treated you shamefully." And he bade her wait until nightfall. When it was dark, he took her to the house of his mother and he asked his mother to leave, saying that he had business, and he allowed no one to enter.

But his mother said, "Why do you hide this thing from me, seeing I am your mother who bore you?" So he suffered his mother to know, but he said, "Tell no one that Wanjiru has returned."

So she abode in the house of his mother. He and his mother slew goats, and Wanjiru ate the fat and grew strong. Then of the skins they made garments for her, so that she was attired most beautifully.

It came to pass that the next day there was a great dance, and her lover went with the throng. But his mother and the girl waited until everyone had assembled at the dance, and all the road was empty. Then they came out of the house and mingled with the crowd. When the relations saw Wanjiru, they said, "Surely that is Wanjiru whom we had lost."

And they pressed to greet her, but her lover beat them off, for he said, "You sold Wanjiru shamefully."

Then she returned to his mother's house. But on the fourth day her family again came and the warrior repented, for he said, "Surely they are her father and her mother and her brothers."

So he paid them the purchase price, and he wedded Wanjiru who had been lost.

[Paul Radin and James Sweeney, eds., *African Folktales and Sculpture* (New York, 1952), p. 272.]

INDONESIA (CERAM): Hainuwele   REVENGE

The Wemale people of Ceram in Indonesia have an origin myth that features the sacrifice of a miraculously born maiden and a form of resurrection that ties the myth archetypally to such stories as the Corn Mother and the Wanjiru narrative.

Among the nine families was the night-man, Ameta, who went hunting with his dog. The dog picked up the scent of a pig, and the two followed the scent to a pond. The pig jumped into the pond and swam away, but soon it could swim no more and drowned. Ameta fished the dead pig from the water and found a coconut impaled on its tusk. Here, surely, was a great treasure, for at the time there were no coconut palms on the earth.

Ameta took his treasure home, wrapped it like a baby, and planted it. Within three days, a coconut palm had sprouted from the ground and grown to its full height. In another three days, it had blossomed. Ameta cut himself by accident, and some of his blood fell on one of the new leaves. Within three days, the maiden Hainuwele grew from the drop of blood, and three days later she had become a maiden of unrivaled feminine richness, bestowing all things beautiful with unceasing generosity.

And thus came about the Maro Dance.

For the men and women of the nine families, held together by a long rope, formed a vast spiral around Hainuwele and slowly danced closer and closer to her, pressing in on her. Eventually, the dancers pressed so close that Hianuwele was pushed into a pit that had been dug beside her in the earth, the chanting of the dancers drowning out her cries. They heaped the earth over her and tamped it down firmly with their dancing feet. They had danced Hainuwele into the earth.

And it was only after this beautiful and generous maiden had been murdered in this fashion that the people could die and be born again. For after she was murdered, Hainuwele grew angry and built a great gate at one of the nine dancing places—a gate in the form of a giant spiral. And since her murder, people have had to die and pass through this gate to the Underworld to see Hainuwele, and only in this manner could the people become human.

To dance the dance of life, they had first to dance the dance of death.

[David A. Leeming and Jake Page, *Goddess* (Oxford University Press, 1994), p. 74.]

INDIA: Rama and Sita

In the Indian epic the *Ramayana*, the wife of the Vishnu avatar and hero Rama is the beautiful Sita, an avatar of Vishnu's wife Lakshmi. We know that Sita is a true member of the hero class because she is born miraculously from the earth when it is ploughed. Sita is captured by the monster Ravana but is eventually rescued by the monkey king Hanuman. Later she would have undergone a sacrifice by fire to preserve the honor of her husband had she not been rescued by her mother, Earth. Sita's scapegoat relatives include Wanjiru and Hainuwele.

Rama and his three brothers grow up in the court of their father, King Dasharatha. Rama and his brother Laksmana are "borrowed" by the sage Visvamitra, to fight against the evil sacrifice-defiling raksasas, followers of the demon Ravana. Only Rama, he says, can defeat them. The reader knows that as an avatar of Vishnu, Rama is indeed the proper defender of the faith, and he succeeds in defeating the raksasas. Rama and his brother then travel on to Mithila, where Rama wins King Janaka's earth-born daughter Sita by succeeding in bending the great bow of the god Shiva, thus revealing himself as a true hero. On his way home, Rama will succeed in still another heroic trial by accepting Parashurama's challenge to bend the bow of Vishnu, a task he also accomplishes. Upon his return home,

Rama's father decides to anoint him heir to the throne, but an intrigue of his stepmother forces the king to honor an old oath and to exile his son to the forest for a number of years. Sita insists on accompanying her husband to the Dandaka (the "punishment forest"). Eventually the evil Ravana abducts Sita from the forest and takes her to his fortress in Lanka. Now begins the essential aspect of the epic, Rama's quest for his Sita, mirroring Vishnu's need of his Shri, his Shakti, or energy source.

Rama is helped in his quest by the monkey god Hanuman and his monkey army. Magically, the monkey troops build a bridge to Lanka, and Rama is able, during a terrible battle, to kill Ravana and thus to rescue Sita. By killing the king of the sacrifice-defiling raksasas, Rama has fulfilled the purpose for which he had been sent as Vishnu's avatar to earth.

Since Sita has been potentially defiled by having been abducted by Ravana, Rama allows a trial by fire in which the innocent Sita climbs upon the funeral pyre in an act of sati but is miraculously refused by the fire god Agni. Rama can now receive her again as his wife. Later his doubts about Sita revive, however, and he exiles her to the forest, where she gives birth to twin sons and stays with the sage Valmiki, who composes the Ramayana and recites it to Rama and Sita's sons. Sita returns to Rama and asks her mother, the earth (Prthivi), to take her back, as proof of her undying innocence. Immediately Prthivi rises on her throne, takes her daughter on her lap, and the earth swallows them. Rama reigns for another one thousand years.

[David A. Leeming, *Oxford Companion to World Mythology* (Oxford University Press, 2005), p. 335.]

INDIA: Draupadi

Another Hindu heroine is Draupadi, the wife of all five Pandava brothers in the epic the *Mahabharata*. Like Sita, Draupadi is an avatar of Lakshmi, the wife of Vishnu. In their gambling match struggle with the Kaurava brothers, the Pandavas, in a shameful act, gamble away Draupadi herself. Draupadi's redemption reveals her as a true hero favored by the gods.

DRAUPADI

The Pandava brothers had lost everything on a few rolls of the dice, and their hostile cousins, the Kauravas, were triumphant. Gone was the Pandava wealth, their gems, their homes, their lands—everything. But Yudhishthira, the leader of the Pandava brothers, could not let the game stop. To the amazement of the other nobles assembled to watch, he put first one, then another of his brothers on the block, and each lost. Finally, only he was left, and he put himself up as a stake and lost again.

Shakuni, the leader of the Kauravas, gloated while the Pandava brothers came to the realization that they were now slaves. But Shakuni was not finished. He leaned over and reminded Yudhishthira that he had one thing more he had not staked against the dice: their wife, the beautiful Draupadi. "Perhaps," he said, "she will bring you good luck."

Sobbing at the thought, but desperate, Yudhishthira cried out his wife's name, "Draupadi! I pledge her!"

All assembled appealed to him not to go through with this shameful dishonoring of a woman, but Yudhishthira was driven to madness. His heart raced as he took the dice one more time.

And again he lost.

"Now Draupadi is our slave!" the Kauravas crowed. "She will sweep the floors of our palace." They sent their charioteer to fetch her from her rooms, but when he arrived with his awful news, Draupadi held her head, with its long black hair, high and refused to go.

"Tell them that Yudhishthira and his brothers were slaves already when he pledged me in his foolish game. As a slave he has no rights, no belongings. They could have no wife to pledge." She gathered up her voluminous skirts of silk and, dark eyes flashing, ordered the charioteer to leave.

When the leader of the Kauravas heard this, he dispatched one of his brothers, who boasted that he would drag the recalcitrant woman out of her apartment through the dust and force her to her knees before her new owners. Arriving at her place, the man chased after Draupadi, who fled into her inner rooms. He finally seized her by the hair and hauled her to the court of the Kauravas, where she was made to kneel.

But Draupadi rose up and haughtily explained to those assembled that she was no slave, since slaves had no possessions to pledge. She excoriated them all for what they had done. Not to be thwarted, the Kaurava brothers gave an order that caused the assembled nobles (and the humiliated Pandavas) to howl. Draupadi would be stripped naked before all those in the court.

For the first time, Draupadi was afraid. There was no one to help her, except perhaps God, to whom she prayed.

And Krishna did come to her aid. For as each garment was ruth-lessly stripped away from her, another appeared in its place, again and again, over and over. The Kaurava brothers were first stunned, and then enraged: they continued to tear away her clothes, only to find that more appeared. An enormous pile of clothes amassed on the floor, and the Kaurava brothers finally exhausted themselves with the unfulfillable task and fell away.

Draupadi then opened her eyes, and the pile of clothes vanished in a column of flames. Draupadi's former husbands stood with their heads hung in shame while, outside, the sky went dark, a storm cloud burst in thunder, and the animals of the fields all shrieked.

The old blind father of the Kaurava brothers was overcome with sadness and shame. He sought to console Draupadi, who now stood, her eyes glittering with the strength of her heart, and demanded the freedom of Yudhishthira and his brothers—her husbands.

"What else can I grant you?" the old man asked. "Make any re-quest. Ask for your husbands' kingdom back, and it will be done."

And Draupadi said, "I will not accept a kingdom from my ene-mies. Let my husbands now reconquer the world. They are free."

But the old man insisted and awarded the Pandavas their king-dom and pleaded with Draupadi to forgive the terrible and dishonor-able things his sons had done. Draupadi said nothing. Instead, she looked at each of her enemies with eyes of scorn, turned on her heel, and left the hall, followed by her five silent husbands.

[David A. Leeming and Jake Page, *Goddess*
(Oxford University Press, 1994), pp. 166–168.]

AUSTRALIA (ABORIGINAL): The Pleiades   PERCIVERANCE

This Aboriginal version of the Pleiades story bears little surface resemblance to the Greek myth about the daughters of Atlas, priestesses of Artemis, being turned into stars. However, in nearly all parts of the ancient world the Pleiades constellation is associated with goddesses who were emanations of the moon goddess. The heroines of the Australian myth, like their sisters of other cul-tures, represent the light that can come from darkness, the renewal and salva-tion that can come from sacrifice, the life that can come from death. They are a representation of the aspect of the hero biography that entails a journey into the darkness.

In various parts of the world and among different races there are traditions that the lustre of the Pleiades is associated with acts in which women were concerned. There is an Australian legend on the subject. According to this story, it was the girls who had reached the age of adolescence who perceived the necessity for bringing the body under subjection to the mind in order to restrain physical appetite and control the effects of pain and fear. They saw that without such control there could be no real racial advancement. Accordingly, they presented themselves to the elders of the tribe in order to undergo the trial by ordeal. The elders explained to the girls that the test that they would have to submit to was a severe one. The girls, however, were firm in their resolve to undergo it. So every morning for three years, in a place apart from their brothers and sisters, the elders, to teach them moderation, gave them a small portion of the usual food, consisting perhaps of a piece of fish or flesh of the emu, kangaroo, or wombat. This they received twice a day, at the hour of sunrise and at the hour of sunset. At the end of the third year they were taken for a long journey through the dense bush, where the thorns scratched their flesh, and across the plains and rivers, travelling during the heat of the day, often almost fainting from fatigue, but ever pressing onward. After a week of such journeying had passed the elders called the girls before them and inquired whether they thought they were better able to control the appetite. To this the girls replied, "Our minds are made up. We will control the appetite." The elders then said, "You are asked to fast for three days, and during this fasting time we will all travel."

So the girls set out with the elders on the journey. The way was long and difficult, and they were weak from lack of food. The blazing sun seemed to them more ruthless and the way more rough and thorny than usual, but they were determined to conquer, and so they kept on their way undaunted. On the evening of the third day they arrived at the appointed camping-ground. The elders prepared the food for them for the following day. On the fourth morning they were given a flint knife and were instructed to cut from the kangaroo or emu the amount of food they required. How tempting was the smell of the roasted flesh to the girls, who had travelled unceasingly for three days without breaking their fast! The temptation to cut a generous portion and satisfy the craving for food was very great. But each cut for herself only an ordinary portion. The elders praised the girls for their restraint. They said, "You have acquitted yourselves well so far; and now there are other appetites, and it is for you to control them as you have controlled your hunger." They replied,

"We are ready to undergo any tests you please. Our minds are made up to subdue appetite and to conquer inclination." They then submitted themselves to various tests in order to learn to control other appetites, each test being more difficult than the former. In every case they were successful.

When the elders told them that it was necessary to overcome pain, they again submitted themselves to their guidance, and the elders decided the particular form of discipline that the girls should undergo. In the presence of the other girls and boys they took the girls away to a selected spot, where all sacred ceremonies were performed. They ordered them to lie upon the ground. Then they took a stone axe and a pointed stick about eight or nine inches long. They told the girls one by one to open their mouths. The elders placed the point of a stick against a front tooth of each, then raised an axe and brought it down upon the stick, breaking the tooth off, and leaving the nerves exposed and quivering. The girls then rose from the ground, and sat awaiting the further commands of the elders. They were asked whether they felt the pain, to which they replied, "Yes, we felt the pain." Then the elders said, "Are you willing to have another tooth knocked out?" And the girls replied, "Yes, our minds are made up. We are going to control pain." And again the elders asked at the conclusion of this test, "Are you willing to undergo more severe testing?" The girls replied as before, "Yes, our minds are made up. We will control pain." They were then led to another camping-ground and commanded to stand in a row. An elder of the tribe approached with a flint knife. He stood before each of the girls for a while, and then drew the knife silently across her breast, and the blood flowed. This he did to each girl in succession. Another elder took the ashes of a particular kind of wood, and rubbed them into the wound. The effect of this was twofold; it intensified the pain, and helped to heal the wound.

A day or two was given to allow the wounds to heal, and then the elders called the girls before them and inquired if they were still willing to submit themselves to further testing. They replied, "Yes, we are willing to go through any tests. Our minds are made up." The elders then went alone through the bush and selected another camping-ground for the girls. At bed-time they were led to the spot, and told, "It is time to retire to rest. This is your camping-ground." The girls, weary and eager for rest, threw their oppossum rugs on the ground. The night was dark and moonless and very warm. They lay there for a little while, and presently they felt things crawling over their bodies. They were afraid, but they refused to give way to fear. It may have been that each girl was afraid of what the others would think of her if she failed, and that thus each helped the others to be brave. By and by they discovered they were lying on a bed of ants. All through the night they lay there with the ants swarming over them. The time seemed very long. These girls had journeyed far, fasting, and their poor bodies were still tender with half-healed wounds. In the morning they presented themselves to the elders, smiling and showing no signs of the terrible night that they had passed.

Still their journey continued, and they underwent further tests, such as the piercing of the nose and the wearing of a stick through it to keep the wound open. Further, they were bidden to lie on a bed of hot cinders. Before each fresh trial they were asked if they were willing to undergo the tests. Their reply, which never varied, was, "Yes, we have made up our minds to conquer pain."

Now the elders were very pleased with the girls, and very proud of the powers of endurance that they showed, but they realized that it was necessary for them to overcome fear as well as the appetites and pain, so they called them together and said, "Girls! You have done very well, and have proved that you possess wonderful courage and endurance. The next stage is the control of fear. Do you wish to continue on the way?" The girls stood there in all their youth, and with glowing eyes; and they repeated the old phrase, "Yes, our minds are made up. We will conquer fear."

On a fresh camping-ground in the dark night, with the campfires gleaming on the trees, and casting dark, gloomy shadows, the elders told them tales about the *bunyip* and the *muldarpe*. This latter is a spirit which assumes many shapes. It may come as a kangaroo, or a wombat, or a lizard. The girls were told fearful stories of these dreadful beings, and of ghosts, to which they listened tremblingly. The more highly strung among them could scarcely refrain from crying out. They found themselves looking over their shoulders, and imagining that the dark shadows were the *bunyip* or the *muldarpe* or other spirits. For hours they listened, until it was time to go to bed. After the elders had made the sign of good-night they told them that the place where they were camping was the burial-place of their great-grandfathers. They lay down to sleep, resolved not to be afraid of any ghosts or spirits.

Then the elders crept round the camp, making weird noises, so that the hair of the girls rose and their blood ran cold. Besides these sounds there were the usual bush-noises, such as the howl of the dingo, the shriek of the owl, and the falling of the decayed branches. But the girls were not to be turned from their purpose, and they lay there until the break of day. Then they rose and presented themselves to the elders, showing no signs of their disturbed night, their faces placid and their eyes clear and shining. The elders knew that the girls had conquered fear, and they rejoiced with pride. They sent out invitations to the adjoining tribes, and they made great rejoicing, and held many corrobberies in honour of the girls.

But the girls were not content with having conquered the appetites and pain and fear. They desired that their sisters should do the same. So the leader of the girls stepped out from the group, and said to the girls of the assembled tribes, "We have passed through the testing that our elders prescribed, and we have endured much pain. Now it is the desire of the Great Spirit that you should go through the same course of testing. You must know that the selfish person is not happy. This is because he thinks only of himself. Happiness comes through thinking of others and forgetting self. Greed and pain and fear are caused by thinking too much of self, and so it is necessary to vanquish self. Will you not go and do as we have done?" The girls of the other tribes eagerly assented, so proud were they of the victory of their sisters.

Then the Great Spirit was so pleased with them that he sent a great star spirit to convey the girls to the heavens without death or further suffering, in order that they might shine there as a pattern and a symbol to their race. And on clear nights ever since that time the aboriginals look into the sky and revere this wonderful constellation, the Seven Sisters, and remember what the girls did, and always think of the story of how there came to be given to them a place in the heavens.

[W. Ramsay Smith, *Myths and Legends of the Australian Aboriginals* (London, 1970), pp. 345–350.]

MESOPOTAMIA: Gilgamesh

One of the earliest-known quest heroes is Gilgamesh. His quest includes a temptation by Ishtar (Inanna), an immortal femme fatale; fights with monsters;

and a descent to the other world. It is a quest for immortality or eternal youth. Gilgamesh is guided by a goddess called Siduri, who reminds us of the later Kalypso in Homer's *Odyssey* and the Sybil in Virgil's *Aeneid*. Gilgamesh's story is found in the earliest of epic poems, a work in fragments that was composed perhaps as early as the second millennium B.C.E. This part of the myth is the story of Gilgamesh's descent into the dark world in search of his dead friend, Enkidu, and the Sumerian Noah, Utnapishtim.

Bitterly Gilgamesh wept for his friend Enkidu; he wandered over the wilderness as a hunter, he roamed over the plains; in his bitterness he cried, "How can I rest, how can I be at peace? Despair is in my heart. What my brother is now, that shall I be when I am dead. Because I am afraid of death I will go as best I can to find Utnapishtim whom they call the Faraway, for he has entered the assembly of the gods." So Gilgamesh travelled over the wilderness, he wandered over the grasslands, a long journey, in search of Utnapishtim, whom the gods took after the deluge; and they set him to live in the land of Dilmun, in the garden of the sun; and to him alone of men they gave everlasting life.

At night when he came to the mountain passes Gilgamesh prayed: "In these mountain passes long ago I saw lions, I was afraid and I lifted my eyes to the moon; I prayed and my prayers went up to the gods, so now, O moon god Sin, protect me." When he had prayed, he lay down to sleep, until he was woken from out of a dream. He saw the lions round him glorying in life; then he took his axe in his hand, he drew his sword from his belt, and he fell upon them like an arrow from the string, and struck and destroyed and scattered them.

So at length Gilgamesh came to Mashu, the great mountains about which he had heard many things, which guard the rising and the setting sun. Its twin peaks are as high as the wall of heaven and its paps reach down to the underworld. At its gate the Scorpions stand guard, half man and half dragon; their glory is terrifying, their stare strikes death into men, their shimmering halo sweeps the mountains that guard the rising sun. When Gilgamesh saw them, he shielded his eyes for the length of a moment only; then he took courage and approached. When they saw him so undismayed, the Man-Scorpion called to his mate, "This one who comes to us now is flesh of the gods." The mate of the Man-Scorpion answered, "Two thirds is god but one third is man."

Then he called to the man Gilgamesh, he called to the child of the gods: "Why have you come so great a journey; for what have you travelled so far, crossing the dangerous waters; tell me the reason for your coming?" Gilgamesh answered, "For Enkidu; I loved him dearly, together we endured all kinds of hardships; on his account I have come, for the common lot of man has taken him. I have wept for him day and night, I would not give up his body for burial, I thought my friend would come back because of my weeping. Since he went, my life is nothing; that is why I have travelled here in search of Utnapishtim my father; for men say he has entered the assembly of the gods, and has found everlasting life. I have a desire to question him concerning the living and the dead." The Man-Scorpion opened his mouth and said, speaking to Gilgamesh, "No man born of woman has done what you have asked, no mortal man has gone into the mountain; the length of it is twelve leagues of darkness; in it there is no light, but the heart is oppressed with darkness. From the rising of the sun to the setting of the sun there is no light." Gilgamesh said, "Although I should go in sorrow and in pain, with sighing and with weeping, still I must go. Open the gate of the mountain." And the Man-Scorpion said, "Go, Gilgamesh, I permit you to pass through the mountain of Mashu and through the high ranges; may your feet carry you safely home. The gate of the mountain is open."

When Gilgamesh heard this, he did as the Man-Scorpion had said, he followed the sun's road to his rising, through the mountain. When he had gone one league, the darkness became thick around him, for there was no light, he could see nothing ahead and nothing behind him. After two leagues the darkness was thick and there was no light, he could see nothing ahead and nothing behind him. After three leagues the darkness was thick, and there was no light, he could see nothing ahead and nothing behind him. After four leagues the darkness was thick and there was no light, he could see nothing ahead and nothing behind him. At the end of five leagues the darkness was thick and there was no light, he could see nothing ahead and nothing behind him. At the end of six leagues the darkness was thick and there was no light, he could see nothing ahead and nothing behind him. When he had gone seven leagues the darkness was thick and there was no light, he could see nothing ahead and nothing behind him. When he had gone eight leagues Gilgamesh gave a great cry, for the darkness was thick and he could see nothing ahead and nothing behind him. After nine leagues he felt the north wind on his face, but the darkness was thick and there was no light, he could see nothing ahead and nothing behind him. After ten leagues the end was near. After eleven leagues the dawn light appeared. At the end of twelve leagues the sun streamed out.

There was the garden of the gods; all round him stood bushes bearing gems. Seeing it, he went down at once, for there was fruit of carnelian with the vine hanging from it, beautiful to look at; lapis lazuli leaves hung thick with fruit, sweet to see. For thorns and this-tles there were haematite and rare stones, agate, and pearls from out of the sea. While Gilgamesh walked in the garden by the edge of the sea, Shamash saw him, and he saw that he was dressed in the skins of animals and ate their flesh. He was distressed, and he spoke and said, "No mortal man has gone this way before, nor will, as long as the winds drive over the sea." And to Gilgamesh he said, "You will never find the life for which you are searching." Gilgamesh said to glorious Shamash, "Now that I have toiled and strayed so far over the wilderness, am I to sleep, and let the earth cover my head for ever? Let my eyes see the sun until they are dazzled with looking. Although I am no better than a dead man, still let me see the light of the sun."

Beside the sea she lives, the woman of the vine, the maker of wine; Siduri sits in the garden at the edge of the sea, with the golden bowl and the golden vats that the gods gave her. She is covered with a veil; and where she sits she sees Gilgamesh coming towards her, wearing skins, the flesh of the gods in his body, but despair in his heart, and his face like the face of one who has made a long journey. She looked, and as she scanned the distance she said in her own heart, "Surely this is some felon; where is he going now?" And she barred her gate against him with the cross-bar and shot home the bolt. But Gilgamesh, hearing the sound of the bolt, threw up his head and lodged his foot in the gate; he called to her, "Young woman, maker of wine, why do you bolt your door; what did you see that made you bar your gate? I will break in your door and burst in your gate, for I am Gilgamesh who seized and killed the Bull of Heaven, I killed the watchman of the cedar forest, I overthrew Humbaba who lived in the forest, and I killed the lions in the passes of the mountain."

Then Siduri said to him, "If you are that Gilgamesh who seized and killed the Bull of Heaven, who killed the watchman of the cedar forest, who overthrew Humbaba that lived in the forest, and killed the lions in the passes of the mountain, why are your cheeks so starved and why is your face so drawn? Why is despair in your heart and your face like the face of one who has made a long journey? Yes, why is your face burned from heat and cold, and why do you come here wandering over the pastures in search of the wind?"

Gilgamesh answered her, "And why should not my cheeks be starved and my face drawn? Despair is in my heart and my face is the face of one who has made a long journey, it was burned with heat and with cold. Why should I not wander over the pastures in search of the wind? My friend, my younger brother, he who hunted the wild ass of the wilderness and the panther of the plains, my friend, my younger brother who seized and killed the Bull of Heaven and overthrew Humbaba in the cedar forest, my friend who was very dear to me and who endured dangers beside me, Enkidu my brother, whom I loved, the end of mortality has overtaken him. I wept for him seven days and nights till the worm fastened on him. Because of my brother I am afraid of death, because of my brother I stray through the wilderness and cannot rest. But now, young woman, maker of wine, since I have seen your face do not let me see the face of death which I dread so much."

She answered, "Gilgamesh, where are you hurrying to? You will never find that life for which you are looking. When the gods created man, they allotted to him death, but life they retained in their own keeping. As for you, Gilgamesh, fill your belly with good things; day and night, night and day, dance and be merry, feast and rejoice. Let your clothes be fresh, bathe yourself in water, cherish the little child that holds your hand, and make your wife happy in your embrace; for this too is the lot of man."

But Gilgamesh said to Siduri, the young woman, "How can I be silent, how can I rest, when Enkidu whom I love is dust, and I too shall die and be laid in the earth. You live by the sea-shore and look into the heart of it; young woman, tell me now, which is the way to Utnapishtim, the son of Ubara-Tutu? What directions are there for the passage; give me, oh, give me directions. I will cross the Ocean if it is possible; if it is not, I will wander still farther in the wilderness." The wine-maker said to him, "Gilgamesh, there is no crossing the Ocean; whoever has come, since the days of old, has not been able to pass that sea. The Sun in his glory crosses the Ocean, but who beside Shamash has ever crossed it? The place and the passage are difficult, and the waters of death are deep which flow between. Gilgamesh, how will you cross the Ocean? When you come to the waters of death, what will you do? But Gilgamesh, down in the woods you will find Urshanabi, the ferryman of Utnapishtim; with him are the holy things, the things of stone. He is fashioning the serpent prow of the boat. Look at him well, and if it is possible, perhaps you will cross the waters with him; but if it is not possible, then you must go back."

When Gilgamesh heard this, he was seized with anger. He took his axe in his hand, and his dagger from his belt. He crept forward and he fell on them like a javelin. Then he went into the forest and sat down. Urshanabi saw the dagger flash and heard the axe, and he beat his head, for Gilgamesh had shattered the tackle of the boat in his rage. Urshanabi said to him, "Tell me, what is your name? I am Urshanabi, the ferryman of Utnapishtim the Faraway." He replied to him, "Gilgamesh is my name, I am from Uruk, from the house of Anu." Then Urshanabi said to him, "Why are your cheeks so starved and your face drawn? Why is despair in your heart and your face like the face of one who has made a long journey; yes, why is your face burned with heat and with cold, and why do you come here wandering over the pastures in search of the wind?"

Gilgamesh said to him, "Why should not my cheeks be starved and my face drawn? Despair is in my heart, and my face is the face of one who has made a long journey. I was burned with heat and with cold. Why should I not wander over the pastures? My friend, my younger brother who seized and killed the Bull of Heaven, and overthrew Humbaba in the cedar forest, my friend who was very dear to me, and who endured dangers beside me, Enkidu my brother whom I loved, the end of mortality has overtaken him. I wept for him seven days and nights till the worm fastened on him. Because of my brother I am afraid of death, because of my brother I stray through the wilderness. His fate lies heavy upon me. How can I be silent, how can I rest? He is dust and I too shall die and be laid in the earth for ever."

[N. K. Sandars, trans., *The Epic of Gilgamesh*, rev. ed. (Harmondsworth, England, 1972), pp. 97–104.]

✦   Chagall's *Orpheus*

GREECE AND ROME: Orpheus and Eurydice

The most poignant of descent rescue stories is that of Orpheus and Eurydice, as retold here by Ovid. Like the myth of Gilgamesh, it suggests human frustration over the inaccessibility of immortality.

ORPHEUS AND EURYDICE

Thence Hymen came, in saffron mantle clad,
At Orpheus' summons through the boundless sky
To Thessaly, but vain the summons proved.
True he was present, but no hallowed words
He brought nor happy smiles nor lucky sign;
Even the torch he held sputtered throughout
With smarting smoke, and caught no living flame
For all his brandishing. The ill-starred rite
Led to a grimmer end. The new-wed bride,
Roaming with her gay Naiads through the grass,
Fell dying when a serpent struck her heel.

And when at last the bard of Rhodope
Had mourned his fill in the wide world above,
He dared descend through Taenarus' dark gate
To Hades to make trial of the shades;
And through the thronging wraiths and grave-spent ghosts
He came to pale Persephone and him,
Lord of the shades, who rules the unlovely realm,
And as he struck his lyre's sad chords he said:
"Ye deities who rule the world below,
Whither we mortal creatures all return,
If simple truth, direct and genuine,
May by your leave be told, I have come down
Not with intent to see the glooms of Hell,
Nor to enchain the triple snake-haired necks
Of Cerberus, but for my dear wife's sake,
In whom a trodden viper poured his venom
And stole her budding years. My heart has sought
Strength to endure; the attempt I'll not deny;
But love has won, a god whose fame is fair
In the world above; but here I doubt, though here
Too, I surmise; and if that ancient tale
Of ravishment is true, you too were joined
In love. Now by these regions filled with fear,
By this huge chaos, these vast silent realms,
Reweave, I implore, the fate unwound too fast
Of my Eurydice. To you are owed
Ourselves and all creation; a brief while
We linger; then we hasten, late or soon,
To one abode; here one road leads us all;
Here in the end is home; over humankind
Your kingdom keeps the longest sovereignty.
She too, when ripening years reach their due term,
Shall own your rule. The favour that I ask
Is but to enjoy her love; and, if the Fates
Will not reprieve her, my resolve is clear
Not to return: may two deaths give you cheer."

    So to the music of his strings he sang,
And all the bloodless spirits wept to hear;
And Tantalus forgot the fleeing water,
Ixion's wheel was tranced; the Danaids

Laid down their urns; the vultures left their feast,
And Sisyphus sat rapt upon his stone.
Then first by that sad singing overwhelmed,
The Furies' cheeks, it's said, were wet with tears;
And Hades' queen and he whose sceptre rules
The Underworld could not deny the prayer,
And called Eurydice. She was among
The recent ghosts and, limping from her wound,
Came slowly forth; and Orpheus took his bride
And with her this compact that, till he reach
The world above and leave Avernus' vale,
He look not back or else the gift would fail.
     The track climbed upwards, steep and indistinct,
Through the hushed silence and the murky gloom;
And now they neared the edge of the bright world,
And, fearing lest she faint, longing to look,
He turned his eyes—and straight she slipped away.
He stretched his arms to hold her—to be held—
And clasped, poor soul, naught but the yielding air.
And she, dying again, made no complaint
(For what complaint had she save she was loved?)
And breathed a faint farewell, and turned again
Back to the land of spirits whence she came.
     The double death of his Eurydice
Stole Orpheus' wits away; (like him who saw
In dread the three-necked hound of Hell with chains
Fast round his middle neck, and never lost
His terror till he lost his nature too
And turned to stone; or Olenos, who took
Upon himself the charge and claimed the guilt
When his ill-starred Lethaea trusted to
Her beauty, hearts once linked so close, and now
Two rocks on runnelled Ida's mountainside).
He longed, he begged, in vain to be allowed
To cross the stream of Styx a second time.
The ferryman repulsed him. Even so
For seven days he sat upon the bank,
Unkempt and fasting, anguish, grief and tears
His nourishment, and cursed Hell's cruelty.
Then he withdrew to soaring Rhodope

And Haemus battered by the northern gales.
    Three times the sun had reached the watery Fish
That close the year, while Orpheus held himself
Aloof from love of women, hurt perhaps
By ill-success or bound by plighted troth.
Yet many a woman burned with passion for
The bard, and many grieved at their repulse.
It was his lead that taught the folk of Thrace
The love for tender boys, to pluck the buds,
The brief springtime, with manhood still to come.
    There was a hill, and on the hill a wide
Level of open ground, all green with grass.
The place lacked any shade. But when the bard,
The heaven-born bard, sat there and touched his strings,
Shade came in plenty. Every tree was there:
Dodona's holy durmast, poplars once
The Sun's sad daughters, oaks with lofty leaves,
Soft limes, the virgin laurel and the beech;
The ash, choice wood for spearshafts, brittle hazels,
The knotless fir, the ilex curving down
With weight of acorns, many-coloured maples,
The social plane, the river-loving willow,
The water-lotus, box for ever green,
Thin tamarisks and myrtles double-hued,
Viburnums bearing berries of rich blue.
Twist-footed ivy came and tendrilled vines,
And vine-clad elms, pitch-pines and mountain-ash,
Arbutus laden with its blushing fruit,
Lithe lofty palms, the prize of victory,
And pines, high-girdled, in a leafy crest,
The favourite of Cybele, the gods'
Great mother, since in this tree Attis doffed
His human shape and stiffened in its trunk.

        [Ovid, *Metamorphoses*, trans. A. D. Melville
        (Oxford University Press, 2008), pp. 225–228.]

GREECE: Odysseus

Before he can achieve his goal of returning home to Ithaca, Homer's Odysseus must meet with the dead. He learns of his destiny and of the nature of death from Tiresias. Having so "descended," he can begin to rise into his true self, in

a motif that relates him and many other heroes to the ancient sun gods, who
seem to die each night only to be reborn each day.

We beached the ship on that shore and put off our sheep. With them
we made our way up the strand of Ocean till we came to the spot
which Circe had described. There Perimedes and Eurylochus held
the victims while I drew the keen blade from my hip, to hollow that
trench of a cubit square and a cubit deep. About it I poured the drink-
offerings to the congregation of the dead, a honey-and-milk draught
first, sweet wine next, with water last of all: and I made a heave-offering
of our glistening barley; invoking the tenuous dead, in general, for
my intention of a heifer-not-in-calf, the best to be found in my
manors when I got back to Ithaca; which should be slain to them and
burnt there on a pyre fed high with treasure: while for Teiresias apart
I vowed an all-black ram, the choicest male out of our flocks.

After I had been thus instant in prayer to the populations of the
grave I took the two sheep and beheaded them across my pit in such
manner that the livid blood drained into it. Then from out of Erebus
they flocked to me, the dead spirits of those who had died. Brides
came and lads; old men and men of sad experience; tender girls
aching from their first agony; and many fighting men showing the
stabbed wounds of brazen spears—war-victims, still in their
blooded arms. All thronged to the trench and ranged restlessly this
side of it and that with an eerie wailing. Pale fear gripped me. Hastily
I called the others and bade them flay and burn with fire the sheep's
bodies which lay there, slaughtered by my pitiless sword. They
obeyed, conjuring without cease the Gods, great Hades, and terrible
Persephone, while I sat over the pit holding out my sharp weapon to
forbid and prevent this shambling legion of the dead from approaching the blood till I had had my answer from Teiresias.

And at last he came, the spirit of Theban Teiresias, gold sceptre
in hand. He knew me and said, "Heaven-born Odysseus, what now?
O son of misfortune, why leave the lambent sunshine for this joy-
less place where only the dead are to be seen? Stand off from the pit
and put up your threatening sword that I may drink blood and declare to you words of truth." So he said and I stepped back, thrusting my silver-hilted sword home into its scabbard: while he drank of
the blackening blood. Then did the blameless seer begin to say: —

"You come here, renowned Odysseus, in quest of a comfortable
way home. I tell you the God will make your way hard. I tell you that

your movements will not remain secret from the Earth-shaker, whose heart is bitter against you for the hurt you did him in blinding the Cyclops, his loved son. Yet have you a chance of surviving to reach Ithaca, despite all obstacles, if you and your followers can master your greed in the island of Thrinacia, when your ship first puts in there for refuge from the lowering sea. For in that island you will find at pasture the oxen and wonderful sheep of Helios our Sun, who oversees and overhears all things. If you are so preoccupied about returning as to leave these beasts unhurt, then you may get back to Ithaca, very toil-worn, after all: but if you meddle with them, then I certify the doom of your men and your ship; and though yourself may escape alive, it will not be till after many days, in a ship of strangers, alone and in sorry plight, that you win back, having suffered the loss of all your company: while in your house you shall find trouble awaiting you, even overbearing men who devour your substance on pretext of courting your worshipful wife and chaffering about her marriage dues. Yet at your coming shall you visit their violence upon them, fatally. After you have killed these suitors, either by cunning within the house or publicly with the stark sword, then go forth under your shapely oar till you come to a people who know not the sea and eat their victuals unsavoured with its salt: a people ignorant of purplé-prowed ships and of the smoothed and shaven oars which are the wings of a ship's flying. I give you this token of them, a sign so plain that you cannot miss it: you have arrived when another wayfarer shall cross you and say that on your doughty shoulder you bear the scatterer of haulms, a winnowing-fan. Then pitch in the earth your polished oar and sacrifice goodly beasts to King Poseidon, a ram and a Bull and a ramping boar. Afterward turn back; and at home offer hecatombs to the Immortal Gods who possess the broad planes of heaven: to all of them in order, as is most seemly. At the last, amidst a happy folk, shall your own death come to you, softly, far from the salt sea, and make an end of one utterly weary of slipping downward into old age. All these things that I relate are true."

So he prophesied and I, answering, said: "O Teiresias, surely these things are threads of destiny woven in the Gods' design. Yet tell to me one other thing. Before me is the ghost of my mother, dead. Lo there, how she crouches by the blood and will not look upon me nor address me one word. Tell me, King, how shall she know that I am her son?" So I said and he replied, "A simple thing for my saying and your learning. Any of these ghosts of the dead, if you permit them to come near the blood, will tell you truth: and to whomsoever you begrudge it, he shall go back, away." The spirit of King Teiresias ended his soothsaying and departed to the House of Hades.

[Homer, *Odyssey*, trans. T. E. Lawrence
(Oxford University Press, 1991), pp. 152–153, 154–156.]

ISRAEL: Jesus

The familiar story of Jesus' life has been the most popular subject of Western painting, music, sculpture, and even architecture during the past two thousand years. It begins with the miraculous birth that establishes the child as a mythological hero—like Perseus and Herakles and Theseus, a "son of God." The story of the hero's death is a full blossoming (with, for some, a historical aspect) of the dying god myth. However, it is a version of the myth that reflects the particular values of the early Christians. The "pagan" sexual elements are gone; the planted seed and the resurrection of the savior king-god result for his followers not so much in the vegetation of spring (though this is a constant Easter theme in ritual if not in myth) as in a spiritual renewal or possibility of returning through Christ—the "New Adam"—to the original state of Adam and Eve before the Fall. Ultimately, immortality is celebrated in this story and in its ritual as it is in the other dying god tales and ceremonies.

The dressing up of Jesus as a mock king of the Jews for his trial suggests the scapegoat element so important in the theology of Jesus in particular and in the tradition of the dying god in general. It has been suggested by Sir James Frazer and others that an ancient tradition of sacrificing a true king in the hope of renewing a tribe was eventually replaced by the tradition of sacrificing a criminal or ordinary citizen who dresses up as a sacrificial "king for a day."

By being resurrected from the dead and ascending on a cloud into heaven, Jesus' herohood is firmly established in the context of Christian belief.

MESO-AMERICA (TOLTEC/AZTEC): Quetzalcoatl

Quetzalcoatl was the feathered serpent god of the Aztec and Toltec cultures. Born miraculously, his life, like that of the Buddha and of Herakles, ends in fire, and he, too, is taken off to the heavens, perhaps as a star. Like King Arthur and Jesus, he is a "once and future king" whose return to earth is expected.

It ended on the beach
It ended with a hulk of serpents formed into a boat
& when he'd made it, sat in it & sailed away
A boat that glided on those burning waters, no one knowing when
    he reached the country of Red Daylight
It ended on the rim of some great sea
It ended with his face reflected in the mirror of its waves
The beauty of his face returned to him
& he was dressed in garments like the sun
It ended with a bonfire on the beach where he would hurl himself
& burn, his ashes rising & the cries of birds
It ended with the linnet, with the birds of turquoise color, birds the
    color of wild sunflowers, red & blue birds
It ended with the birds of yellow feathers in a riot of bright gold
Circling till the fire had died out
Circling while his heart rose through the sky
It ended with his heart transformed into a star
It ended with the morning star with dawn & evening
It ended with his journey to Death's Kingdom with seven days of
    darkness
With his body changed to light
A star that burns forever in that sky
    [From "The Flight of Quetzalcoatl," trans. Jerome Rothenberg, in
    Shaking the Pumpkin: Traditional Poetry of the Indian North Americas, ed.
    Jerome Rothenberg (New York, 1972), pp. 122–123.]

EUROPE: Mary

The early Christian people felt an instinctive desire to recognize the Great Mother, even though that concept was thoroughly removed from the young Church's official doctrine. They created an elaborate myth around the figure of Mary, stressing the idea of the Immaculate Conception, in which Mary is seen as having been conceived without original sin, and the idea of her bodily assumption into heaven to reign there as queen. Both ideas would eventually become doctrine.

Mary was also closely associated with the Great Goddess of Ephesus, whose temples she took over. In the 5th century an Ephesian priest named Proclus delivered a sermon on the multiform nature of Mary, calling her "the living bush, which was not burnt by the fire of the divine birth . . . virgin and heaven, the only bridge between God and men, the awesome loom . . . on which the garment of union was woven."

Much was made of the reversal of Mary's Latin *Ave* and the name of Eve (Eva). Mystics said Mary was Eve's purified reincarnation, as Jesus was the similar reincarnation of Adam. Somehow, theologians failed to recognize that the new incarnations apparently reversed the parent–child relationship. Then again, as Adam and Eve were spouses, so the relationship of Mary and Jesus sometimes verged on the sexual or conjugal. In a legend ascribed to St. John, Jesus welcomed Mary into heaven with the words, "Come, my chosen, and I shall set thee in my seat, for I have coveted the beauty of thee."

The Church's doctrine of the assumption of Mary was explained in a number of ways. Early churchmen declared that Jesus visited Mary's tomb—variously located in Ephesus, Bethlehem, Gethsemane, or Josaphat—and raised up her corpse, which he made to live again; then he personally escorted her into heaven as a live woman. She was not a soul or a spirit but an immortal person in her own original body. This became the official modern view when the doctrine of the assumption was declared an article of faith in 1950, when Pope Pius XII pronounced that "the immaculate mother of God, the ever Virgin Mary, when the course of her earthly life was run, was assumed in body and in soul to heavenly glory." But the point had already been argued for more than a thousand years.

The Church's problem was to take advantage of popular reverence for Mary but at the same time prevent her literal deification. Some theologians of the 13th century claimed Mary's mortality should bring more women to obey the Church, because the king of heaven "is no mere man but a mere woman is its queen. It is not a mere man who is set above the angels and all the rest of the heavenly court, but a mere woman is; nor is anyone who is merely man as powerful there as a mere woman."

Always the theologians feared to impute too much power and glory to Mary. Pope John XXIII, presuming to know Mary's inner thoughts, announced: "The Madonna is not pleased when she is put above her Son," though in fact it was the church who was not pleased. Catholic doctrines themselves attributed to her two of the three basic characteristics of divinity: she was immortal by reason of the assumption, and sinless by reason of the Immaculate Conception.

The third requirement of divinity, omniscience, was conceded to her by popular belief.

[Barbara G. Walker, *The Woman's Encyclopedia of Myths and Secrets* (San Francisco, 1983), pp. 605–606.]

GREECE: Alcestis

Alcestis, the wife of the selfish Admetus, is the heroine of the myth told by Euripides in his *Alcestis* and by several other classical writers. She agrees to die for her husband, only to be brought back from the underworld by Herakles.

Alcestis, the most beautiful of Pelias's daughters, was asked in marriage by many kings and princes. Not wishing to endanger his political position by refusing any of them, and yet clearly unable to satisfy more than one, Pelias let it be known that he would marry Alcestis to the man who could yoke a wild boar and a lion to his chariot and drive them around the race-course. At this, Admetus King of Pherae summoned Apollo, whom Zeus had bound to him for one year as a herdsman, and asked: "Have I treated you with the respect due to your godhead?" "You have indeed," Apollo assented, "and I have shown my gratitude by making all your ewes drop twins." "As a final favour, then," pleaded Admetus, "pray help me to win Alcestis, by enabling me to fulfil Pelias's conditions." "I shall be pleased to do so," replied Apollo. Heracles lent him a hand with the taming of the wild beasts and presently Admetus was driving his chariot around the race-course at Iolcus, drawn by this savage team.

It is not known why Admetus omitted the customary sacrifice to Artemis before marrying Alcestis, but the goddess was quick enough to punish him. When, flushed with wine, anointed with essences and garlanded with flowers, he entered the bridal chamber that night, he recoiled in horror. No lovely naked bride awaited him on the marriage couch, but a tangled knot of hissing serpents. Admetus ran shouting for Apollo, who kindly intervened with Artemis on his behalf. The neglected sacrifice having been offered at once, all was well, Apollo even obtaining Artemis's promise that, when the day of Admetus's death came, he should be spared on condition that a member of his family died voluntarily for love of him.

This fatal day came sooner than Admetus expected. Hermes flew into the palace one morning and summoned him to Tartarus. General consternation prevailed; but Apollo gained a little time for Admetus by making the Three Fates drunk, and thus delayed the fatal scission of his life's thread. Admetus ran in haste to his old parents, clasped their knees, and begged each of them in turn to surrender him the butt-end of existence. Both roundly refused, saying that they still derived much enjoyment from life, and that he should be content with his appointed lot, like everyone else.

Then, for love of Admetus, Alcestis took poison and her ghost descended to Tartarus; but Persephone considered it an evil thing that a wife should die instead of a husband. "Back with you to the upper air!" she cried.

Some tell the tale differently. They say that Hades came in person to fetch Admetus and that, when he fled, Alcestis volunteered to take his place; but Herakles arrived unexpectedly with a new wild-olive club, and rescued her.

[Robert Graves, *The Greek Myths*, vol. 1
(Baltimore, MD, 1955), pp. 223–224.]

BIBLIOGRAPHY

✦

A classic work on the archetypal hero biography is Joseph Campbell's *The Hero with a Thousand Faces* (New York, 1949). *Mythology: The Voyage of the Hero* (New York, 1981), by David Leeming, is a collection of hero myths arranged according to a reworking of Campbell. *The Hero in Literature* (New York, 1969), edited by Victor Brombert, contains several essays on various kinds of literary heroes. Otto Rank's *The Myth of the Birth of the Hero* (New York, 1959) is a Freudian interpretation of the hero motif. Other useful works on the hero are Lewis R. Farnell's *Greek Hero Cults and Ideas of Immortality* (Oxford University Press, 1970) and Theodor Gaster's "Heroes" in *The Encyclopedia of Religion*, vol. 6, pp. 302–305. For an examination of the concept of a "new-age hero," see Carol Pearson's *The Hero Within: Six Archetypes We Live By* (San Francisco: HarperOne, 1998). For emphasis on the female hero, see Valerie Estelle Frankel's *From Girl to Goddess: The Heroine's Journey Through Myth and Legend* (McFarland, 2010) and Maureen Murdock's *The Heroine's Journey* (Shambala Press, 1990).

✦ Delphi omphalos

PART 4 ✦

PLACE
AND OBJECT
MYTHS

I n the world of myth, objects and places are endowed with properties of the sacred, the "other." This is logical because myths are religious and assume the existence of a meaningful cosmos that is literally charged with the informing energy of the creator. In the modern literary or psychological sense, places and objects in myth are symbols, and like other mythological motifs—the descent into the underworld, the Supreme Being, the femme fatale, and so on—they have archetypal significance. The student of mythology understands quickly that a tree, a garden, a castle, or a city is a material reality that expresses a particular place or culture and at the same time a connotative one that transcends place and time. The cross is at once the one on which Jesus hangs at Golgotha and the sacred tree on which Attis and Odin hang as "victims" who bridge the world of death and the world of eternity. The rock out of which Arthur pulls his sword is also the maternal rock that is Jesus' tomb or Mithras' birth cave or the altar on which Isaac is nearly sacrificed.

It is this connotative or archetypally symbolic nature of certain places and objects that makes them, like other archetypes, so useful to the creative artist. When the child hero of the fairy tale enters the dark wood, we know in the depths of our collective being exactly where he or she is. And we recognize the tree that stands alone in the center of the grove or garden. Even in our nonmythological age, the poet can, by making use of such symbols, awaken understandings that still sleep in our collective unconscious. As Mircea Eliade writes, "It is through symbols that man finds his way out of his particular situation and 'opens himself' to the general and the universal" (*The Sacred and the Profane*, p. 211). This process of "opening" is a common concern of the religious person and the creative artist.

The sacred places and objects considered briefly here are only a very few of many. To make the archetypal character of these places and objects clear, they have been arranged according to type.

THE WORLD OF AFTERLIFE

The belief in some sort of afterlife is ubiquitous. The human being finds the concept of total dissipation of self after death more difficult to accept than the notion of conscious existence after death. The Land of the Dead need not be pleasant; one of the earliest literary examples of an afterlife is the one recorded in Homer's *Odyssey*. The Land of the Dead that Odysseus visits is a place of darkness, sadness, and despair. Yet it is not primarily a place of punishment. The religious cultures that stress the struggle between good and evil in this world are the ones that divide the afterworld into areas of suffering and bliss. The Christian and Muslim concept of heaven and hell is only one example of this tendency. In the more mystical religions that stress the illusory nature of life, the afterlife may be a distinctly nonphysical realm, even a place where self loses its individual identity in a larger Self. In fact, such concepts as nirvana do not include a sense of place and are not properly thought of as myths of the afterlife, any more than is the Christian idea of the Kingdom of God. In one way or another, all afterlife myths, and even the lack of such myths, reflect cultural perceptions of this world.

Part of the need for belief in an afterlife can probably be traced to humanity's experience of the cycles of nature. As a functioning part of the organism called Earth, we do not like to be left out. The paths of the sun and the moon, the rhythms of the tides, the menstrual process, and the seasons all suggest a natural return of whatever is lost and lead naturally to the concept of life after death and ultimately some kind of restoration of life.

Perhaps an even more important factor is consciousness itself. Of all species, only humans are capable of conceiving of life as a complete process, including birth and death. It might be said that consciousness of the total life process—of life's beginning, middle, and end as a single plot—is our defining characteristic. Without that consciousness, existence itself—certainly our existence—is threatened. That being the case, it is perhaps ultimately impossible to conceive of the permanent loss of consciousness. Even if we do not go so far as to believe in the physical restoration of our individual lives, we tend to have difficulty conceiving of life without the consciousness by which we perceive it. The afterlife is an almost inevitable result. And it should be noted that more often than not, the souls in the various underworlds—the heavens and hells of world mythology—are nearly always, in death, freed from the restrictions on knowledge of the future that are necessarily associated with the physical life—with mortality itself. In the afterlife individual consciousness comes into its own as part of a larger consciousness that informs all things and all actions.

EGYPT: Osiris

Given its general emphasis on death and rebirth, it is not surprising that in ancient Egyptian civilization the afterlife is a predominant theme. Osiris, the resurrection god, is the central figure in the afterlife myth and in Egyptian mythology as a whole. To die and be properly prepared for the other life is to become one with Osiris in the underworld over which he rules. Thus, at a funeral, the name Osiris was attached to the name of the mummified dead person. In this new identity the individual could be reborn as a soul. Our sources for the Egyptian afterlife myth are the Pyramid and Coffin Texts and the *Book of the Dead*. R. T. Rundle Clark creates a single narrative from these sources.

> The ancients thought of death as the essential prelude to life. The two form a polarity; one is meaningless without the other, and they alternate in all spheres of nature—among men, animals, vegetation and stars. Death is a passing from one kind of time to another—from life yesterday to life tomorrow. What is in the Underworld belongs to death, but it is in a state of becoming, where the "form" or shape of things is given in which they will later "appear." Life can be seen, becoming is hidden. The chief instance of this great process is the sun, which must somehow be refitted or remoulded beneath the earth or beyond the visible sky. The place where these things happened was called by the Egyptians the Dat, which for convenience is called the Under-world. The Egyptians, however, do not seem to have given a fixed location to the Dat; it is usually under the earth but sometimes beyond the visible sky vault ("the belly of Nut") or in the waters which they imagined to extend everywhere beneath the land. The Dat is without light and beyond the reach of man. It is the place of the formation of the living out of the dead and the past, the true meeting-place of time before and after. Being mysterious, the anxieties of the living were easily transposed. If it was the source of new life, it was also the lair of demons who symbolized the forces of annihilation which threatened re-creation in the early and crucial stages. The demons must be kept at bay, so the gates of the Underworld are protected by still more grisly creatures, the tamed forces of chaos, represented by the authors of the Under-world literature as poisonous fire-spitting serpents, lions, lakes of fire, and dragons of mixed form.

Osiris is the spirit of becoming, but in the Dat he has largely lost his accidental characteristics. He is no longer the Dead King, Fertility Daimon, or Inundation Spirit but the personification of the coming into being of all things. He is generalized as the secret of what lies beneath the surface and is represented as a mummy figure without any distinguishing marks, the symbol which the Egyptians called "irw"—"form." He is the embodiment of the positive aspect of the Dat. A journey to the Underworld is a descent either to the recumbent Osiris or to view the various stages through which he has to go to be reconstituted.

During the Middle Kingdom the Underworld became a much more frightening place than had been imagined by the authors of the Pyramid Texts. It was divided into sections, each of which was guarded by fearful monsters. The earliest of the special works which deal with these horrors must date from before the Twelfth Dynasty. One of them, the so-called Book of the Two Ways, is a guide through the subterranean paths to the places where the sun and moon are reconstituted, apparently in the far north beneath the world axis. The second is Spell 336 of the Coffin Texts, which divides up the Underworld journey into a series of obstacles or gates which must be passed through by means of magical formulae. In these early Underworld texts the journey is made by the soul, but in the developed works which appear on the tombs of the New Kingdom, the theme is the night journey of the sun. As the latter goes through the subterranean ways it lights up the denizens of the dark. It has been the custom of recent commentators to dismiss these sombre productions as trivial expressions of fear and deficient imagination. This is to misunderstand their intention and overlooks the fact that they remained popular until almost the end of the civilization. When the sun passes along, it illumines all the forms which must be in the Underworld and belong to the past or future. As an imaginative exercise, it is also a journey into the inner reaches of the mind and an attempt to penetrate to the reality which underlies phenomena. The temptation to people the darkness with the unredeemed dead has appealed to nearly every culture—witness the Underworlds of Homer and Virgil. The Egyptians, too, thought it a place destitute of light and hope, the domain of unregulated power, phantoms, and terror. Nevertheless, the Underworld is one of the abiding symbols of mankind. Life must come from elsewhere and revival of the heavenly

bodies must take place beyond human knowledge. The Underworld
may be a limbo or a hell, but it is also the source of new life.

[R. T. Rundle Clark, *Myth and Symbol in Ancient Egypt*
(London, 1959, 1978), pp. 165–167.]

GREECE AND ROME: Lands of the Dead

In Homer's *Odyssey* (Book XI) Odysseus visits the Land of the Dead, providing
us with the most complete vision of the Greek concept of the afterlife. The
great hero Achilles has become lord over this land, but he reminds the visiting
Odysseus that life in any form is better than death: "Would that I were on earth
a menial, bound to some insubstantial man who must pinch and scrape to keep
alive! Life so were better than King of Kings among these dead men who have
had their day and died" (*Odyssey*, trans. Lawrence, 165). The Land of the Dead
is a place marked by emptiness and despair, a land in which the shades of
heroes wander aimlessly, longing for a life lost to them forever.

But another view of the afterlife, which Homer also knew, emerged in the
Greek world. In Book IV of the *Odyssey* we hear of the Elysian Field, where
Menelaos, as the husband of a daughter of Zeus (Helen), will be privileged to
spend his afterlife:

> The Deathless Ones [will] carry you to the Elysian plain, the place
> beyond the world, where is the fair-haired Rhadamanthus and where
> the lines of life run smoothest for mortal men. In that land there is
> no snow-fall, nor much winter, nor any storm of rain: but from the
> river of earth the west wind ever sings soft and thrillingly to re-
> animate the souls of men.
>
> [*The Odyssey of Homer*, trans. T.E. Lawrence (New York and Oxford,
> Oxford University Press, 1991), Book IV, pp. 60–61.]

Gradually this underworld, in which Rhadamanthos, a former king of Crete and
son of Zeus and Europa, was to become a judge, would emerge as a place where the
dead would be punished or rewarded for their lives on earth. This is the familiar
classical Hades, reached when the river Acheron, the River of Woe, is crossed by
means of Charon's ferry. Other rivers, such as Lethe, the River of Forgetfulness,
and the mysterious Styx, must also be crossed. Hades is presided over by the brother
of Zeus, who is himself called Hades. The gates of Hades are guarded by the
monster Cerberus. The reader will find a comic version of Hades in Aristophanes'
The Frogs, where Herakles describes the underworld to the god Dionysos.

The Roman Virgil's epic the *Aeneid* (Book VI) contains a vision of the afterlife
that places emphasis on reward and punishment. It is an extension of the two

visions of the underworld provided by Homer, the *Aeneid* itself being in a sense a Roman version of the *Iliad* and the *Odyssey*. The Roman afterlife reflects the Roman view of an orderly, law-abiding culture dominated by a sense of justice.

In Virgil's story Aeneas travels under the guidance of the Virgin Sybil (as he and the Virgin Beatrice will guide Dante in the *Divine Comedy*), allowing us to share his experience of an underworld in which sins are appropriately punished and virtues rewarded. The next stage in Western civilization's view of the afterlife is found in the Bible.

NATIVE NORTH AMERICA (Hopi): The Kachinas

Nearly every Native American tribe has its highly complex version of the after-life. One such version is this Hopi Indian myth as told to Alice Marriott and Carol Rachlin by two Hopi "informants" who, given the Hopi tendency to be secretive with outsiders about religious matters, were willing to reveal only a part of the story. The context of this myth includes the land of the good spirits (*Kachinas*), whom the single-hearted (i.e., good) Hopis will join in death, and the Hopi hell, known as the "Country of the Two Hearts" (two hearts signify-ing falseness—a deviation from single-heartedness), where evil people go.

> The San Francisco Peaks stand north of Flagstaff, Arizona, and for many centuries they have been the most sacred places known to the Hopis, except parts of the Grand Canyon.
>
> Within the San Francisco Peaks, the kachinas[1] live. They have a very beautiful world. The corn grows thickly every year; the squashes and melons grow at every joint of the vines; nobody knows how many different kinds of beans the kachinas have. There are lakes of water—there are springs, too, like those on the mesas—but there are really lakes of water, where the cattails grow tall and sweet.
>
> The hills are covered with all the plants the Hopis use: wild spin-ach and wild potatoes for food, rabbit brush and yucca for baskets, and all the plants the Hopis need to make dyes for their basketry.
>
> Highest up of all grow the sacred trees, blue spruce and juniper and mountain mahogany and piñon. The kachinas can go out when-ever they like and gather everything they need for their ceremonies.

---

[1] A kachina may be one of the forces of nature: life, death, fire, flood, or famine. A kachina may be the spirit of a much-loved ancestor who, as the Hopis say, has "passed beyond." A kachina may be man dancing to impersonate one of these spirits. Or a kachina, as is most frequently said, may be what the Hopis call a "kachin tihu"—a doll carved and painted to represent a spirit. These dolls are given to children as a combination toy-catechism book, with which they play but from which they also learn the essentials of their religion.

During the growing months, from February to July, the kachinas live in the villages with the Hopis. Nobody can see them, except when they come out of the kivas to dance in the plaza, but the Hopis know the kachinas are there, and they feel that they and their crops are safe.

Late in July, the kachinas go home to the San Francisco Peaks. They dance for the people one last time, and give presents to all the children. Then the kachinas go over the edge of the mesa, and you can see the tall rain columns marching across the desert to the San Francisco Peaks.

Naturally, every Hopi wishes to join the spirits of his loved ones who have passed beyond. To that end he keeps his heart pure and is kind and generous to other people.

When a bad person—one who is known as ka-Hopi, or not Hopi—dies, his fate is very different. The Two Hearts, or witches, take him by the hand as soon as the breath is out of his body, and they lead him away to their own country. The country of the Two Hearts is as bad as they are themselves. You may live in a village all your life with a Two Heart, and the only way that you can tell he is a witch is that the people in his family keep dying off. Every time a Two Heart works his wickedness and hurts somebody else, he must give up one of his own kinfolk.

The country of the Two Hearts is a desert. It is dry, dry, and it has no water holes. The ka-Hopi must crawl through it on his hands and knees; when he is too weak, he crawls on his belly. Sometimes the ka-Hopi has a vision of someone he loved and he begs and pleads for water, for shade, for rest. But no matter how much his loved one wants to help the ka-Hopi, he cannot do so.

That is what happens to Hopis who do wrong, and who are self-ish and cruel. No Hopi wants to suffer that way.

There was a young couple who married, many years ago. Naturally, the husband went to live in his wife's mother's house. At first everything went very well, but then the husband began to feel nervous. He felt as if someone were looking at him all the time. He glanced here and there, over his shoulder, up at the sky, down at the earth, but he could see nobody.

They lived on the very top of the mesa, and down at its foot was the old cemetery. When people were wrapped in their blankets, their faces covered over with cloud cotton, and they were buried, their relatives smashed pottery bowls on their graves, and gave away everything the dead ones had owned. Nobody ever went near the cemetery at any other time, unless he took the burro trails from the spring that led past its outer edge. Only Two Hearts went there, to gather more power to hurt people.

Presently the young husband noticed that his wife's relatives were dying off. They were young people, hard workers, and lived good lives, but they would sicken and die, leaving their children to be taken care of by the women of the children's clans.

The young wife did not mourn aloud—that is not the Hopi way. But often in the night her husband woke to find his wife's body shaking with sobs, at his side. When the husband asked her what was wrong, the wife told him that she was crying because they had no children. That was true, although they loved each other very much, and wanted children, and tried to have them.

This went on for a long time—about four years. The husband grew more and more disturbed. Once he went back to his mother's house, in another village, but his wife followed him, crying and begging him to come home, so at last he gave up and went with her.

One night it was getting dark, and the wife said to her husband, "I wonder where my mother is? I don't think she should be out so late."

"I don't know where she's gone," the husband answered. "I've been in the fields all day. How would I know what you women are doing?"

"Well, I wish you'd go and look for her," his wife said.

"Not till I eat my dinner," the husband answered.

She gave him beans boiled with mutton, and some baked corn, and a cup of coffee. When he had finished he got up and said, "That was a good meal. I'll go and look for your mother now."

"All right," said his wife. "Will you take the water canteen with you and fill it at the spring? I'm almost out of water."

The husband grumbled a little, but he finally took the flat-sided canteen and slung it with a strap across his forehead, the way a woman would carry it. It was dark, and none of the other men would see him carrying water the way a woman would.

The young man climbed down the track toward the spring, feeling his way very carefully, because the pebbles were rough under his moccasins. He reached the spring safely, and held the canteen under its trickle until the jar was full. Then he slung it across his forehead and down his back, and started back toward the village to look for his wife's mother. He thought she might be visiting some relatives.

Just as he reached the edge of the old cemetery, something struck him in the back, and he felt legs locked around his hips.

"I'm going to take you," a voice hissed in his ear. The man couldn't tell if it was a man's or a woman's. "I'm going to take you right now, away from here. All of us Two Hearts are holding a meeting, and it's my turn, to bring in a new member. I'm going to take you to the Two Heart kiva and make you one of us. If I don't, they'll kill me."

"You can't do that," the man answered. "I'm a kachina priest, and the kachinas will protect me."

"I'm going to ride you like a mule," the Two Heart hissed. It began beating him with a clump of yucca. "Do what I tell you and go where I tell you to go. I've captured you, and now you'll be one of us."

"The kachinas will protect me," the man insisted.

Again the Two Heart beat him with the yucca. "Do what I say," it insisted.

The man struggled again, and tried to throw the Two Heart off, but in vain. It only beat him more, and at last he gave up and followed its directions to the Two Heart kiva. In his heart he was praying to the kachinas, telling them he had tried to be a good man and take care of his family, that he was studying to be their priest, and that he believed that their power was stronger than that of the Two Hearts.

At last the wall of the mesa loomed in front of them. The Two Heart slipped from the man's back, and knocked four times against the rock. It opened in front of them. Inside, the man saw many people he knew sitting in council. Outside, in the dim light from the fire in the kiva, when he turned his head, he saw his wife's mother. Between the man and his mother-in-law stood the Sun God kachina, the strongest of all the good kachinas.

"Go home to your wife," said the Sun God. "You will always be safe."

The husband, with his water canteen still on his back, went home. "I couldn't find your mother anywhere," was all that he said as he put it down.

They went to bed, then, and late at night they heard the door open and the old lady come in. She slipped into her own bed very quietly, but they knew she was there. The husband prayed to the kachinas all night; he dared not sleep with a Two Heart in the house.

From that day on, the old woman withered and shriveled. The younger members of the family grew round and strong and healthy again, but she wasted away. The only time she spoke she cried for water, but when they gave it to her she could not swallow it, not even when they tried to drop it into her mouth with a yucca blade. Within the year she died.

[Alice Marriott and Carol K. Rachlin, *American Indian Mythology* (New York, 1968), pp. 233–237.]

THE MOUNTAIN

The sacred mountain is the *mons veneris* of Mother Earth. It is the cosmic center on which the temple or the city is placed. It is the spot, nearest to the supreme sky god, where the word—the cosmic energy—can be received by Earth. It is Mount Parnassus, where the oracle of Delphi delivers dire predictions. It is the hill on which Athena builds her acropolis and temple in Athens. It is the mountain on which Moses receives the Ten Commandments, the mountain on which Jesus is "transfigured" (Mark 9). In India it is the Golden Mountain, Meru— the *axis mundi* where Shiva sits, the place from which the sacred rivers such as Ganga (the Ganges) flow.

INDIA: Mount Meru

Mount Meru (Mahâmeru, the cosmic mountain) began with its base at the center of an earth island known as Jambudvîpa (rose-apple tree island). Meru, or Mahâmeru, was shaped like a banyan tree, smaller at its base and larger above. In the upper regions of Mount Meru were the regions for the gods and their respective palaces (lokas). All had names—Brahmâloka, Indraloka or Svarga, Vaikuntha (this name was also given to the watery realm where Vishnu rested on the serpent Ananta, or Śesha), Kailâsa (for Śiva), Mahodaya (for Kubera), Śraddhâvatî (for Varuna), and so on.

Jambudvîpa was either the island at the center of a series of concentric islands or the first of seven donut-shaped islands with Meru at the center; in either case, Meru was at its center. Each island had an ocean filled with a different liquid surrounding it (salt, sugar-cane juice, wine, ghee, buttermilk, milk, and sweet water). Some sages and kings were said to have wandered until they reached the Himâlayas and then finally Mount Meru. Others needed divine transport to reach it. Not only could the occasional human reach Meru, but also many other beings: animals (some divine like Hanuman and others who were just companions or vehicles of the gods), semi-divine beings (apsaras and gandharvas), and demons—even armies of them could invade Meru.

[George M. Williams, *Handbook of Hindu Mythology*
(New York: Oxford University Press, 2003), p. 40.]

THE CITY

The city, whether Troy, Jerusalem, Thebes, or Uruk, is humanity's stand against chaos. Like so many other constructs in this world, it is feminine in nature—a representation of nourishment and protection, the gateways of which must be guarded against potential invaders. The city is our "mother," and her fall or corruption is among the most moving of tragedies.

GREECE AND ROME: Troy

Virgil describes the fall of Troy in the *Aeneid*. The Greek Sinon has convinced the Trojans that the giant wooden horse left outside their gates by the Greeks is a peace offering. Despite the warnings of Laocoön, a priest of Apollo, who is killed by serpents sent from the sea by Poseidon, the Trojans receive the horse into their city. It is filled with Greek warriors. When they take the city, order gives way to chaos, experienced here through the eyes of Aeneas, the Trojan who will escape to found the "new Troy," Rome.

> The horse emitted men; gladly they dropped. . . .
> . . .
> Into the darkened city, buried deep
> In sleep and wine, they made their way,
> Cut the few sentries down,
> Let in their fellow soldiers at the gate,
> And joined their combat companies as planned.
> That time of night it was when the first sleep,
> Gift of the gods, begins for ill mankind,
> Arriving gradually, delicious rest.
> In sleep, in dream, Hector appeared to me,
> Gaunt with sorrow, streaming tears, all torn—
> As by the violent car on his death day—
> And black with bloody dust,
> His puffed-out feet cut by the rawhide thongs.
> Ah god, the look of him! How changed
> From that proud Hector who returned to Troy

Wearing Achilles' armor, or that one
Who pitched the torches on Danaan ships;
His beard all filth, his hair matted with blood,
Showing the wounds, the many wounds, received
Outside his father's city walls. I seemed
Myself to weep and call upon the man
In grieving speech, brought from the depth of me:
"Light of Dardania, best hope of Troy,
What kept you from us for so long, and where?
From what far place, O Hector, have you come,
Long, long awaited? After so many deaths
Of friends and brothers, after a world of pain
For all our folk and all our town, at last,
Boneweary, we behold you! What has happened
To ravage your serene face? Why these wounds?"
He wasted no reply on my poor questions
But heaved a great sigh from his chest and said:
"Ai! Give up and go, child of the goddess,
Save yourself, out of these flames. The enemy
Holds the city walls, and from her height
Troy falls in ruin. Fatherland and Priam
Have their due; if by one hand our towers
Could be defended, by this hand, my own,
They would have been. Her holy things, her gods
Of hearth and household Troy commends to you.
Accept them as companions of your days;
Go find for them the great walls that one day
You'll dedicate, when you have roamed the sea."
As he said this, he brought out from the sanctuary
Chaplets and Vesta, Lady of the Hearth,
With her eternal fire.
. . . The ancient city falls, after dominion
Many long years. In windrows on the streets,
In homes, on solemn porches of the gods,
Dead bodies lie. And not alone the Trojans
Pay the price with their heart's blood; at times
Manhood returns to fire even the conquered
And Danaan conquerors fall. Grief everywhere,
Everywhere terror, and all shapes of death.
That was the end

Of Priam's age, the doom that took him off,
With Troy in flames before his eyes, his towers
Headlong fallen—he that in other days
Had ruled in pride so many lands and peoples,
The power of Asia.
On the distant shore
The vast trunk headless lies without a name.

[Virgil, *Aeneid*, trans. Robert Fitzgerald
(New York, 1983), pp. 40–52.]

ISRAEL-PALESTINE: Jerusalem

Jerusalem has traditionally been the "beloved of God," sacred to Christians
and Muslims as well as to Jews. For some, the holy city takes on a purely metaphorical rather than physical form—the "heavenly Jerusalem" or the "new
Jerusalem," which might be anywhere or might simply be a phrase to describe
the newly discovered Kingdom of God. The feminine nature of Jerusalem is
clear in the Old Testament's Lamentations of Jeremiah, written perhaps during
the exile of the Jews in Babylon.

How doth the city sit solitary, that was full of people! how is she become as a
widow! she that was great among the nations, and princess among the provinces,
how is she become tributary!

2 She weepeth sore in the night, and her tears are on her cheeks: among all her
   lovers she hath none to comfort her: all her friends have dealt treacherously
   with her, they are become her enemies.

3 Judah is gone into captivity because of affliction, and because of great servi-
   tude: she dwelleth among the heathen, she findeth no rest: all her persecutors
   overtook her between the straits.

4 The ways of Zion do mourn, because none come to the solemn feasts: all
   her gates are desolate: her priests sigh, her virgins are afflicted, and she is in
   bitterness.

5 Her adversaries are the chief, her enemies prosper; for the Lord hath afflicted
   her for the multitude of her transgressions: her children are gone into captivity
   before the enemy.

6 And from the daughter of Zion all her beauty is departed: her princes are
   become like harts that find no pasture, and they are gone without strength
   before the pursuer.

7 Jerusalem remembered in the days of her affliction and of her miseries all her pleasant things that she had in the days of old, when her people fell into the hand of the enemy, and none did help her: the adversaries saw her, and did mock at her sabbaths.

8 Jerusalem hath grievously sinned; therefore she is removed: all that honoured her despise her, because they have seen her nakedness: yea, she sigheth, and turneth backward.

9 Her filthiness is in her skirts; she remembereth not her last end; therefore she came down wonderfully: she had no comforter. O Lord, behold my affliction: for the enemy hath magnified himself.

10 The adversary hath spread out his hand upon all her pleasant things: for she hath seen that the heathen entered into her sanctuary, whom thou didst command that they should not enter into thy congregation.

11 All her people sigh, they seek bread; they have given their pleasant things for meat to relieve the soul: see, O Lord, and consider; for I am become vile.

12 Is it nothing to you, all ye that pass by? behold, and see if there be any sorrow like unto my sorrow, which is done unto me, wherewith the Lord hath afflicted me in the day of his fierce anger.

13 From above hath he sent fire into my bones, and it prevaileth against them: he hath spread a net for my feet, he hath turned me back: he hath made me desolate and faint all the day.

14 The yoke of my transgressions is bound by his hand: they are wreathed, and come up upon my neck: he hath made my strength to fall, the Lord hath delivered me into their hands, from whom I am not able to rise up.

15 The Lord hath trodden under foot all my mighty men in the midst of me: he hath called an assembly against me to crush my young men: the Lord hath trodden the virgin, the daughter of Judah, as in a wine-press.

16 For these things I weep; mine eye, mine eye runneth down with water, because the comforter that should relieve my soul is far from me: my children are desolate, because the enemy prevailed.

17 Zion spreadeth forth her hands, and there is none to comfort her; the Lord hath commanded concerning Jacob, that his adversaries should be round about him: Jerusalem is as a menstruous woman among them.

18 The Lord is righteous; for I have rebelled against his commandment: hear, I pray you, all people, and behold my sorrow: my virgins and my young men are gone into captivity.

19 I called for my lovers, but they deceived me: my priests and mine elders gave up the ghost in the city, while they sought their meat to relieve their souls.

20 Behold, O Lord; for I am in distress: my bowels are troubled; mine heart is turned within me; for I have grievously rebelled: abroad the sword bereaveth, at home there is as death.

21 They have heard that I sigh; there is none to comfort me: all mine enemies have heard of my trouble; they are glad that thou hast done it: thou wilt bring the day that thou hast called, and they shall be like unto me.

22 Let all their wickedness come before thee; and do unto them, as thou hast done unto me for all my transgressions: for my sighs are many, and my heart is faint.

[Lamentations of Jeremiah 1.]

GREECE: Delphi

Although a sacred precinct rather than a city, Delphi, like the great cities and temples of the ancient world, is the navel or omphalos—the very center—of the world. The conical stone in Apollo's temple at Delphi is the navel that gives significance to Earth herself. The chasm in the earth at the sacred precinct gave access to the very womb of Mother Earth.

But the most celebrated of the Grecian oracles was that of Apollo at Delphi, a city built on the slopes of Parnassus in Phocis.

It had been observed at a very early period that the goats feeding on Parnassus were thrown into convulsions when they approached a certain long deep cleft in the side of the mountain. This was owing to a peculiar vapor arising out of the cavern, and one of the goatherds was induced to try its effects upon himself. Inhaling the intoxicating air, he was affected in the same manner as the cattle had been, and the inhabitants of the surrounding country, unable to explain the circumstance, imputed the convulsive ravings to which he gave utterance while under the power of the exhalations to a divine inspiration. The fact was speedily circulated widely, and a temple was erected on the spot. The prophetic influence was at first variously attributed to the goddess Earth, to Neptune, Themis, and others, but it was at length assigned to Apollo, and to him alone. A priestess was appointed whose office it was to inhale the hallowed air, and who was named the Pythia. She was prepared for this duty by previous ablution at the fountain of Castalia, and being crowned with laurel, was seated upon a tripod similarly adorned, which was placed over the chasm whence the divine afflatus proceeded. Her inspired words while thus situated were interpreted by the priests.

[Thomas Bulfinch, *Bulfinch's Mythology: The Age of Fable* (New York, 1962), p. 337.]

THE TEMPLE

The temple is a microcosmic version of the city. It, too, is feminine, representative also of the Mother Mountain, the maternal womb into which the hero enters and plants his seed. The great cathedrals of Europe are the body of Christ on the horizontal plane and a representation of the cavernous and monumental Mother Mountain on the vertical. Often named after Mary, the Christian version of the Great Mother, they are architectural depictions of the union of the hero and the mother-wife—Mother Church, the church as the bride of the Lamb. The symbols within the church building reinforce this theme: the feminine font into which the pascal candle is plunged on Holy Saturday, the feminine altar-tomb-throne that is the place of the lover-god's sacrifice. The pyramids of Egypt, the Ziggurat of Babylon at the top of which the king marries the Goddess, the towering *gopuram* of the Tamilnad temples to Shiva and Vishnu and the Goddess, the Chapel Perilous where Galahad rediscovers the blood vessel, the Holy Grail—all are symbols of the feminine cosmic mound, the primeval mound of Earth from which life itself is born.

EUROPE: The Chapel Perilous

The Chapel Perilous is perhaps related to the Seat (or Siege) Perilous. It is one form of the "Mount of Joy," the maternal place where the womb symbol and later Christian symbol called the Holy Grail was kept. The virginal *puer aeternus* Galahad may sit in the chapel in his quest for the Holy Grail, just as over the main doors of so many cathedrals the Christ Child as king is depicted seated on the lap of Mary, who thus, like the altar and the church itself, becomes the feminine throne for the seed-bearing hero. The Chapel Perilous appears in several versions of the Grail myth, not always in connection with Galahad.

Students of the Grail romances will remember that in many of the versions the hero—sometimes it is a heroine—meets with a strange and terrifying adventure in a mysterious Chapel, an adventure which, we are given to understand, is fraught with extreme peril to life. The details vary: sometimes there is a Dead Body laid on the altar; sometimes a Black Hand extinguishes the tapers; there are strange and threatening voices, and the general impression is that this is an adventure in which supernatural, and evil, forces are engaged.

Such an adventure befalls Gawain on his way to the Grail castle. He is overtaken by a terrible storm, and coming to a Chapel, standing at a crossways in the middle of a forest, enters for shelter. The altar is bare, with no cloth, or covering, nothing is thereon but a great golden candlestick with a tall taper burning within it. Behind the altar is a window, and as Gawain looks a Hand, black and hideous, comes through the window, and extinguishes the taper, while a voice makes lamentation loud and dire, beneath which the very building rocks. Gawain's horse shies for terror, and the knight, making the sign of the Cross, rides out of the Chapel, to find the storm abated, and the great wind fallen. Thereafter the night was calm and clear.

[Jessie L. Weston, From Ritual to Romance: An Account
of the Holy Grail from Ancient Ritual to Christian Symbol
(New York, 1920, 1957), p. 175.]

THE GENITALS

As we have seen in the myth of the dying god, the loss of genitals is directly associated with the god's role as seed planted in the earth-womb of the Great Goddess. The conjunction of genitals in this case, as in the case of the many Indian depictions of sex acts between Shiva and Parvati—his feminine soul, or *Shakti* (anima)—and between Vishnu and his spouse, is a symbol of union or wholeness. The Shiva phallus, or *lingam* (often painted blood red), standing within the temple inner sanctum, the *yoni* or Great Goddess vulva, is the iconographic correlative of the essence of the Shivite cult. It is related to the ritual of the flower-bedecked maypole or such mythological images as the Christian *Pietà*, in which the mythic son-lover is joined with the mother-wife after the Crucifixion. The archetypal image of Arthur's sword in the rock takes another form in the little stone *lingam-yoni* combinations that are to be found in and around Shiva temples.

GREECE: Tiresias

The rather bizarre story of Tiresias must have its roots in the archetype of the Androgyny, the person of both sexes who becomes another version of the yin-yang/lingam-yoni unity, which carries with it the powers of prophecy.

(See Ovid's version of the story in the collection of miscellaneous stories of the gods and lesser spirits in Part II of this book.)

NATIVE NORTH AMERICA (APACHE): The Vagina Girls

This Apache tale is almost certainly a patriarchal myth of the taming of the female powers associated in other traditions—India's, for example—with the destructive nature of the Great Goddess of death and rebirth.

Long ago, nearer to the beginning of this world than now, a malevolent and powerful being named Kicking Monster roamed the earth. Kicking Monster had four daughters who were in the shape of women, but in reality they were vaginas. They were the only beings on earth that possessed vaginas, though they lived in a house—all four of them—that itself had vaginas hanging on the walls. But the vagina girls had legs and other body parts and could walk around.

Not surprisingly, knowledge of the vagina girls' existence spread far and wide, and many men of the Haisndayin, the people who came from below, eagerly traveled the road to their house. But as they approached, they were ambushed by Kicking Monster and kicked into the house, from which they never returned.

Then a young hero, little more than a boy and called Killer-of-Enemies, already known for ridding the world of many monsters, heard about this alluring snare and decided to set things right. He outwitted Kicking Monster, slipping past him and entering the house, where he was set upon by the four vagina girls, hungry for intercourse.

Before they could lavish their attentions on him, Killer-of-Enemies asked them the whereabouts of all the men whom the monster had kicked into the house. The girls replied that they had eaten the men, which they liked to do. And they reached lustfully out for the boy hero.

Killer-of-Enemies shouted for them to stop: "Stay away from me! That's no way to use a vagina." He knew that these four vaginas yearning for him were lined with teeth, with which he too would be chewed and devoured.

He told the vagina girls that first, before any love-making could take place, he had to give them some medicine made from four kinds of berries. It was sour medicine, he warned them, and unlike anything they had tasted before, but it would make their vaginas sweet. Tantalized, the girls ate the medicine and liked it very much.

Its sourness puckered up their mouths so much that they could not chew with their teeth, but could only swallow. Indeed, it made them feel just as though Killer-of Enemies were thrusting into them, and they were bedazzled with ecstasy.

And the medicine not only fooled the vagina girls, but destroyed their teeth altogether. So it was that the boy-hero tamed the toothed vaginas so that they would always thereafter behave in a proper manner.

[David A. Leeming and Jake Page, *Goddess* (Oxford University Press, 1994), pp. 126–127.]

THE STONE

In myth, the stone is often a place of sacrifice. Again, the symbolism seems to be maternal, or at least feminine. Arthur proves his powers by pulling the phallic sword from the maternal rock. Theseus does the same by removing the sword and sandals from under the rock.

ASIA MINOR (PHRYGIA): The Agdos Rock

The Phrygian earth religion, in which Cybele, the Great Goddess, is central, contains this tale in which the mother is identified with the rock. This myth also makes use of the genital archetype and is a virgin birth story.

The Agdos rock—so the story runs—had assumed the shape of the Great Mother. [The Phrygian sky-god, Papas] . . . fell asleep upon it. As he slept, or as he strove with the goddess, his semen fell upon the rock. In the tenth month the Agdos rock bellowed and brought forth an untamable, savage being, of twofold sex and twofold lust, named Agdistis. With cruel joy Agdistis plundered, murdered and destroyed whatever it chose, cared for neither gods nor men, and held nothing mightier on earth or in heaven than itself. The gods often consulted together as to how this insolence could be tamed. When they all hesitated, Dionysos took over the task. There was a certain spring to which Agdistis came to assuage its thirst when it was overheated with sport and hunting. Dionysos turned the springwater into wine. Agdistis came running up, impelled by thirst, greedily drank the strange liquor and fell perforce into deepest sleep. Dionysos was on the watch. He adroitly made a cord of hair, and with it bound Agdistis's male member to a tree. Awakened from its drunkenness, the monster sprang up and castrated itself by its own strength. The earth drank the flowing blood, and with it the torn-off parts. From these at once arose a fruit-bearing tree: an almond-tree or— according to another tale—a pomegranate-tree. Nana, the daughter of the king or river-god Sangarios (Nana is another name for the great goddess of Asia Minor), saw the beauty of the fruit, plucked it and hid it in her lap. The fruit vanished, and Nana conceived a child of it. Her father imprisoned her, as a woman deflowered, and condemned her to death by starvation. The Great Mother fed her on fruits and on the foods of the gods. She gave birth to a little boy. Sangarios had the child left out in the open to perish. A he-goat tended the suckling, who, when he was found, was fed upon a liquor called "he-goat's milk." He was named Attis, either because attis is Lydian for a handsome boy or because attagus was Phrygian for a he-goat.

[C. Kerenyi, *The Gods of the Greeks*
(London, 1951), pp. 89–90.]

AUSTRALIA (ABORIGINAL): Erathipa

This fertility stone has a feminine opening on one side.

The tribes of central Australia have . . . a huge rock known as Erathipa which has an opening in one side from which the souls of the children imprisoned in it watch for a woman to pass by so that they may be reborn in her. When women who do not want children go near the rock, they pretend to be old, and walk as if leaning on a stick, crying: "Don't come to me, I am an old woman!" . . .

The idea implicit in all these rites is that certain stones have the power to make sterile women fruitful, either because of the spirits of the ancestors that dwell in them, or because of their shape (the pregnant woman, "woman stone"), or because of their origin (svayaṁm bhū, "autogenesis").

[Mircea Eliade, *Patterns in Comparative Religion*
(New York, 1958), pp. 220–221.]

THE TREE

The roots of the sacred tree extend to the depths of the earth, and its branches reach to the heavens. It brings together the temporal and the eternal. Furthermore, it is a symbol of life and of wholeness. The cross of the Crucifixion is a tree; the Buddha found enlightenment under the Bodhi Tree; Osiris was found in a tree; Adonis was born of a tree. Many cultures possess world trees or axle trees, which, like temples and primeval mounds, are the center of the world.

INDIA: The Cosmic Tree

In the ancient Upanishads the cosmic tree, Asvattha, represents Brahman itself, the cosmos in full bloom. In the *Bhagavad-Gita* it incorporates the world of humanity.

Indian tradition, according to its earliest writings, represents the cosmos in the form of a giant tree. This idea is defined fairly formally in the Upanisads: the Universe is an inverted tree, burying its roots in the sky and spreading its branches over the whole earth. (It is not impossible that this image was suggested by the downpouring of the sun's rays. Cf. ṚgVeda: "The branches grow towards what is low, the roots are on high, that its rays may descend upon us!") The Katha-Upanisad describes it like this: "This eternal Aśvattha, whose roots rise on high, and whose branches grow low, is the pure [śukram], is the Brahman, is what we call the Non-Death. All the worlds rest in it!" The aśvattha tree here represents the clearest possible manifestation of Brahman in the Cosmos, represents, in other words, creation as a descending movement. Other texts from the Upanisads restate still more clearly this notion of the cosmos as a tree. "Its branches are the ether, the air, fire, water, earth," etc. The natural elements are the expression of this "Brahman whose name is Aśvattha."

In the Bhagavad-Gitā, the cosmic tree comes to express not only the universe, but also man's condition in the world: "It is said that there is an indestructible tree, its roots above, its branches below, its leaves the hymns of the Veda; whoever knows it knows the Veda also. Its branches increase in height and depth, growing on the gunas; its buds are the objects of sense; its roots spread out from below, bound to actions in the world of men. In this world one cannot perceive the shape, nor the end, nor the beginning, nor the expanse of it. With the strong weapon of renunciation, one must first cut down this aśvattha with its powerful roots, and then seek the place from which one never returns. . . ." The whole universe, as well as the experience of man who lives in it and is not detached from it, are here symbolized by the cosmic tree. By everything in himself which corresponds with the cosmos or shares in its life, man merges into the same single and immense manifestation of Brahman. "To cut the tree at its roots" means to withdraw man from the cosmos, to cut him off from the things of sense and the fruits of his actions. We find the same motif of detachment from the life of the cosmos, of withdrawal into oneself and recollection as man's only way of transcending himself and becoming free, in a text from the Mahābhārata. "Sprung from the Unmanifested, arising from it as only support, its trunk is bodhi, its inward cavities the channels of the sense, the great elements its branches, the objects of the senses its leaves, its fair flowers good and evil [dharmādharmav], pleasure and pain the consequent fruits. This eternal Brahma-tree [brahma-vrksa] is the source of life [abjīva] for all beings. . . . Having cut asunder and broken the tree with the weapon of gnosis [jananēna], and thenceforth taking pleasure in the Spirit, none returneth thither again.

[Mircea Eliade, *Patterns in Comparative Religion* (New York, 1958), pp. 273–274.]

CHINA: Fusang

Fusang (literally meaning "Leaning Mulberry") is a world-tree in the east where the ten suns stay, bathe, and rise. It is also known as Fumu (Leaning Tree.)

Fusang is one of the most famous Chinese world-trees. According to texts from Shanhaijing, Fusang grew in the water of the Tang Valley. The tree was very high; its trunk reached 300 li (100 miles) in height, and its leaves were like the leaves of the mustard plant. The ten suns stayed on the tree and bathed in the valley. Nine of them stayed on the lower branches of Fusang while the sun that was going to rise stayed on its top branch. The ten suns rose from the Fusang tree one by one. As soon as one sun came back from crossing the sky, another sun went up. Each sun was carried by a crow. In an account from Huainanzi, the sun is said to rise from the Yang Valley (the same as the Tang Valley) and be bathed in the Xian Pool. When the sun swept past Fusang, it was called First Dawn. When it climbed up Fusang and was prepared to begin its journey, it was called Daybreak.

In some later versions, Fusang is described as a large tree in the east. Its top reached heaven while its trunk curved down and reached the Three Springs of the earth. However, according to Shizhouji (A Record of Ten Mythic Islets, said to have been written during the Han dynasty but probably written in the Six Dynasties era), Fusang seemed to be not only a kind of tree but also a mythical place that was located in the middle of the Blue Sea. It was thousands of miles in circumference with a palace for an immortal built on it. Fusang trees grew here. Their leaves were like those of the mulberry, and they also produced the same fruit. The biggest one of them was more than 100,000 feet high and 2,000 wei wide (one wei is equal to the diameter of a circle created by a person's arms). Since the trees grew in pairs, every pair of them shared the same root and their trunks leaned toward each other; therefore they received the name "Leaning Mulberry." Though the trees were extremely large, their fruits were rare, because the trees produced fruit only once every 9,000 years. The fruit was red, and it tasted very sweet and savory. When the immortals ate the fruit, their bodies would turn a golden color, and they were able to fly and float in the air.

Other legends state that there were Heaven Chickens on the Fusang tree. The chickens nested in the top of the mythical tree and crowed at midnight each night. Every time they crowed, the crows inside the suns followed them. And then all the chickens in the world would follow and crow loudly.

[Yang et al., *Handbook of Chinese Mythology*
(Oxford University Press, 2005), pp. 117–118.]

ICELAND (NORSE): Yggdrasil

The most famous cosmic tree is the Norse Yggdrasil, which is not only the Tree of Wisdom or Knowledge but also the Tree of Life.

Yggdrasill is a mighty ash tree; between the tips of its branches and the ends of its roots it comprises the entire cosmos; it ever has and it ever shall. The most beautiful of trees is ever green, and has three great roots: one reaches down into Asgard, one world on the plane of the gods and light elves; one courses down beyond, to Jotunheim, in the middle plane, that men, giants, dark elves, and dwarfs call home; one spirals far, far below, to Niflheim, on the bottom level, the land of cold and mist, where the dead languish under the dreadful care of Hel, and where the dragon Nidhogg hatefully sups upon the root of the greatest of trees. Thus Yggdrasill connects all three planes of the cosmos—which are stacked one above the other—and the nine worlds of the Norse universe. All life springs from this source, and it sustains its own life, as well; four stags feast upon its tender shoots, and the dew that drips from its branches is the stuff of honey. Its fruit is treasured by pregnant women, as it promises safe delivery. Just so, after Ragnarok, Lif and Lifthrasit will emerge from its bark as if reborn, to renew the race of men.

A well lies beneath each root. The well of Urd in Asgard is at the base of the first root, where the Norns stand watch and sprinkle water and mud from the spring onto the World Ash, thus curing its ills; here also the gods meet in conclave. The spring of Mimir in Jotunheim, home of great wisdom, is the source of the second root. At the bottom of this spring Odin's pawned orb glistens and glitters next to Heimdalr's horn. Into the spring of Hvergelmir in Niflheim, source of eleven great floods, thrusts the third root; here is home to hungry Nidhogg and his host of slithering kin. An eagle sits in the topmost branches, a hawk perched upon his beak; Ratatoskr—old drill-tooth—that incorrigible ne'er do well, is a squirrel who runs along the branches and down the roots, bringing insults from eagle above to dragon below. So he shall continue, until Yggdrasill's branches tremble with the coming of Ragnarok, and the world is ended and begun anew.

[Christopher Fee and David A. Leeming, *Gods Heroes and Kings* (New York: Oxford University Press, 2001), pp. 112–113.]

THE GARDEN, THE GROVE, AND THE CAVE

The garden, the grove, and the cave are sacred spaces in myth. Their connotative energy derives from the fact that they are originally associated with the Mother Goddess. They are places of birth (Jesus, the Buddha, Dionysos in some stories). They are places of withdrawal for meditation, which can lead to a second birth (Muhammad, Jesus in Gethsemane). They are enclosed, protective places that, like temples and walled cities, are metaphors for cosmos in the face of chaos. The Tree of Life and other forms of the Cosmic Tree are often found in gardens (the Bodhi Tree, the Tree of Knowledge), forming still another version of union in the tradition of the lingam-yoni conjunction, the tree being the standing phallus in the womb-garden.

ARABIA: Muhammad's Cave

The prophet retires to the cave to receive the word of Allah.

Mohammad was now approaching his fortieth year. Always pensive, he had of late become even more thoughtful and retiring. Contemplation and reflection engaged his mind. The debasement of his people pressed heavily on him; the dim and imperfect shadows of Judaism and Christianity excited doubts without satisfying them; and his soul was perplexed with uncertainty as to what was the true religion. Thus burdened, he frequently retired to seek relief in meditation amongst the solitary valleys and rocks near Mecca. His favourite spot was a cave in the declivities at the foot of mount Hira, a lofty conical hill two or three miles north of Mecca. Thither he would retire for days at a time; and his faithful wife sometimes accompanied him. The continued solitude, instead of stilling his anxiety, magnified into sterner and more impressive shapes the solemn realities which agitated his soul. Close by was the grave of the aged Zeid, who, after spending a lifetime in the same inquiries, had now passed into the state of certainty;—might he himself not reach the same assurance without crossing the gate of death?

All around was bleak and rugged. To the east and south, the vision from the cave of Hira is bounded by lofty mountain ranges, but to the north and west the weary prospect is thus described by Burckhardt:— "The country before us had a dreary aspect, not a single green spot being visible; barren, black, and grey hills, and white sandy valleys, were the only objects in sight." There was harmony here between external nature, and the troubled world within. By degrees the impulsive and susceptible mind of Mohammad was wrought up to the highest pitch of excitement; and he would give vent to his agitation in wild rhapsodical language, enforced often with incoherent oaths, the counterpart of inward struggling after truth. The following fragments [from the Koran] belong probably to this period:

> By the declining day I swear!
> Verily, man is in the way of ruin;
> Excepting such as possess faith,
> And do the things which are right,
> And stir up one another unto truth and steadfastness.

And again—

> By the rushing panting steeds!
> Striking fire with flashing hoof,

That scour the land at early morn!
And, darkening it with dust,
Cleave thereby the Enemy!
Verily Man is to his Lord ungrateful,
And he himself is witness of it.
Verily he is keen after this world's good.
Ah! witteth he not that when what is in the graves shall be brought forth,
And that which is in men's breasts laid bare;—
Verily in that day shall the Lord be well informed of them.

Nor was he wanting in prayer for guidance to the great Being who, he felt, alone could give it. The following petitions (though probably adapted subsequently to public worship) contain perhaps the germ of frequent prayer at this early period.

Praise be to God, the Lord of creation,
The most merciful, the most compassionate!
Ruler of the day of Reckoning!
Thee we worship, and invoke for help.
Lead us in the straight path;—
The path of those towards whom Thou hast been gracious;
Not of those against whom Thy wrath is kindled, or that
    walk in error.
   . . .

Several years after, Mohammad thus alludes in the Koran to the position of himself and his friend [Abu Bekr] in the cave of mount Thaur:

If ye will not assist the Prophet, verily God assisted him aforetime when the Unbelievers cast him forth, in the company of a Second only; when they two were in the cave alone, when the Prophet said unto his companion, Be not cast down, for verily God is with us. And God caused to descend tranquillity upon him, and strengthened him with hosts which ye saw not, and made the word of the Unbelievers to be abased; and the word of the Lord, that is exalted, for God is mighty and wise.

The "sole companion," or in Arabic phraseology The Second of the Two, became one of Abu Bekr's most honoured titles. Hassan, the contemporary poet of Medina, thus sings of him:—

And the Second of the two in the glorious Cave, while the foes were
searching around, and they two had ascended the mountain;
And the Prophet of the Lord, they well knew, loved him,—more
    than all
the world; he held no one equal unto him.

Legends cluster around the cave. A spider wove its web across the
entrance. Branches sprouted, covering it in on every side. Wild pigeons
settled on the trees to divert attention, and so forth. Whatever may
have been the real peril, Mohammad and his companion felt it,
no doubt, to be a time of jeopardy. Glancing upwards at a crevice
through which the morning light began to break, Abu Bekr whispered: "What if one were to look through the chink, and see us
underneath his very feet." "Think not thus, Abu Bekr!" said the
Prophet; "We are two, but God is in the midst a third."

[Sir William Muir, *The Life of Mohammad*
(New York, 1923, 1975), pp. 37–38, 138–139.]

THE LABYRINTH

The labyrinth appears in the myths of many cultures, but most prominently in
the story of Theseus. The word derives from the Greek *labrys*, ax. Presumably,
in Crete, where the labyrinth was built in the form of a double ax by Daedalus
to house the half-bull Minotaur, it referred to the sacred double ax used there
for sacrifices. The labyrinth has always connoted the idea of a difficult journey
into the unknown. To escape from it and from the monster within is to have
faced death and been reborn (see the Theseus story in the Hero Myths section
of this book).

GREECE: Daedalus and Icarus

An outgrowth of the labyrinth myth is the tragic story of Daedalus and Icarus,
who longed to escape Crete and the Labyrinth, which Daedalus himself had
designed and built. The labyrinth of Crete is the direct result of the strange
story of Minos and Pasiphae.

DAEDALUS AND MINOS

Daedalus was son or grandson of Metion, younger brother of
Cecrops, and therefore a member of the Athenian royal house. He
was a skilled craftsman and inventor; his assistant was his nephew
Perdix. One day Perdix invented the saw, getting the idea from a

fish's backbone. In a fit of jealousy, Daedalus hurled him from a rock. As he fell, he was turned into a partridge, which still bears the name perdix. Being now guilty of homicide, Daedalus had to leave Athens. He went to Crete, where his skill was employed by Minos and Pasiphaë.

Now Minos had prayed to Poseidon to send him a Bull from the sea for sacrifice; when Poseidon answered his prayer, Minos was so covetous that he sacrificed another, less beautiful Bull, keeping Poseidon's animal for himself. As a punishment, Poseidon caused his wife, Pasiphaë, to fall in love with the Bull. To satisfy her passion, Daedalus constructed a lifelike hollow cow in which Pasiphaë was shut up to mate with the Bull. Her offspring was the Minotaur. It had a man's body and the head of a Bull, and was held captive in the Labyrinth, a mazelike prison of Daedalus' devising. We have already seen how Theseus destroyed it. The famous discoveries at Cnossus in Crete have shown that the Bull played a significant part in Cretan ritual, and that a common sacred object was the labrys, or double-headed ax, which is certainly to be connected with the word labyrinth. The idea of the maze has plausibly been thought to have its origin in the huge and complex palace of Cnossus, with its many passageways and endless series of rooms. Minos and Pasiphaë, like their daughters Ariadne and Phaedra, are probably divine figures; Minos was son and friend of Zeus, while Pasiphaë was the daughter of Helius.

THE FLIGHT OF ICARUS

Daedalus eventually tired of his life in Crete, but Minos would not let him go. He therefore contrived feathered wings, held together by wax, by means of which he and his son Icarus could escape. As they flew high above the sea, Icarus ignored his father's warning not to fly too close to the sun . . . and as the wax on his wings melted he fell into the sea, which thereafter was called Mare Icarium. The story is told by Ovid (Metamorphoses 8):

When Daedalus the craftsman had finished [making the wings], he balanced his body between the twin wings and by moving them hung suspended in air. He also gave instructions to his son, saying: "Icarus, I advise you to take a middle course. If you fly too low, the sea will soak the wings; if you fly too high, the sun's heat will burn them. Fly between sea and sun! Take the course along which I shall lead you."

As he gave the instructions for flying, he fitted the novel wings to Icarus' shoulders. While he worked and gave his advice, the old man's face was wet with tears, and his hands trembled with a father's anxiety. For the last time, he kissed his son and rose into the air upon his wings. He led the way in flight and was anxious for his companion, like a bird that leads its young from the nest into the air. He encouraged Icarus to follow and showed him the skills that were to destroy him; he moved his wings and looked back at those of his son. Some fisherman with trembling rod, or shepherd leaning on his crook, or farmer resting on his plow saw them and was amazed, and believed that those who could travel through the air were gods.

Now Juno's Samos was on the left (they had already passed Delos and Paros), and Lebinthos and Calymne, rich in honey, were on the right, when the boy began to exult in his bold flight. He left his guide and, drawn by a desire to reach the heavens, took his course too high. The burning heat of the nearby sun softened the scented wax that fastened the wings. The wax melted; Icarus moved his arms, now uncovered, and without the wings to drive him on, vainly beat the air. Even as he called upon his father's name the sea received him and from him took its name.

Daedalus himself reached Sicily, where Cocalus, king of the city of Camicus received him. Here he was pursued by Minos, who discovered him by the ruse of carrying round a spiral shell, which he asked Cocalus to have threaded. Cocalus gave the shell to Daedalus, who alone of men was ingenious enough to succeed. Minos knew that Daedalus was there when Cocalus gave him back the threaded shell. However, Daedalus still stayed out of Minos' reach, for the daughters of Cocalus drowned Minos in boiling water. There is no reliable legend about the further history or death of Daedalus.

[Morford et al., *Classical Mythology*
(Oxford University Press, 2011), pp. 609–612.]

BIBLIOGRAPHY

✦

Among the most stimulating discussions of sacred places and objects are those of Mircea Eliade, particularly in his *Patterns in Comparative Religion* (New York, 1958) and *The Sacred and the Profane* (New York, 1959). For useful discussions of biblical places and objects, see Walter Beltz, *God and the Gods: Myths of the Bible* (Baltimore, MD, 1983). Rebecca Hind's *Sacred Places: Sites of Spirituality and Faith* (Overlook, 2008) is a good overview of the subject. For a strong and convincing feminist analysis of sacred places and objects and much of mythology in general, see Barbara Walker, *The Woman's Encyclopedia of Myths and Secrets* (New York, 1983). Jessie Weston's *From Ritual to Romance* (New York, 1957) is still the most exciting analysis of the Holy Grail myth. For the poetic and philosophical implications of sacred space, places, and objects, see Gaston Bachelard, *The Poetics of Space* (Boston, 1969). Moyre Caldecott's *Myths of the Sacred Tree* (Destiny Books, 1993) and Edwin Bernbaum's *Sacred Mountains of the World* (University of California Press, 1998) contain helpful material. Richard Cavendish's *Visions of Heaven and Hell* (London, 1977) contains useful commentary and an excellent bibliography. James Mew's *Traditional Aspects of Hell* (Michigan, 1903, 1971) and Christopher Moreman's *Beyond the Threshold: Afterlife Beliefs and Experience in World Religion* (Rowman and Littlefied, 2010) are valuable works on the subject of the afterlife.

GLOSSARY

✦

The list below contains terms commonly used by scholars in their discussions of mythology.

Androgyny: Referring to the combination of male and female genders in one person. An androgyne is such a person and in mythology and religion can sometimes symbolize psychological or spiritual wholeness.

Animistic myths: Myths that reflect understandings of the world based in the concept that everything contains soul (*animus*) or spiritual significance. Many African and Native American myths and religions are animistic. World parent creation myths can be said to be animistic because they are based on the assumption that everything in creation was once part of the world parent.

Anthropology: Literally, the study of humans. Anthropologists study human cultures.

Apocalypse: An apocalypse is the end of everything. Apocalypse myths are myths of the end of the world. Since we have not experienced the end of the world, such myths are revelations rather than facts.

Archetype: A universal symbol or pattern. The term is used primarily in psychology by Carl Jung and his followers, in religious studies by Mircea Eliade and his followers, and in literary criticism by scholars such as Northrop Frye. The heroic *monomyth* (see below) is concerned with the hero archetype.

Aryans: The term is sometimes used in connection with the Indo-Iranians who descended from the north into India and Iran in ancient times, bringing with them Indo-European linguistic, cultural, and religious traditions.

Chaos: A term used to characterize the undifferentiated, un-ordered reality—before creation.

Chaos creation: Creation from chaos is one of the major archetypes (see above) of creation, in which the world emerges from elements already in existence but not yet ordered or differentiated.

Cosmogony: The study of the coming into existence of the cosmos (Greek *kosmos*, order + *genesis*, birth), that is, of creation. A cosmogonic myth is a cosmogony, and so is the modern big bang theory.

Creatrix: A term used to distinguish a female creator from a male one.

Cuneiform: Perhaps the first form of writing, invented by the ancient Sumerians of Mesopotamia (Iraq). It consisted of a system of pictographs carved into clay tablets.

Dualism: Some religions and their myths reflect a belief in dualism, the sense that the world is dominated by a struggle between two opposites, for example, good and evil, spiritual and physical. See, for example, the Zoroastrian myths.

Earth diver creation: One of the primary archetypes of creation, the earth diver myth involves the diving into the primordial waters to find the material with which to create the world. The archetype is ubiquitous among eastern Native Americans.

Emergence creation: One of the primary archetypes of creation, the emergence myth involves the coming of the first people from within the earth. The archetype is popular among southwestern Native Americans.

Eschatological myths: Myths that deal with the end of things. The Norse Ragnarök story, like all apocalypse stories, is eschatological, as is the belief in the "Last Judgment."

Etiological myths: Etiology is the study of origins. Etiological myths are those that explain traditions and natural phenomena. Creation myths have etiological aspects.

Ex nihilo creation: One of the primary archetypes of creation, the ex nihilo (from nothing) myths tell, for example, of the creation of the world by the creator's words or thoughts at a time when time and space was simply an empty void.

Hero: In mythology a hero is a human male or female who embodies the aspirations of a people and has special powers, usually derived from some direct relationship with the divine.

Matriarchal: Matriarchal societies are those in which matriarchs (women leaders) are dominant.

Matrilineal: Matrilineal societies (as opposed to more common patrilineal ones) are those in which a person's name and significance and sometimes property rights come from the female rather than male line.

Metaphor: In myths, characters and events can often be seen as metaphorical, that is, as representations or symbols of a culture's ideas and beliefs rather than as factual reality.

Monism: The belief that reality is contained in one being that has many manifestations. Hindus who believe in the concept of Brahman, the single, all-encompassing reality as revealed, for instance, by Shiva, Vishnu, and other deities, can be called monists.

Monomyth: A term coined by James Joyce and used primarily by mythologist Joseph Campbell to refer to the universal or archetypal pattern of hero myths around the world. The monomyth contains such elements as the miraculous conception, the search for the father, the quest, and the descent to the underworld.

Monotheism: The belief in a single god such as the Hebrew/Jewish Yahweh, the Christian God, and the Muslim Allah. These three religions are usually referred to when people speak of the monotheists.

Myth: A narrative, usually religious in nature, which explains reality and expresses a sense of a culture's place in reality, but which to some within and outside the culture is more metaphorical and symbolic than literal. Myths are eschatological, etiological, ontological, or teleological (see these terms above and below).

Mythology: The study of myths, sometimes called *mythography,* and also a collection of myths. We can study the concept of myths, and we can, for instance, study Greek mythology or Egyptian mythology or world mythology.

Mythos: The Greek term from which our word *myth* is derived.

Ontological myths: Ontology is the study of being. Ontological myths explain the nature of being or existence.

Pagan: A term commonly applied—often in a derogative manner—to nonmonotheistic beliefs, especially pantheism (see below).

Pantheism: The belief in many deities. The ancient Greek religion was pantheistic, and most would argue that animistic (see above) religions and myths are pantheistic.

Pantheon: A pantheon *(pan,* all + *theos,* gods*)* is a collection of deities belonging to a particular cult or religion. The Olympians make up the ancient Greek pantheon. The gods of the Ennead make up the Egyptian pantheon of the Heliopolis tradition.

Patriarchal: Cultures and traditions dominated by male as opposed to female leaders. The opposite of *matriarchal* (see above).

Primal: A word used in mythology to refer to original forms such as the primal waters out of which creation came about in some creation myths.

Primeval: Used synonymously with *primal* in mythological descriptions.

Primordial: Used synonymously with *primal* and *primeval* in mythological descriptions.

Resurrection: The act of returning to life after a period of death. Osiris in Egypt and Jesus both experience resurrection as opposed to "rebirth."

Ritual: An ordered form of actions (or rite) to celebrate or reenact a mythological act or belief.

Scapegoat: An archetypal aspect of the lives of certain heroes—Sita and Jesus are examples—in which the hero pays a significant price (usually death) in some sense to save the lives of others or of a whole society.

Shaman: A holy person—called a "Medicine Man" or "Medicine Woman" by some Native Americans—who communicates, by way of a radical change in the state of consciousness, with the spirit world and has the power to cure.

Structuralism: A system of thought that assumes consistent underlying patterns in all forms of human experience, whether so-called civilized or primitive.

Symbol: Something that represents an idea. A church steeple might be seen as a symbol of the idea of reaching up to the deity. Myths are full of symbols. Thor's hammer, for instance, is a symbol of power.

Teleological myths: Myths that stress or suggest the connection between natural processes and a final purpose or design. Monotheistic myths tend to be teleological.

Theism: The belief in gods or a god, particularly personal ones as opposed to mere concepts.

Triad: The concept of three dominant gods, as in the case of Hinduism's Shiva, Vishnu, and Brahma or Shiva, Vishnu, and Devi. This differs from the Christian dogma of the *Trinity*, in which God has three aspects, Creator, Redeemer, and Spirit.

Virgin birth: In the heroic *monomyth* (see above) the hero is sometimes marked clearly by a miraculous conception and birth, such as having been conceived without sexual intercourse and having been born of a mother who was a virgin.

Void, the: In the *ex nihilo creation* myths (see above), the creator exists in a state of no-thing-ness or void before he or she creates the universe. Such is the case of Yahweh in the biblical book of Genesis.

World parent creation: Creation in which a *primal* (see above) being is in some way turned into the elements of reality, as in the Norse creation.

INDEX

✦

- Pele – MANY PEOPLE IN KILAUEA'S SHADOW
  WERE THANKFUL FOR ERUPTION
  EVEN THO IT DESTROYED THEIR HOMES

  - EXTRADITED TO THE STATES

  - FORCED TO FLEE BC SHE TRIED
    TO SEDUCE HER BRO IN LAW

  - PELE IS FIRE DIETY, CONTROLS LAVA
    HIGHEST DIETY IN HWAIIE

RAVEN CLAN